THE ZINCALI - AN ACCOUNT OF THE GYPSIES OF SPAIN

ISBN: 1-4264-0085-3

GEORGE BORROW

THE ZINCALI - AN ACCOUNT OF THE GYPSIES OF SPAIN

BIBLIOBAZAAR

THE ZINCALI - AN ACCOUNT OF THE GYPSIES OF SPAIN

PREFACE

IT is with some diffidence that the author ventures to offer the present work to the public.

The greater part of it has been written under very peculiar circumstances, such as are not in general deemed at all favourable for literary composition: at considerable intervals, during a period of nearly five years passed in Spain - in moments snatched from more important pursuits - chiefly in ventas and posadas, whilst wandering through the country in the arduous and unthankful task of distributing the Gospel among its children.

Owing to the causes above stated, he is aware that his work must not unfrequently appear somewhat disjointed and unconnected, and the style rude and unpolished: he has, nevertheless, permitted the tree to remain where he felled it, having, indeed, subsequently enjoyed too little leisure to make much effectual alteration.

At the same time he flatters himself that the work is not destitute of certain qualifications to entitle it to approbation. The author's acquaintance with the Gypsy race in general dates from a very early period of his life, which considerably facilitated his intercourse with the Peninsular portion, to the elucidation of whose history and character the present volumes are more particularly devoted. Whatever he has asserted, is less the result of reading than of close observation, he having long since come to the conclusion that the Gypsies are not a people to be studied in books, or at least in such books as he believes have hitherto been written concerning them.

Throughout he has dealt more in facts than in theories, of which he is in general no friend. True it is, that no race in the world affords, in many points, a more extensive field for theory and conjecture than the Gypsies, who are certainly a very mysterious people come from some distant land, no mortal knows why, and who made their first appearance in Europe at a dark period, when events were not so accurately recorded as at the present time.

But if he has avoided as much as possible touching upon subjects which must always, to a certain extent, remain shrouded in obscurity; for example, the, original state and condition of the Gypsies, and the causes which first brought them into Europe; he has stated what they are at the present day, what he knows them to be from a close scrutiny of their ways and habits, for which, perhaps, no one ever enjoyed better opportunities; and he has, moreover, given - not a few words culled expressly for the purpose of supporting a theory, but one entire dialect of their language, collected with much trouble and difficulty; and to this he humbly calls the attention of the learned, who, by comparing it with certain languages, may decide as to the countries in which the Gypsies have lived or travelled.

With respect to the Gypsy rhymes in the second volume, he wishes to make one observation which cannot be too frequently repeated, and which he entreats the reader to bear in mind: they are GYPSY COMPOSITIONS, and have little merit save so far as they throw light on the manner of thinking and speaking of the Gypsy people, or rather a portion of them, and as to what they are capable of effecting in the way of poetry. It will, doubtless, be said that the rhymes are TRASH; - even were it so, they are original, and on that account, in a philosophic point of view, are more valuable than the most brilliant compositions pretending to describe Gypsy life, but written by persons who are not of the Gypsy sect. Such compositions, however replete with fiery sentiments, and allusions to freedom and independence, are certain to be tainted with affectation. Now in the Gypsy rhymes there is no affectation, and on that very account they are different in every respect from the poetry of those interesting personages who figure, under the names of Gypsies, Gitanos, Bohemians, etc., in novels and on the boards of the theatre.

It will, perhaps, be objected to the present work, that it contains little that is edifying in a moral or Christian point of view: to such an objection the author would reply, that the Gypsies are not a Christian people, and that their morality is of a peculiar kind, not calculated to afford much edification to what is generally termed the respectable portion of society. Should it be urged that certain individuals have found them very different from what they are represented in these volumes, he would frankly say that he yields no credit to the presumed fact, and at the same time he would refer to the vocabulary contained in the second volume, whence it will appear that the words HOAX and HOCUS have been immediately derived from the language of the Gypsies, who, there is good reason to believe, first introduced the system into Europe, to which those words belong.

The author entertains no ill-will towards the Gypsies; why should he, were he a mere carnal reasoner? He has known them for upwards of twenty years, in various countries, and they never injured a hair of his head, or deprived him of a shred of his raiment; but he is not deceived as to the motive of their forbearance: they thought him a ROM, and on this supposition they hurt him not, their love of 'the blood' being their most distinguishing characteristic. He derived considerable assistance from them in Spain, as in various instances they officiated as colporteurs in the distribution of the Gospel: but on that account he is not prepared to say that they entertained any love for the Gospel or that they circulated it for the honour of Tebleque the Saviour. Whatever they did for the Gospel in Spain, was done in the hope that he whom they conceived to be their brother had some purpose in view which was to contribute to the profit of the Cales, or Gypsies, and to terminate in the confusion and plunder of the Busne, or Gentiles. Convinced of this, he is too little of an enthusiast to rear, on such a foundation, any fantastic edifice of hope which would soon tumble to the ground.

The cause of truth can scarcely be forwarded by enthusiasm, which is almost invariably the child of ignorance and error. The author is anxious to direct the attention of the public towards the Gypsies; but he hopes to be able to do so without any romantic appeals in their behalf, by concealing the truth, or by warping the truth until it becomes falsehood. In the following pages he has depicted the Gypsies as he has found them, neither aggravating their crimes nor gilding them with imaginary virtues. He has not expatiated on 'their gratitude towards good people, who treat them kindly and take an interest in their welfare'; for he believes that of all beings in the world they are the least susceptible of such a feeling. Nor has he ever done them injustice by attributing to them licentious habits, from which they are, perhaps, more free than any race in the creation.

PREFACE TO THE SECOND EDITION

I CANNOT permit the second edition of this work to go to press without premising it with a few words.

When some two years ago I first gave THE ZINCALI to the world, it was, as I stated at the time, with considerable hesitation and diffidence: the composition of it and the collecting of Gypsy words had served as a kind of relaxation to me whilst engaged in the circulation of the Gospel in Spain. After the completion of the work, I had not the slightest idea that it possessed any peculiar merit, or was calculated to make the slightest impression upon the reading world. Nevertheless, as every one who writes feels a kind of affection, greater or less, for the productions of his pen, I was averse, since the book was written, to suffer it to perish of damp in a lumber closet, or by friction in my travelling wallet. I committed it therefore to the press, with a friendly 'Farewell, little book; I have done for you all I can, and much more than you deserve.'

My expectations at this time were widely different from those of my namesake George in the VICAR OF WAKEFIELD when he published his paradoxes. I took it as a matter of course that the world, whether learned or unlearned, would say to my book what they said to his paradoxes, as the event showed, - nothing at all. To my utter astonishment, however, I had no sooner returned to my humble retreat, where I hoped to find the repose of which I was very much in need, than I was followed by the voice not only of England but of the greater part of Europe, informing me that I had achieved a feat - a work in the nineteenth century with some pretensions to originality. The book was speedily reprinted in America, portions of it were translated into French and Russian, and a fresh edition demanded.

In the midst of all this there sounded upon my ears a voice which I recognised as that of the Maecenas of British literature:

'Borromeo, don't believe all you hear, nor think that you have accomplished anything so very extraordinary: a great portion of your book is very sorry trash indeed - Gypsy poetry, dry laws, and compilations from dull Spanish authors: it has good points, however, which show that you are capable of something much better: try your hand again - avoid your besetting sins; and when you have accomplished something which will really do credit to - Street, it will be time enough to think of another delivery of these GYPSIES.'

Mistos amande: 'I am content,' I replied; and sitting down I commenced the BIBLE IN SPAIN. At first I proceeded slowly - sickness was in the land, and the face of nature was overcast - heavy rain-clouds swam in the heavens, - the blast howled amid the pines which nearly surround my lonely dwelling, and the waters of the lake which lies before it, so quiet in general and tranquil, were fearfully agitated. 'Bring lights hither, O Hayim Ben Attar, son of the miracle! ' And the Jew of Fez brought in the lights, for though it was midday I could scarcely see in the little room where I was writing. . . .

A dreary summer and autumn passed by, and were succeeded by as gloomy a winter. I still proceeded with the BIBLE IN SPAIN. The winter passed, and spring came with cold dry winds and occasional sunshine, whereupon I arose, shouted, and mounting my horse, even Sidi Habismilk, I scoured all the surrounding district, and thought but little of the BIBLE IN SPAIN.

So I rode about the country, over the heaths, and through the green lanes of my native land, occasionally visiting friends at a distance, and sometimes, for variety's sake, I stayed at home and amused myself by catching huge pike, which lie perdue in certain deep ponds skirted with lofty reeds, upon my land, and to which there is a communication from the lagoon by a deep and narrow watercourse. - I had almost forgotten the BIBLE IN SPAIN.

Then came the summer with much heat and sunshine, and then I would lie for hours in the sun and recall the sunny days I had spent in Andalusia, and my thoughts were continually reverting to Spain, and at last I remembered that the BIBLE IN SPAIN was still unfinished; whereupon I arose and said: 'This loitering profiteth nothing' - and I hastened to my summer-house by the side of the lake, and there I thought and wrote, and every day I repaired to the same place, and thought and wrote until I had finished the BIBLE IN SPAIN.

And at the proper season the BIBLE IN SPAIN was given to the world; and the world, both learned and unlearned, was delighted with the BIBLE IN SPAIN, and the highest authority [1] said, 'This is a much better book than the GYPSIES'; and the next great authority[2] said, 'something betwixt Le Sage and Bunyan.' 'A far more entertaining work than DON QUIXOTE,' exclaimed a literary lady. 'Another GIL BLAS,' said the cleverest writer in Europe.[3] 'Yes,' exclaimed the cool sensible SPECTATOR,[4] 'a GIL BLAS in water-colours.'

And when I heard the last sentence, I laughed, and shouted, 'KOSKO PENNESE PAL!'[5] It pleased me better than all the rest. Is there not a text in a certain old book which says: Woe unto you when all men shall speak well of you! Those are awful words, brothers; woe is me!

'Revenons a nos Bohemiens!' Now the BIBLE IN SPAIN is off my hands, I return to 'these GYPSIES'; and here you have, most kind, lenient, and courteous public, a fresh delivery of them. In the present edition, I have attended as much as possible to the suggestions of certain individuals, for whose opinion I cannot but entertain the highest respect. I have omitted various passages from Spanish authors, which the world has objected to as being quite out of place, and serving for no other purpose than to swell out the work. In lieu thereof, I have introduced some original matter relative to the Gypsies, which is, perhaps, more calculated to fling light over their peculiar habits than anything which has yet appeared. To remodel the work, however, I have neither time nor inclination, and must therefore again commend it, with all the imperfections which still cling to it, to the generosity of the public.

A few words in conclusion. Since the publication of the first edition, I have received more than one letter, in which the writers complain that I, who seem to know so much of what has been written concerning the Gypsies,[6] should have taken no notice of a theory entertained by many, namely, that they are of Jewish origin, and that they are neither more nor less than the descendants of the two lost tribes of Israel. Now I am not going to enter into a discussion upon this point, for I know by experience, that the public cares nothing for discussions, however learned and edifying, but will take the present opportunity to relate a little adventure of mine, which bears not a little upon this matter.

So it came to pass, that one day I was scampering over a heath, at some distance from my present home: I was mounted upon the good horse Sidi Habismilk, and the Jew of Fez, swifter than the wind, ran by the side of the good horse Habismilk, when what should I see at a corner of the heath but the encampment of certain friends of mine; and the chief of that camp, even Mr. Petulengro, stood before the encampment, and his adopted daughter, Miss Pinfold, stood beside him.

MYSELF. - 'Kosko divvus[7], Mr. Petulengro! I am glad to see you: how are you getting on?'

MR. PETULENGRO. - 'How am I getting on? as well as I can. What will you have for that nokengro [8]?'

Thereupon I dismounted, and delivering the reins of the good horse to Miss Pinfold, I took the Jew of Fez, even Hayim Ben Attar, by the hand, and went up to Mr. Petulengro, exclaiming, 'Sure ye are two brothers.' Anon the Gypsy passed his hand over the Jew's face, and stared him in the eyes: then turning to me he said, 'We are not dui palor [9]; this man is no Roman; I believe him to be a Jew; he has the face of one; besides, if he were a Rom, even from Jericho, he could rokra a few words in Rommany.'

Now the Gypsy had been in the habit of seeing German and English Jews, who must have been separated from their African brethren for a term of at least 1700 years; yet he recognised the Jew of Fez for what he was - a Jew, and without hesitation declared that he was 'no Roman.' The Jews, therefore, and the Gypsies have each their peculiar and distinctive countenance, which, to say nothing of the difference of language, precludes the possibility of their having ever been the same people.

MARCH 1, 1843.

NOTICE TO THE FOURTH EDITION

THIS edition has been carefully revised by the author, and some few insertions have been made. In order, however, to give to the work a more popular character, the elaborate vocabulary of the Gypsy tongue, and other parts relating to the Gypsy language and literature, have been omitted. Those who take an interest in these subjects are referred to the larger edition in two vols.[10]

THE GYPSIES - INTRODUCTION

THROUGHOUT my life the Gypsy race has always had a peculiar interest for me. Indeed I can remember no period when the mere mention of the name of Gypsy did not awaken within me feelings hard to be described. I cannot account for this - I merely state a fact.

Some of the Gypsies, to whom I have stated this circumstance, have accounted for it on the supposition that the soul which at present animates my body has at some former period tenanted that of one of their people; for many among them are believers in metempsychosis, and, like the followers of Bouddha, imagine that their souls, by passing through an infinite number of bodies, attain at length sufficient purity to be admitted to a state of perfect rest and quietude, which is the only idea of heaven they can form.

Having in various and distant countries lived in habits of intimacy with these people, I have come to the following conclusions respecting them: that wherever they are found, their manners and customs are virtually the same, though somewhat modified by circumstances, and that the language they speak amongst themselves, and of which they are particularly anxious to keep others in ignorance, is in all countries one and the same, but has been subjected more or less to modification; and lastly, that their countenances exhibit a decided family resemblance, but are darker or fairer according to the temperature of the climate, but invariably darker, at least in Europe, than those of the natives of the countries in which they dwell, for example, England and Russia, Germany and Spain.

The names by which they are known differ with the country, though, with one or two exceptions, not materially for example, they are styled in Russia, Zigani; in Turkey and Persia, Zingarri; and in Germany, Zigeuner; all which words apparently spring from the same etymon, which there is no improbability in supposing to be 'Zincali,' a term by which these people, especially those of Spain, sometimes designate themselves, and the meaning of which is believed to be, THE BLACK MEN OF ZEND OR IND. In England and Spain they are commonly known as Gypsies and Gitanos, from a general belief that they were originally Egyptians, to which the two words are tantamount; and in France as Bohemians, from the circumstance that Bohemia was one of the first countries in civilised Europe where they made their appearance.

But they generally style themselves and the language which they speak, Rommany. This word, of which I shall ultimately have more to say, is of Sanscrit origin, and signifies, The Husbands, or that which pertaineth unto them. From whatever motive this appellation may have originated, it is perhaps more applicable than any other to a sect or caste like them, who have no love and no affection beyond their own race; who are capable of making great sacrifices for each other, and who gladly prey upon all the rest of the human species, whom they detest, and by whom they are hated and despised. It will perhaps not be out of place to observe here, that there is no reason for supposing that the word Roma or Rommany is derived from the Arabic word which signifies Greece or Grecians, as some people not much acquainted with the language of the race in question have imagined.

I have no intention at present to say anything about their origin. Scholars have asserted that the language which they speak proves them to be of Indian stock, and undoubtedly a great number of their words are Sanscrit. My own opinion upon this subject will be found in a subsequent article. I shall here content myself with observing that from whatever country they come, whether from India or Egypt, there can be no doubt that they are human beings and have immortal souls; and it is in the humble hope of drawing the attention of the Christian philanthropist towards them, especially that degraded and unhappy portion of them, the Gitanos of Spain, that the present little work has been undertaken. But before proceeding to speak of the latter, it will perhaps not be amiss to afford some account of the Rommany as I have seen them in other countries; for there is scarcely a part of the habitable world where they are not to be found: their tents are alike pitched on the heaths of Brazil and the ridges of the Himalayan hills, and their language is heard at Moscow and Madrid, in the streets of London and Stamboul.

THE ZIGANI, OR RUSSIAN GYPSIES

They are found in all parts of Russia, with the exception of the government of St. Petersburg, from which they have been banished. In most of the provincial towns they are to be found in a state of half-civilisation, supporting themselves by trafficking in horses, or by curing the disorders incidental to those animals; but the vast majority reject this manner of life, and traverse the country in bands, like the ancient Hamaxobioi; the immense grassy plains of Russia affording pasturage for their herds of cattle, on which, and the produce of the chase, they chiefly depend for subsistence. They are, however, not destitute of money, which they obtain by various means, but principally by curing diseases amongst the cattle of the mujiks or peasantry, and by telling fortunes, and not unfrequently by theft and brigandage.

Their power of resisting cold is truly wonderful, as it is not uncommon to find them encamped in the midst of the snow, in slight canvas tents, when the temperature is twenty-five or thirty degrees below the freezing-point according to Reaumur; but in the winter they generally seek the shelter of the forests, which afford fuel for their fires, and abound in game.

The race of the Rommany is by nature perhaps the most beautiful in the world; and amongst the children of the Russian Zigani are frequently to be found countenances to do justice to which would require the pencil of a second Murillo; but exposure to the rays of the burning sun, the biting of the frost, and the pelting of the pitiless sleet and snow, destroys their beauty at a very early age; and if in infancy their personal advantages are remarkable, their ugliness at an advanced age is no less so, for then it is loathsome, and even appalling.

A hundred years, could I live so long, would not efface from my mind the appearance of an aged Ziganskie Attaman, or Captain of Zigani, and his grandson, who approached me on the meadow before Novo Gorod, where stood the encampment of a numerous horde. The boy was of a form and face which might have entitled him to represent Astyanax, and Hector of Troy might have pressed him to his bosom, and called him his pride; but the old man was, perhaps, such a shape as Milton has alluded to, but could only describe as execrable - he wanted but the dart and kingly crown to have represented the monster who opposed the progress of Lucifer, whilst careering in burning arms and infernal glory to the outlet of his hellish prison.

But in speaking of the Russian Gypsies, those of Moscow must not be passed over in silence. The station to which they have attained in society in that most remarkable of cities is so far above the sphere in which the remainder of their race pass their lives, that it may be considered as a phenomenon in Gypsy history, and on that account is entitled to particular notice.

Those who have been accustomed to consider the Gypsy as a wandering outcast, incapable of appreciating the blessings of a settled and civilised life, or - if abandoning vagabond propensities, and becoming stationary - as one who never ascends higher than the condition of a low trafficker, will be surprised to learn, that amongst the Gypsies of Moscow there are not a few who inhabit stately houses, go abroad in elegant equipages, and are behind the higher orders of the Russians neither in appearance nor mental acquirements. To the power of song alone this phenomenon is to be attributed. From time immemorial the female Gypsies of Moscow have been much addicted to the vocal art, and bands or quires of them have sung for pay in the halls of the nobility or upon the boards of the theatre. Some first-rate songsters have been produced among them, whose merits have been acknowledged, not only by the Russian public, but by the most fastidious foreign critics. Perhaps the highest compliment ever paid to a songster was paid by Catalani herself to one of these daughters of Roma. It is well known throughout Russia that the celebrated Italian was so enchanted with the voice of a Moscow Gypsy (who, after the former had displayed her noble talent before a splendid audience in the old Russian capital, stepped forward and poured forth one of her national strains), that she tore from her own shoulders a shawl of cashmire, which had been presented to her by the Pope, and, embracing the Gypsy, insisted on her acceptance of the splendid gift, saying, that it had been intended for the matchless songster, which she now perceived she herself was not.

The sums obtained by many of these females by the exercise of their art enable them to support their relatives in affluence and luxury: some are married to Russians, and no one who has visited Russia can but be aware that a lovely and accomplished countess, of the noble and numerous family of Tolstoy, is by birth a Zigana, and was originally one of the principal attractions of a Rommany choir at Moscow.

But it is not to be supposed that the whole of the Gypsy females at Moscow are of this high and talented description; the majority of them are of far lower quality, and obtain their livelihood by singing and dancing at taverns, whilst their husbands in general follow the occupation of horse-dealing.

Their favourite place of resort in the summer time is Marina Rotze, a species of sylvan garden about two versts from Moscow, and thither, tempted by curiosity, I drove one fine evening. On my arrival the Ziganas came flocking out from their little tents, and from the tractir or inn which has been erected for the accommodation of the public. Standing on the seat of the calash, I addressed them in a loud voice in the English dialect of the Rommany, of which I have some knowledge. A shrill scream of wonder was instantly raised, and welcomes and blessings were poured forth in floods of musical Rommany, above all of which predominated the cry of KAK CAMENNA TUTE PRALA - or, How we love you, brother! - for at first they mistook me for one of their wandering brethren from the distant lands, come over the great panee or ocean to visit them.

After some conversation they commenced singing, and favoured me with many songs, both in Russian and Rommany: the former were modern popular pieces, such as are accustomed to be sung on the boards of the theatre; but the latter were evidently of great antiquity, exhibiting the strongest marks of originality, the metaphors bold and sublime, and the metre differing from anything of the kind which it has been my fortune to observe in Oriental or European prosody.

One of the most remarkable, and which commences thus:

'Za mateia rosherroro odolata
Bravintata,'

(or, Her head is aching with grief, as if she had tasted wine) describes the anguish of a maiden separated from her lover, and who calls for her steed:

'Tedjav manga gurraoro' -

that she may depart in quest of the lord of her bosom, and share his joys and pleasures.

A collection of these songs, with a translation and vocabulary, would be no slight accession to literature, and would probably throw more light on the history of this race than anything which has yet appeared; and, as there is no want of zeal and talent in Russia amongst the cultivators of every branch of literature, and especially philology, it is only surprising that such a collection still remains a desideratum.

The religion which these singular females externally professed was the Greek, and they mostly wore crosses of copper or gold; but when I questioned them on this subject in their native language, they laughed, and said it was only to please the Russians. Their names for God and his adversary are Deval and Bengel, which differ little from the Spanish Un-debel and Bengi, which signify the same. I will now say something of

THE HUNGARIAN GYPSIES, OR CZIGANY

Hungary, though a country not a tenth part so extensive as the huge colossus of the Russian empire, whose tzar reigns over a hundred lands, contains perhaps as many Gypsies, it not being uncommon to find whole villages inhabited by this race; they likewise abound in the suburbs of the towns. In Hungary the feudal system still exists in all its pristine barbarity; in no country does the hard hand of this oppression bear so heavy upon the lower classes - not even in Russia. The peasants of Russia are serfs, it is true, but their condition is enviable compared with that of the same class in the other country; they have certain rights and privileges, and are, upon the whole, happy and contented, whilst the Hungarians are ground to powder. Two classes are free in Hungary to do almost what they please - the nobility and - the Gypsies; the former are above the law - the latter below it: a toll is wrung from the hands of the hard-working labourers, that most meritorious class, in passing over a bridge, for example at Pesth, which is not demanded from a well-dressed person - nor from the Czigany, who have frequently no dress at all - and whose insouciance stands in striking contrast with the trembling submission of the peasants. The Gypsy, wherever you find him, is an incomprehensible being, but nowhere more than in Hungary, where, in the midst of slavery, he is free, though apparently one step lower than the lowest slave. The habits of the Hungarian Gypsies are abominable; their hovels appear sinks of the vilest poverty and filth, their dress is at best rags, their food frequently the vilest carrion, and occasionally, if report be true, still worse - on which point, when speaking of the Spanish Gitanos, we shall have subsequently more to say: thus they live in filth, in rags, in nakedness, and in merriness of heart, for nowhere is there more of song and dance than in an Hungarian Gypsy village. They are very fond of music, and some of them are heard to touch the violin in a manner wild, but of peculiar excellence. Parties of them have been known to exhibit even at Paris.

In Hungary, as in all parts, they are addicted to horse-dealing; they are likewise tinkers, and smiths in a small way. The women are fortune-tellers, of course - both sexes thieves of the first water. They roam where they list - in a country where all other people are held under strict surveillance, no one seems to care about these Parias. The most remarkable feature, however, connected with the habits of the Czigany, consists in their foreign excursions, having plunder in view, which frequently endure for three or four years, when, if no mischance has befallen them, they return to their native land - rich; where they squander the proceeds of their dexterity in mad festivals. They wander in bands of twelve and fourteen through France, even to Rome. Once, during my own wanderings in Italy, I rested at nightfall by the side of a kiln, the air being piercingly cold; it was about four leagues from Genoa. Presently arrived three individuals to take advantage of the warmth - a man, a woman, and a lad. They soon began to discourse - and I found that they were Hungarian Gypsies; they spoke of what they had been doing, and what they had amassed - I think they mentioned nine hundred crowns. They had companions in the neighbourhood, some of whom they were expecting; they took no notice of me, and conversed in their own dialect; I did not approve of their propinquity, and rising, hastened away.

When Napoleon invaded Spain there were not a few Hungarian Gypsies in his armies; some strange encounters occurred on the field of battle between these people and the Spanish Gitanos, one of which is related in the second part of the present work. When quartered in the Spanish towns, the Czigany invariably sought out their peninsular brethren, to whom they revealed themselves, kissing and embracing most affectionately; the Gitanos were astonished at the proficiency of the strangers in thievish arts, and looked upon them almost in the light of superior beings: 'They knew the whole reckoning,' is still a common expression amongst them. There was a Cziganian soldier for some time at Cordoba, of whom the Gitanos of the place still frequently discourse, whilst smoking their cigars during winter nights over their braseros.

The Hungarian Gypsies have a peculiar accent when speaking the language of the country, by which they can be instantly distinguished; the same thing is applicable to the Gitanos of Spain when speaking Spanish. In no part of the world is the Gypsy language preserved better than in Hungary.

The following short prayer to the Virgin, which I have frequently heard amongst the Gypsies of Hungary and Transylvania, will serve as a specimen of their language.-

Gula Devla, da me saschipo. Swuntuna Devla, da me bacht t' aldaschis cari me jav; te ferin man, Devla, sila ta niapaschiata, chungale manuschendar, ke me jav ande drom ca hin man traba; ferin man, Devia; ma mek man Devla, ke manga man tre Devies-key.

Sweet Goddess, give me health. Holy Goddess, give me luck and grace wherever I go; and help me, Goddess, powerful and immaculate, from ugly men, that I may go in the road to the place I purpose: help me, Goddess; forsake me not, Goddess, for I pray for God's sake.

WALLACHIA AND MOLDAVIA

In Wallachia and Moldavia, two of the eastern-most regions of Europe, are to be found seven millions of people calling themselves Roumouni, and speaking a dialect of the Latin tongue much corrupted by barbarous terms, so called. They are supposed to be in part descendants of Roman soldiers, Rome in the days of her grandeur having established immense military colonies in these parts. In the midst of these people exist vast numbers of Gypsies, amounting, I am disposed to think, to at least two hundred thousand. The land of the Roumouni, indeed, seems to have been the hive from which the West of Europe derived the Gypsy part of its population. Far be it from me to say that the Gypsies sprang originally from Roumouni-land. All I mean is, that it was their grand resting-place after crossing the Danube. They entered Roumouni-land from Bulgaria, crossing the great river, and from thence some went to the north- east, overrunning Russia, others to the west of Europe, as far as Spain and England. That the early Gypsies of the West, and also those of Russia, came from Roumouni-land, is easily proved, as in all the western Gypsy dialects, and also in the Russian, are to be found words belonging to the Roumouni speech; for example, primavera, spring; cheros, heaven; chorab, stocking; chismey, boots; - Roum - primivari, cherul, chorapul, chisme. One might almost be tempted to suppose that the term Rommany, by which the Gypsies of Russia and the West call themselves, was derived from Roumouni, were it not for one fact, which is, that Romanus in the Latin tongue merely means a native of Rome, whilst the specific meaning of Rome still remains in the dark; whereas in Gypsy Rom means a husband, Rommany the sect of the husbands; Romanesti if married. Whether both words were derived originally from the same source, as I believe some people have supposed, is a question which, with my present lights, I cannot pretend to determine.

THE ENGLISH GYPSIES

No country appears less adapted for that wandering life, which seems so natural to these people, than England. Those wildernesses and forests, which they are so attached to, are not to be found there; every inch of land is cultivated, and its produce watched with a jealous eye; and as the laws against trampers, without the visible means of supporting themselves, are exceedingly severe, the possibility of the Gypsies existing as a distinct race, and retaining their original free and independent habits, might naturally be called in question by those who had not satisfactorily verified the fact. Yet it is a truth that, amidst all these seeming disadvantages, they not only exist there, but in no part of the world is their life more in accordance with the general idea that the Gypsy is like Cain, a wanderer of the earth; for in England the covered cart and the little tent are the houses of the Gypsy, and he seldom remains more than three days in the same place.

At present they are considered in some degree as a privileged people; for, though their way of life is unlawful, it is connived at; the law of England having discovered by experience, that its utmost fury is inefficient to reclaim them from their inveterate habits.

Shortly after their first arrival in England, which is upwards of three centuries since, a dreadful persecution was raised against them, the aim of which was their utter extermination; the being a Gypsy was esteemed a crime worthy of death, and the gibbets of England groaned and creaked beneath the weight of Gypsy carcases, and the miserable survivors were literally obliged to creep into the earth in order to preserve their lives. But these days passed by; their persecutors became weary of pursuing them; they showed their heads from the holes and caves where they had hidden themselves, they ventured forth, increased in numbers, and, each tribe or family choosing a particular circuit, they fairly divided the land amongst them.

In England, the male Gypsies are all dealers in horses, and sometimes employ their idle time in mending the tin and copper utensils of the peasantry; the females tell fortunes. They generally pitch their tents in the vicinity of a village or small town by the road side, under the shelter of the hedges and trees. The climate of England is well known to be favourable to beauty, and in no part of the world is the appearance of the Gypsies so prepossessing as in that country; their complexion is dark, but not disagreeably so; their faces are oval, their features regular, their foreheads rather low, and their hands and feet small. The men are taller than the English peasantry, and far more active. They all speak the English language with fluency, and in their gait and demeanour are easy and graceful; in both points standing in striking contrast with the peasantry, who in speech are slow and uncouth, and in manner dogged and brutal.

The dialect of the Rommany, which they speak, though mixed with English words, may be considered as tolerably pure, from the fact that it is intelligible to the Gypsy race in the heart of Russia. Whatever crimes they may commit, their vices are few, for the men are not drunkards, nor are the women harlots; there are no two characters which they hold in so much abhorrence, nor do any words when applied by them convey so much execration as these two.

The crimes of which these people were originally accused were various, but the principal were theft, sorcery, and causing disease among the cattle; and there is every reason for supposing that in none of these points they were altogether guiltless.

With respect to sorcery, a thing in itself impossible, not only the English Gypsies, but the whole race, have ever professed it; therefore, whatever misery they may have suffered on that account, they may be considered as having called it down upon their own heads.

Dabbling in sorcery is in some degree the province of the female Gypsy. She affects to tell the future, and to prepare philtres by means of which love can be awakened in any individual towards any particular object; and such is the credulity of the human race, even in the most enlightened countries, that the profits arising from these practices are great. The following is a case in point: two females, neighbours and friends, were tried some years since, in England, for the murder of their husbands. It appeared that they were in love with the same individual, and had conjointly, at various times, paid sums of money to a Gypsy woman to work charms to captivate his affections. Whatever little effect the charms might produce, they were successful in their principal object, for the person in question carried on for some time a criminal intercourse with both. The matter came to the knowledge of the husbands, who, taking means to break off this connection, were respectively poisoned by their wives. Till the moment of conviction these wretched females betrayed neither emotion nor fear, but then their consternation was indescribable; and they afterwards confessed that the Gypsy, who had visited them in prison, had promised to shield them from conviction by means of her art. It is therefore not surprising that in the fifteenth and sixteenth centuries, when a belief in sorcery was supported by the laws of all Europe, these people were regarded as practisers of sorcery, and punished as such, when, even in the nineteenth, they still find people weak enough to place confidence in their claims to supernatural power.

The accusation of producing disease and death amongst the cattle was far from groundless. Indeed, however strange and incredible it may sound in the present day to those who are unacquainted with this caste, and the peculiar habits of the Rommanees, the practice is still occasionally pursued in England and many other countries where they are found. From this practice, when they are not detected, they derive considerable advantage. Poisoning cattle is exercised by them in two ways: by one, they merely cause disease in the animals, with the view of receiving money for curing them upon offering their services; the poison is generally administered by powders cast at night into the mangers of the animals: this way is only practised upon the larger cattle, such as horses and cows. By the other, which they practise chiefly on swine, speedy death is almost invariably produced, the drug administered being of a highly intoxicating nature, and affecting the brain. They then apply at the house or farm where the disaster has occurred for the carcase of the animal, which is generally given them without suspicion, and then they feast on the flesh, which is not injured by the poison, which only affects the head.

The English Gypsies are constant attendants at the racecourse; what jockey is not? Perhaps jockeyism originated with them, and even racing, at least in England. Jockeyism properly implies THE MANAGEMENT OF A WHIP, and the word jockey is neither more nor less than the term slightly modified, by which they designate the formidable whips which they usually carry, and which are at present in general use amongst horse-traffickers, under the title of jockey whips. They are likewise fond of resorting to the prize-ring, and have occasionally even attained some eminence, as principals, in those disgraceful and brutalising exhibitions called pugilistic combats. I believe a great deal has been written on the subject of the English Gypsies, but the writers have dwelt too much in generalities; they have been afraid to take the Gypsy by the hand, lead him forth from the crowd, and exhibit him in the area; he is well worth observing. When a boy of fourteen, I was present at a prize-fight; why should I hide the truth? It took place on a green meadow, beside a running stream, close by the old church of E-, and within a league of the ancient town of N-, the capital of one of the eastern counties. The terrible Thurtell was present, lord of the concourse; for wherever he moved he was master, and whenever he spoke, even when in chains, every other voice was silent. He stood on the mead, grim and pale as usual, with his bruisers around. He it was, indeed, who GOT UP the fight, as he had previously done twenty others; it being his frequent boast that he had first introduced bruising and bloodshed amidst rural scenes, and transformed a quiet slumbering town into a den of Jews and metropolitan thieves. Some time before the commencement of the combat, three men, mounted on wild-looking horses, came dashing down the road in the direction of the meadow, in the midst of which they presently showed themselves, their horses clearing the deep ditches with wonderful alacrity. 'That's Gypsy Will and his gang,' lisped a Hebrew pickpocket; 'we shall have another fight.' The word Gypsy was always sufficient to excite my curiosity, and I looked attentively at the newcomers.

I have seen Gypsies of various lands, Russian, Hungarian, and Turkish; and I have also seen the legitimate children of most countries of the world; but I never saw, upon the whole, three more remarkable individuals, as far as personal appearance was concerned, than the three English Gypsies who now presented themselves to my eyes on that spot. Two of them had dismounted, and were holding their horses by the reins. The tallest, and, at the first glance, the most interesting of the two, was almost a giant, for his height could not have been less than six feet three. It is impossible for the imagination to conceive anything more perfectly beautiful than were the features of this man, and the most skilful sculptor of Greece might have taken them as his model for a hero and a god. The forehead was exceedingly lofty, - a rare thing in a Gypsy; the nose less Roman than Grecian, - fine yet delicate; the eyes large, overhung with long drooping lashes, giving them almost a melancholy expression; it was only when the lashes were elevated that the Gypsy glance was seen, if that can be called a glance which is a strange stare, like nothing else in this world. His complexion was a beautiful olive; and his teeth were of a brilliancy uncommon even amongst these people, who have all fine teeth. He was dressed in a coarse waggoner's slop, which, however, was unable to conceal altogether the proportions of his noble and Herculean figure. He might be about twenty-eight. His companion and his captain, Gypsy Will, was, I think, fifty when he was hanged, ten years subsequently (for I never afterwards lost sight of him), in the front of the jail of Bury St. Edmunds. I have still present before me his bushy black hair, his black face, and his big black eyes fixed and staring. His dress consisted of a loose blue jockey coat, jockey boots and breeches; in his hand was a huge jockey whip, and on his head (it struck me at the time for its singularity) a broad-brimmed, high-peaked Andalusian hat, or at least one very much resembling those generally worn in that province. In stature he was shorter than his more youthful companion, yet he must have measured six feet at least, and was stronger built, if possible. What brawn! - what bone! - what legs! - what thighs! The third Gypsy, who remained on horseback, looked more like a phantom than any thing human. His complexion was the colour of pale dust, and of that same colour was all that pertained to him, hat and clothes. His boots were dusty of course, for it was midsummer, and his very horse was of a dusty dun. His features were whimsically ugly, most of his teeth were gone, and as to his age, he might be thirty or sixty. He was somewhat lame and halt, but an unequalled rider when once upon his steed, which he was naturally not very solicitous to quit. I subsequently discovered that he was considered the wizard of the gang.

I have been already prolix with respect to these Gypsies, but I will not leave them quite yet. The intended combatants at length arrived; it was necessary to clear the ring, - always a troublesome and difficult task. Thurtell went up to the two Gypsies, with whom he seemed to be acquainted, and with his surly smile, said two or three words, which I, who was standing by, did not understand. The Gypsies smiled in return, and giving the reins of their animals to their mounted companion, immediately set about the task which the king of the flash-men had, as I conjecture, imposed upon them; this they soon accomplished. Who could stand against such fellows and such whips? The fight was soon over - then there was a pause. Once more Thurtell came up to the Gypsies and said something - the Gypsies looked at each other and conversed; but their words then had no meaning for my ears. The tall Gypsy shook his head - 'Very well,' said the other, in English. 'I will - that's all.'

Then pushing the people aside, he strode to the ropes, over which he bounded into the ring, flinging his Spanish hat high into the air.

GYPSY WILL. - 'The best man in England for twenty pounds!'

'THURTELL. - 'I am backer!'

Twenty pounds is a tempting sum, and there men that day upon the green meadow who would have shed the blood of their own fathers for the fifth of the price. But the Gypsy was not an unknown man, his prowess and strength were notorious, and no one cared to encounter him. Some of the Jews looked eager for a moment; but their sharp eyes quailed quickly before his savage glances, as he towered in the ring, his huge form dilating, and his black features convulsed with excitement. The Westminster bravoes eyed the Gypsy askance; but the comparison, if they made any, seemed by no means favourable to themselves. 'Gypsy! rum chap. - Ugly customer, - always in training.' Such were the exclamations which I heard, some of which at that period of my life I did not understand.

No man would fight the Gypsy. - Yes! a strong country fellow wished to win the stakes, and was about to fling up his hat in defiance, but he was prevented by his friends, with - 'Fool! he'll kill you!'

As the Gypsies were mounting their horses, I heard the dusty phantom exclaim -

'Brother, you are an arrant ring-maker and a horse-breaker; you'll make a hempen ring to break your own neck of a horse one of these days.'

They pressed their horses' flanks, again leaped over the ditches, and speedily vanished, amidst the whirlwinds of dust which they raised upon the road.

The words of the phantom Gypsy were ominous. Gypsy Will was eventually executed for a murder committed in his early youth, in company with two English labourers, one of whom confessed the fact on his death-bed. He was the head of the clan Young, which, with the clan Smith, still haunts two of the eastern counties.

SOME FURTHER PARTICULARS RESPECTING THE ENGLISH GYPSIES

It is difficult to say at what period the Gypsies or Rommany made their first appearance in England. They had become, however, such a nuisance in the time of Henry the Eighth, Philip and Mary, and Elizabeth, that Gypsyism was denounced by various royal statutes, and, if persisted in, was to be punished as felony without benefit of clergy; it is probable, however, that they had overrun England long before the period of the earliest of these monarchs. The Gypsies penetrate into all countries, save poor ones, and it is hardly to be supposed that a few leagues of intervening salt water would have kept a race so enterprising any considerable length of time, after their arrival on the continent of Europe, from obtaining a footing in the fairest and richest country of the West.

It is easy enough to conceive the manner in which the Gypsies lived in England for a long time subsequent to their arrival: doubtless in a half-savage state, wandering about from place to place, encamping on the uninhabited spots, of which there were then so many in England, feared and hated by the population, who looked upon them as thieves and foreign sorcerers, occasionally committing acts of brigandage, but depending chiefly for subsistence on the practice of the 'arts of Egypt,' in which cunning and dexterity were far more necessary than courage or strength of hand.

It would appear that they were always divided into clans or tribes, each bearing a particular name, and to which a particular district more especially belonged, though occasionally they would exchange districts for a period, and, incited by their characteristic love of wandering, would travel far and wide. Of these families each had a sher-engro, or head man, but that they were ever united under one Rommany Krallis, or Gypsy King, as some people have insisted, there is not the slightest ground for supposing.

It is possible that many of the original Gypsy tribes are no longer in existence: disease or the law may have made sad havoc among them, and the few survivors have incorporated themselves with other families, whose name they have adopted. Two or three instances of this description have occurred within the sphere of my own knowledge: the heads of small families have been cut off, and the subordinate members, too young and inexperienced to continue Gypsying as independent wanderers, have been adopted by other tribes.

The principal Gypsy tribes at present in existence are the Stanleys, whose grand haunt is the New Forest; the Lovells, who are fond of London and its vicinity; the Coopers, who call Windsor Castle their home; the Hernes, to whom the north country, more especially Yorkshire, belongeth; and lastly, my brethren, the Smiths, - to whom East Anglia appears to have been allotted from the beginning.

All these families have Gypsy names, which seem, however, to be little more than attempts at translation of the English ones:- thus the Stanleys are called Bar-engres[11], which means stony-fellows, or stony-hearts; the Coopers, Wardo-engres, or wheelwrights; the Lovells, Camo-mescres, or amorous fellows the Hernes (German Haaren) Balors, hairs, or hairy men; while the Smiths are called Petul-engres, signifying horseshoe fellows, or blacksmiths.

It is not very easy to determine how the Gypsies became possessed of some of these names: the reader, however, will have observed that two of them, Stanley and Lovell, are the names of two highly aristocratic English families; the Gypsies who bear them perhaps adopted them from having, at their first arrival, established themselves on the estates of those great people; or it is possible that they translated their original Gypsy appellations by these names, which they deemed synonymous. Much the same may be said with respect to Herne, an ancient English name; they probably sometimes officiated as coopers or wheelwrights, whence the cognomination. Of the term Petul-engro, or Smith, however, I wish to say something in particular.

There is every reason for believing that this last is a genuine Gypsy name, brought with them from the country from which they originally came; it is compounded of two words, signifying, as has been already observed, horseshoe fellows, or people whose trade is to manufacture horseshoes, a trade which the Gypsies ply in various parts of the world, - for example, in Russia and Hungary, and more particularly about Granada in Spain, as will subsequently be shown. True it is, that at present there are none amongst the English Gypsies who manufacture horseshoes; all the men, however, are tinkers more or less, and the word Petul-engro is applied to the tinker also, though the proper meaning of it is undoubtedly what I have already stated above. In other dialects of the Gypsy tongue, this cognomen exists, though not exactly with the same signification; for example, in the Hungarian dialect, PINDORO, which is evidently a modification of Petul-engro, is applied to a Gypsy in general, whilst in Spanish Pepindorio is the Gypsy word for Antonio. In some parts of Northern Asia, the Gypsies call themselves Wattul[12], which seems to be one and the same as Petul.

Besides the above-named Gypsy clans, there are other smaller ones, some of which do not comprise more than a dozen individuals, children included. For example, the Bosviles, the Browns, the Chilcotts, the Grays, Lees, Taylors, and Whites; of these the principal is the Bosvile tribe.

After the days of the great persecution in England against the Gypsies, there can be little doubt that they lived a right merry and tranquil life, wandering about and pitching their tents wherever inclination led them: indeed, I can scarcely conceive any human condition more enviable than Gypsy life must have been in England during the latter part of the seventeenth, and the whole of the eighteenth century, which were likewise the happy days for Englishmen in general; there was peace and plenty in the land, a contented population, and everything went well. Yes, those were brave times for the Rommany chals, to which the old people often revert with a sigh: the poor Gypsies, say they, were then allowed to SOVE ABRI (sleep abroad) where they listed, to heat their kettles at the foot of the oaks, and no people grudged the poor persons one night's use of a meadow to feed their cattle in. TUGNIS AMANDE, our heart is heavy, brother, - there is no longer Gypsy law in the land, - our people have become negligent, - they are but half Rommany, - they are divided and care for nothing, - they do not even fear Pazorrhus, brother.

Much the same complaints are at present made by the Spanish Gypsies. Gypsyism is certainly on the decline in both countries. In England, a superabundant population, and, of late, a very vigilant police, have done much to modify Gypsy life; whilst in Spain, causes widely different have produced a still greater change, as will be seen further on.

Gypsy law does not flourish at present in England, and still less in Spain, nor does Gypsyism. I need not explain here what Gypsyism is, but the reader may be excused for asking what is Gypsy law. Gypsy law divides itself into the three following heads or precepts:-

Separate not from THE HUSBANDS.
Be faithful to THE HUSBANDS.
Pay your debts to THE HUSBANDS.

By the first section the Rom or Gypsy is enjoined to live with his brethren, the husbands, and not with the gorgios[13] or gentiles; he is to live in a tent, as is befitting a Rom and a wanderer, and not in a house, which ties him to one spot; in a word, he is in every respect to conform to the ways of his own people, and to eschew those of gorgios, with whom he is not to mix, save to tell them HOQUEPENES (lies), and to chore them.

The second section, in which fidelity is enjoined, was more particularly intended for the women: be faithful to the ROMS, ye JUWAS, and take not up with the gorgios, whether they be RAIOR or BAUOR (gentlemen or fellows). This was a very important injunction, so much so, indeed, that upon the observance of it depended the very existence of the Rommany sect, - for if the female Gypsy admitted the gorgio to the privilege of the Rom, the race of the Rommany would quickly disappear. How well this injunction has been observed needs scarcely be said; for the Rommany have been roving about England for three centuries at least, and are still to be distinguished from the gorgios in feature and complexion, which assuredly would not have been the case if the juwas had not been faithful to the Roms. The gorgio says that the juwa is at his disposal in all things, because she tells him fortunes and endures his free discourse; but the Rom, when he hears the boast, laughs within his sleeve, and whispers to himself, LET HIM TRY.

The third section, which relates to the paying of debts, is highly curious. In the Gypsy language, the state of being in debt is called PAZORRHUS, and the Rom who did not seek to extricate himself from that state was deemed infamous, and eventually turned out of the society. It has been asserted, I believe, by various gorgio writers, that the Roms have everything in common, and that there is a common stock out of which every one takes what he needs; this is quite a mistake, however: a Gypsy tribe is an epitome of the world; every one keeps his own purse and maintains himself and children to the best of his ability, and every tent is independent of the other. True it is that one Gypsy will lend to another in the expectation of being repaid, and until that happen the borrower is pazorrhus, or indebted. Even at the present time, a Gypsy will make the greatest sacrifices rather than remain pazorrhus to one of his brethren, even though he be of another clan; though perhaps the feeling is not so strong as of old, for time modifies everything; even Jews and Gypsies are affected by it. In the old time, indeed, the Gypsy law was so strong against the debtor, that provided he could not repay his brother husband, he was delivered over to him as his slave for a year and a day, and compelled to serve him as a hewer of wood, a drawer of water, or a beast of burden; but those times are past, the Gypsies are no longer the independent people they were of yore, - dark, mysterious, and dreaded wanderers, living apart in the deserts and heaths with which England at one time abounded. Gypsy law has given place to common law; but the principle of honour is still recognised amongst them, and base indeed must the Gypsy be who would continue pazorrhus because Gypsy law has become too weak to force him to liquidate a debt by money or by service.

Such was Gypsy law in England, and there is every probability that it is much the same in all parts of the world where the Gypsy race is to be found. About the peculiar practices of the Gypsies I need not say much here; the reader will find in the account of the Spanish Gypsies much that will afford him an idea of Gypsy arts in England. I have already alluded to CHIVING DRAV, or poisoning, which is still much practised by the English Gypsies, though it has almost entirely ceased in Spain; then there is CHIVING LUVVU ADREY PUVO, or putting money within the earth, a trick by which the females deceive the gorgios, and which will be more particularly described in the affairs of Spain: the men are adepts at cheating the gorgios by means of NOK-ENGROES and POGGADO-BAVENGROES (glandered and broken-winded horses). But, leaving the subject of their tricks and Rommany arts, by no means an agreeable one, I will take the present opportunity of saying a few words about a practice of theirs, highly characteristic of a wandering people, and which is only extant amongst those of the race who still continue to wander much; for example, the Russian Gypsies and those of the Hungarian family, who stroll through Italy on plundering expeditions: I allude to the PATTERAN or TRAIL.

It is very possible that the reader during his country walks or rides has observed, on coming to four cross-roads, two or three handfuls of grass lying at a small distance from each other down one of these roads; perhaps he may have supposed that this grass was recently plucked from the roadside by frolicsome children, and flung upon the ground in sport, and this may possibly have been the case; it is ten chances to one, however, that no children's hands plucked them, but that they were strewed in this manner by Gypsies, for the purpose of informing any of their companions, who might be straggling behind, the route which they had taken; this is one form of the patteran or trail. It is likely, too, that the gorgio reader may have seen a cross drawn at the entrance of a road, the long part or stem of it pointing down that particular road, and he may have thought nothing of it, or have supposed that some sauntering individual like himself had made the mark with his stick: not so, courteous gorgio; ley tiro solloholomus opre lesti, YOU MAY TAKE YOUR OATH UPON IT that it was drawn by a Gypsy finger, for that mark is another of the Rommany trails; there is no mistake in this. Once in the south of France, when I was weary, hungry, and penniless, I observed one of these last patterans, and following the direction pointed out, arrived at the resting-place of 'certain Bohemians,' by whom I was received with kindness and hospitality, on the faith of no other word of recommendation than patteran. There is also another kind of patteran, which is more particularly adapted for the night; it is a cleft stick stuck at the side of the road, close by the hedge, with a little arm in the cleft pointing down the road which the band have taken, in the manner of a signpost; any stragglers who may arrive at night where cross-roads occur search for this patteran on the left-hand side, and speedily rejoin their companions.

By following these patterans, or trails, the first Gypsies on their way to Europe never lost each other, though wandering amidst horrid wildernesses and dreary defiles. Rommany matters have always had a peculiar interest for me; nothing, however, connected with Gypsy life ever more captivated my imagination than this patteran system: many thanks to the Gypsies for it; it has more than once been of service to me.

The English Gypsies at the present day are far from being a numerous race; I consider their aggregate number, from the opportunities which I have had of judging, to be considerably under ten thousand: it is probable that, ere the conclusion of the present century, they will have entirely disappeared. They are in general quite strangers to the commonest rudiments of education; few even of the most wealthy can either read or write. With respect to religion, they call themselves members of the Established Church, and are generally anxious to have their children baptized, and to obtain a copy of the register. Some of their baptismal papers, which they carry about with them, are highly curious, going back for a period of upwards of two hundred years. With respect to the essential points of religion, they are quite careless and ignorant; if they believe in a future state they dread it not, and if they manifest when dying any anxiety, it is not for the soul, but the body: a handsome coffin, and a grave in a quiet country churchyard, are invariably the objects of their last thoughts; and it is probable that, in their observance of the rite of baptism, they are principally influenced by a desire to enjoy the privilege of burial in consecrated ground. A Gypsy family never speak of their dead save with regret and affection, and any request of the dying individual is attended to, especially with regard to interment; so much so, that I have known a corpse conveyed a distance of nearly one hundred miles, because the deceased expressed a wish to be buried in a particular spot.

Of the language of the English Gypsies, some specimens will be given in the sequel; it is much more pure and copious than the Spanish dialect. It has been asserted that the English Gypsies are not possessed of any poetry in their own tongue; but this is a gross error; they possess a great many songs and ballads upon ordinary subjects, without any particular merit, however, and seemingly of a very modern date.

THE GYPSIES OF THE EAST, OR ZINGARRI

What has been said of the Gypsies of Europe is, to a considerable extent, applicable to their brethren in the East, or, as they are called, Zingarri; they are either found wandering amongst the deserts or mountains, or settled in towns, supporting themselves by horse-dealing or jugglery, by music and song. In no part of the East are they more numerous than in Turkey, especially in Constantinople, where the females frequently enter the harems of the great, pretending to cure children of 'the evil eye,' and to interpret the dreams of the women. They are not unfrequently seen in the coffee-houses, exhibiting their figures in lascivious dances to the tune of various instruments; yet these females are by no means unchaste, however their manners and appearance may denote the contrary, and either Turk or Christian who, stimulated by their songs and voluptuous movements, should address them with proposals of a dishonourable nature, would, in all probability, meet with a decided repulse.

Among the Zingarri are not a few who deal in precious stones, and some who vend poisons; and the most remarkable individual whom it has been my fortune to encounter amongst the Gypsies, whether of the Eastern or Western world, was a person who dealt in both these articles. He was a native of Constantinople, and in the pursuit of his trade had visited the most remote and remarkable portions of the world. He had traversed alone and on foot the greatest part of India; he spoke several dialects of the Malay, and understood the original language of Java, that isle more fertile in poisons than even 'far Iolchos and Spain.' From what I could learn from him, it appeared that his jewels were in less request than his drugs, though he assured me that there was scarcely a Bey or Satrap in Persia or Turkey whom he had not supplied with both. I have seen this individual in more countries than one, for he flits over the world like the shadow of a cloud; the last time at Granada in Spain, whither he had come after paying a visit to his Gitano brethren in the presidio of Ceuta.

Few Eastern authors have spoken of the Zingarri, notwithstanding they have been known in the East for many centuries; amongst the few, none has made more curious mention of them than Arabschah, in a chapter of his life of Timour or Tamerlane, which is deservedly considered as one of the three classic works of Arabian literature. This passage, which, while it serves to illustrate the craft, if not the valour of the conqueror of half the world, offers some curious particulars as to Gypsy life in the East at a remote period, will scarcely be considered out of place if reproduced here, and the following is as close a translation of it as the metaphorical style of the original will allow.

'There were in Samarcand numerous families of Zingarri of various descriptions: some were wrestlers, others gladiators, others pugilists. These people were much at variance, so that hostilities and battling were continually arising amongst them. Each band had its chief and subordinate officers; and it came to pass that Timour and the power which he possessed filled them with dread, for they knew that he was aware of their crimes and disorderly way of life. Now it was the custom of Timour, on departing upon his expeditions, to leave a viceroy in Samarcand; but no sooner had he left the city, than forth marched these bands, and giving battle to the viceroy, deposed him and took possession of the government, so that on the return of Timour he found order broken, confusion reigning, and his throne overturned, and then he had much to do in restoring things to their former state, and in punishing or pardoning the guilty; but no sooner did he depart again to his wars, and to his various other concerns, than they broke out into the same excesses, and this they repeated no less than three times, and he at length laid a plan for their utter extermination, and it was the following:- He commenced building a wall, and he summoned unto him the people small and great, and he allotted to every man his place, and to every workman his duty, and he stationed the Zingarri and their chieftains apart; and in one particular spot he placed a band of soldiers, and he commanded them to kill whomsoever he should send to them; and having done so, he called to him the heads of the people, and he filled the cup for them and clothed them in splendid vests; and when the turn came to the Zingarri, he likewise pledged one of them, and bestowed a vest upon him, and sent him with a message to the soldiers, who, as soon as he arrived, tore from him his vest, and stabbed him, pouring forth the gold of his heart into the pan of destruction,[14] and in this way they continued until the last of them was destroyed; and by that blow he exterminated their race, and their traces, and from that time forward there were no more rebellions in Samarcand.'

It has of late years been one of the favourite theories of the learned, that Timour's invasion of Hindostan, and the cruelties committed by his savage hordes in that part of the world, caused a vast number of Hindoos to abandon their native land, and that the Gypsies of the present day are the descendants of those exiles who wended their weary way to the West. Now, provided the above passage in the work of Arabschah be entitled to credence, the opinion that Timour was the cause of the expatriation and subsequent wandering life of these people, must be abandoned as untenable. At the time he is stated by the Arabian writer to have annihilated the Gypsy hordes of Samarcand, he had but just commenced his career of conquest and devastation, and had not even directed his thoughts to the invasion of India; yet at this early period of the history of his life, we find families of Zingarri established at Samarcand, living much in the same manner as others of the race have subsequently done in various towns of Europe and the East; but supposing the event here narrated to be a fable, or at best a floating legend, it appears singular that, if they left their native land to escape from Timour, they should never have mentioned in the Western world the name of that scourge of the human race, nor detailed the history of their flight and sufferings, which assuredly would have procured them sympathy; the ravages of Timour being already but too well known in Europe. That they came from India is much easier to prove than that they fled before the fierce Mongol.

Such people as the Gypsies, whom the Bishop of Forli in the year 1422, only sixteen years subsequent to the invasion of India, describes as a 'raging rabble, of brutal and animal propensities,' [15] are not such as generally abandon their country on foreign invasion.

PART I

CHAPTER I

GITANOS, or Egyptians, is the name by which the Gypsies have been most generally known in Spain, in the ancient as well as in the modern period, but various other names have been and still are applied to them; for example, New Castilians, Germans, and Flemings; the first of which titles probably originated after the name of Gitano had begun to be considered a term of reproach and infamy. They may have thus designated themselves from an unwillingness to utter, when speaking of themselves, the detested expression 'Gitano,' a word which seldom escapes their mouths; or it may have been applied to them first by the Spaniards, in their mutual dealings and communication, as a term less calculated to wound their feelings and to beget a spirit of animosity than the other; but, however it might have originated, New Castilian, in course of time, became a term of little less infamy than Gitano; for, by the law of Philip the Fourth, both terms are forbidden to be applied to them under severe penalties.

That they were called Germans, may be accounted for, either by the supposition that their generic name of Rommany was misunderstood and mispronounced by the Spaniards amongst whom they came, or from the fact of their having passed through Germany in their way to the south, and bearing passports and letters of safety from the various German states. The title of Flemings, by which at the present day they are known in various parts of Spain, would probably never have been bestowed upon them but from the circumstance of their having been designated or believed to be Germans, - as German and Fleming are considered by the ignorant as synonymous terms.

Amongst themselves they have three words to distinguish them and their race in general: Zincalo, Romano, and Chai; of the first two of which something has been already said.

They likewise call themselves 'Cales,' by which appellation indeed they are tolerably well known by the Spaniards, and which is merely the plural termination of the compound word Zincalo, and signifies, The black men. Chai is a modification of the word Chal, which, by the Gitanos of Estremadura, is applied to Egypt, and in many parts of Spain is equivalent to 'Heaven,' and which is perhaps a modification of 'Cheros,' the word for heaven in other dialects of the Gypsy language. Thus Chai may denote, The men of Egypt, or, The sons of Heaven. It is, however, right to observe, that amongst the Gitanos, the word Chai has frequently no other signification than the simple one of 'children.'

It is impossible to state for certainty the exact year of their first appearance in Spain; but it is reasonable to presume that it was early in the fifteenth century; as in the year 1417 numerous bands entered France from the north-east of Europe, and speedily spread themselves over the greatest part of that country. Of these wanderers a French author has left the following graphic description:[16]

'On the 17th of April 1427, appeared in Paris twelve penitents of Egypt, driven from thence by the Saracens; they brought in their company one hundred and twenty persons; they took up their quarters in La Chapelle, whither the people flocked in crowds to visit them. They had their ears pierced, from which depended a ring of silver; their hair was black and crispy, and their women were filthy to a degree, and were sorceresses who told fortunes.'

Such were the people who, after traversing France and scaling the sides of the Pyrenees, poured down in various bands upon the sunburnt plains of Spain. Wherever they had appeared they had been looked upon as a curse and a pestilence, and with much reason. Either unwilling or unable to devote themselves to any laborious or useful occupation, they came like flights of wasps to prey upon the fruits which their more industrious fellow-beings amassed by the toil of their hands and the sweat of their foreheads; the natural result being, that wherever they arrived, their fellow-creatures banded themselves against them. Terrible laws were enacted soon after their appearance in France, calculated to put a stop to their frauds and dishonest propensities; wherever their hordes were found, they were attacked by the incensed rustics or by the armed hand of justice, and those who were not massacred on the spot, or could not escape by flight, were, without a shadow of a trial, either hanged on the next tree, or sent to serve for life in the galleys; or if females or children, either scourged or mutilated.

The consequence of this severity, which, considering the manners and spirit of the time, is scarcely to be wondered at, was the speedy disappearance of the Gypsies from the soil of France.

Many returned by the way they came, to Germany, Hungary, and the woods and forests of Bohemia; but there is little doubt that by far the greater portion found a refuge in the Peninsula, a country which, though by no means so rich and fertile as the one they had quitted, nor offering so wide and ready a field for the exercise of those fraudulent arts for which their race had become so infamously notorious, was, nevertheless, in many respects, suitable and congenial to them. If there were less gold and silver in the purses of the citizens to reward the dexterous handler of the knife and scissors amidst the crowd in the market-place; if fewer sides of fatted swine graced the ample chimney of the labourer in Spain than in the neighbouring country; if fewer beeves bellowed in the plains, and fewer sheep bleated upon the hills, there were far better opportunities afforded of indulging in wild independence. Should the halberded bands of the city be ordered out to quell, seize, or exterminate them; should the alcalde of the village cause the tocsin to be rung, gathering together the villanos for a similar purpose, the wild sierra was generally at hand, which, with its winding paths, its caves, its frowning precipices, and ragged thickets, would offer to them a secure refuge where they might laugh to scorn the rage of their baffled pursuers, and from which they might emerge either to fresh districts or to those which they had left, to repeat their ravages when opportunity served.

After crossing the Pyrenees, a very short time elapsed before the Gypsy hordes had bivouacked in the principal provinces of Spain. There can indeed be little doubt, that shortly after their arrival they made themselves perfectly acquainted with all the secrets of the land, and that there was scarcely a nook or retired corner within Spain, from which the smoke of their fires had not arisen, or where their cattle had not grazed. People, however, so acute as they have always proverbially been, would scarcely be slow in distinguishing the provinces most adapted to their manner of life, and most calculated to afford them opportunities of practising those arts to which they were mainly indebted for their subsistence; the savage hills of Biscay, of Galicia, and the Asturias, whose inhabitants were almost as poor as themselves, which possessed no superior breed of horses or mules from amongst which they might pick and purloin many a gallant beast, and having transformed by their dexterous scissors, impose him again upon his rightful master for a high price, - such provinces, where, moreover, provisions were hard to be obtained, even by pilfering hands, could scarcely be supposed to offer strong temptations to these roving visitors to settle down in, or to vex and harass by a long sojourn.

Valencia and Murcia found far more favour in their eyes; a far more fertile soil, and wealthier inhabitants, were better calculated to entice them; there was a prospect of plunder, and likewise a prospect of safety and refuge, should the dogs of justice be roused against them. If there were the populous town and village in those lands, there was likewise the lone waste, and uncultivated spot, to which they could retire when danger threatened them. Still more suitable to them must have been La Mancha, a land of tillage, of horses, and of mules, skirted by its brown sierra, ever eager to afford its shelter to their dusky race. Equally suitable, Estremadura and New Castile; but far, far more, Andalusia, with its three kingdoms, Jaen, Granada, and Seville, one of which was still possessed by the swarthy Moor, - Andalusia, the land of the proud steed and the stubborn mule, the land of the savage sierra and the fruitful and cultivated plain: to Andalusia they hied, in bands of thirties and sixties; the hoofs of their asses might be heard clattering in the passes of the stony hills; the girls might be seen bounding in lascivious dance in the streets of many a town, and the beldames standing beneath the eaves telling the 'buena ventura' to many a credulous female dupe; the men the while chaffered in the fair and market-place with the labourers and chalanes, casting significant glances on each other, or exchanging a word or two in Rommany, whilst they placed some uncouth animal in a particular posture which served to conceal its ugliness from the eyes of the chapman. Yes, of all provinces of Spain, Andalusia was the most frequented by the Gitano race, and in Andalusia they most abound at the present day, though no longer as restless independent wanderers of the fields and hills, but as residents in villages and towns, especially in Seville.

CHAPTER II

HAVING already stated to the reader at what period and by what means these wanderers introduced themselves into Spain, we shall now say something concerning their manner of life.

It would appear that, for many years after their arrival in the Peninsula, their manners and habits underwent no change; they were wanderers, in the strictest sense of the word, and lived much in the same way as their brethren exist in the present day in England, Russia, and Bessarabia, with the exception perhaps of being more reckless, mischievous, and having less respect for the laws; it is true that their superiority in wickedness in these points may have been more the effect of the moral state of the country in which they were, than of any other operating cause.

Arriving in Spain with a predisposition to every species of crime and villainy, they were not likely to be improved or reclaimed by the example of the people with whom they were about to mix; nor was it probable that they would entertain much respect for laws which, from time immemorial, have principally served, not to protect the honest and useful members of society, but to enrich those entrusted with the administration of them. Thus, if they came thieves, it is not probable that they would become ashamed of the title of thief in Spain, where the officers of justice were ever willing to shield an offender on receiving the largest portion of the booty obtained. If on their arrival they held the lives of others in very low estimation, could it be expected that they would become gentle as lambs in a land where blood had its price, and the shedder was seldom executed unless he was poor and friendless, and unable to cram with ounces of yellow gold the greedy hands of the pursuers of blood, - the alguazil and escribano? therefore, if the Spanish Gypsies have been more bloody and more wolfishly eager in the pursuit of booty than those of their race in most other regions, the cause must be attributed to their residence in a country unsound in every branch of its civil polity, where right has ever been in less esteem, and wrong in less disrepute, than in any other part of the world.

However, if the moral state of Spain was not calculated to have a favourable effect on the habits and pursuits of the Gypsies, their manners were as little calculated to operate beneficially, in any point of view, on the country where they had lately arrived. Divided into numerous bodies, frequently formidable in point of number, their presence was an evil and a curse in whatever quarter they directed their steps. As might be expected, the labourers, who in all countries are the most honest, most useful, and meritorious class, were the principal sufferers; their mules and horses were stolen, carried away to distant fairs, and there disposed of, perhaps, to individuals destined to be deprived of them in a similar manner; whilst their flocks of sheep and goats were laid under requisition to assuage the hungry cravings of these thievish cormorants.

It was not uncommon for a large band or tribe to encamp in the vicinity of a remote village scantily peopled, and to remain there until, like a flight of locusts, they had consumed everything which the inhabitants possessed for their support; or until they were scared away by the approach of justice, or by an army of rustics assembled from the surrounding country. Then would ensue the hurried march; the women and children, mounted on lean but spirited asses, would scour along the plains fleeter than the wind; ragged and savage-looking men, wielding the scourge and goad, would scamper by their side or close behind, whilst perhaps a small party on strong horses, armed with rusty matchlocks or sabres, would bring up the rear, threatening the distant foe, and now and then saluting them with a hoarse blast from the Gypsy horn:-

'O, when I sit my courser bold,
My bantling in my rear,
And in my hand my musket hold -
O how they quake with fear!'

Let us for a moment suppose some unfortunate traveller, mounted on a handsome mule or beast of some value, meeting, unarmed and alone, such a rabble rout at the close of eve, in the wildest part, for example, of La Mancha; we will suppose that he is journeying from Seville to Madrid, and that he has left at a considerable distance behind him the gloomy and horrible passes of the Sierra Morena; his bosom, which for some time past has been contracted with dreadful forebodings, is beginning to expand; his blood, which has been congealed in his veins, is beginning to circulate warmly and freely; he is fondly anticipating the still distant posada and savoury omelet. The sun is sinking rapidly behind the savage and uncouth hills in his rear; he has reached the bottom of a small valley, where runs a rivulet at which he allows his tired animal to drink; he is about to ascend the side of the hill; his eyes are turned upwards; suddenly he beholds strange and uncouth forms at the top of the ascent - the sun descending slants its rays upon red cloaks, with here and there a turbaned head, or long streaming hair. The traveller hesitates, but reflecting that he is no longer in the mountains, and that in the open road there is no danger of banditti, he advances. In a moment he is in the midst of the Gypsy group, in a moment there is a general halt; fiery eyes are turned upon him replete with an expression which only the eyes of the Roma possess, then ensues a jabber in a language or jargon which is strange to the ears of the traveller; at last an ugly urchin springs from the crupper of a halting mule, and in a lisping accent entreats charity in the name of the Virgin and the Majoro. The traveller, with a faltering hand, produces his purse, and is proceeding to loosen its strings, but he accomplishes not his purpose, for, struck violently by a huge knotted club in an unseen hand, he tumbles headlong from his mule. Next morning a naked corse, besmeared with brains and blood, is found by an arriero; and within a week a simple cross records the event, according to the custom of Spain.

'Below there in the dusky pass
Was wrought a murder dread;
The murdered fell upon the grass,
way the murderer fled.'

To many, such a scene, as above described, will appear purely imaginary, or at least a mass of exaggeration, but many such anecdotes are related by old Spanish writers of these people; they traversed the country in gangs; they were what the Spanish law has styled Abigeos and Salteadores de Camino, cattle-stealers and highwaymen; though, in the latter character, they never rose to any considerable eminence. True it is that they would not hesitate to attack or even murder the unarmed and defenceless traveller, when they felt assured of obtaining booty with little or no risk to themselves; but they were not by constitution adapted to rival those bold and daring banditti of whom so many terrible anecdotes are related in Spain and Italy, and who have acquired their renown by the dauntless daring which they have invariably displayed in the pursuit of plunder.

Besides trafficking in horses and mules, and now and then attacking and plundering travellers upon the highway, the Gypsies of Spain appear, from a very early period, to have plied occasionally the trade of the blacksmith, and to have worked in iron, forming rude implements of domestic and agricultural use, which they disposed of, either for provisions or money, in the neighbourhood of those places where they had taken up their temporary residence. As their bands were composed of numerous individuals, there is no improbability in assuming that to every member was allotted that branch of labour in which he was most calculated to excel. The most important, and that which required the greatest share of cunning and address, was undoubtedly that of the chalan or jockey, who frequented the fairs with the beasts which he had obtained by various means, but generally by theft. Highway robbery, though occasionally committed by all jointly or severally, was probably the peculiar department of the boldest spirits of the gang; whilst wielding the hammer and tongs was abandoned to those who, though possessed of athletic forms, were perhaps, like Vulcan, lame, or from some particular cause, moral or physical, unsuited for the other two very respectable avocations. The forge was generally placed in the heart of some mountain abounding in wood; the gaunt smiths felled a tree, perhaps with the very axes which their own sturdy hands had hammered at a former period; with the wood thus procured they prepared the charcoal which their labour demanded. Everything is in readiness; the bellows puff until the coal is excited to a furious glow; the metal, hot, pliant, and ductile, is laid on the anvil, round which stands the Cyclop group, their hammers upraised; down they descend successively, one, two, three, the sparks are scattered on every side. The sparks -

'More than a hundred lovely daughters I see produced at one time, fiery as roses: in one moment they expire gracefully circumvolving.'[17]

The anvil rings beneath the thundering stroke, hour succeeds hour, and still endures the hard sullen toil.

One of the most remarkable features in the history of Gypsies is the striking similarity of their pursuits in every region of the globe to which they have penetrated; they are not merely alike in limb and in feature, in the cast and expression of the eye, in the colour of the hair, in their walk and gait, but everywhere they seem to exhibit the same tendencies, and to hunt for their bread by the same means, as if they were not of the human but rather of the animal species, and in lieu of reason were endowed with a kind of instinct which assists them to a very limited extent and no farther.

In no part of the world are they found engaged in the cultivation of the earth, or in the service of a regular master; but in all lands they are jockeys, or thieves, or cheats; and if ever they devote themselves to any toil or trade, it is assuredly in every material point one and the same. We have found them above, in the heart of a wild mountain, hammering iron, and manufacturing from it instruments either for their own use or that of the neighbouring towns and villages. They may be seen employed in a similar manner in the plains of Russia, or in the bosom of its eternal forests; and whoever inspects the site where a horde of Gypsies has encamped, in the grassy lanes beneath the hazel bushes of merry England, is generally sure to find relics of tin and other metal, avouching that they have there been exercising the arts of the tinker or smith. Perhaps nothing speaks more forcibly for the antiquity of this sect or caste than the tenacity with which they have uniformly preserved their peculiar customs since the period of their becoming generally known; for, unless their habits had become a part of their nature, which could only have been effected by a strict devotion to them through a long succession of generations, it is not to be supposed that after their arrival in civilised Europe they would have retained and cherished them precisely in the same manner in the various countries where they found an asylum.

Each band or family of the Spanish Gypsies had its Captain, or, as he was generally designated, its Count. Don Juan de Quinones, who, in a small volume published in 1632, has written some details respecting their way of life, says: 'They roam about, divided into families and troops, each of which has its head or Count; and to fill this office they choose the most valiant and courageous individual amongst them, and the one endowed with the greatest strength. He must at the same time be crafty and sagacious, and adapted in every respect to govern them. It is he who settles their differences and disputes, even when they are residing in a place where there is a regular justice. He heads them at night when they go out to plunder the flocks, or to rob travellers on the highway; and whatever they steal or plunder they divide amongst them, always allowing the captain a third part of the whole.'

These Counts, being elected for such qualities as promised to be useful to their troop or family, were consequently liable to be deposed if at any time their conduct was not calculated to afford satisfaction to their subjects. The office was not hereditary, and though it carried along with it partial privileges, was both toilsome and dangerous. Should the plans for plunder, which it was the duty of the Count to form, miscarry in the attempt to execute them; should individuals of the gang fall into the hand of justice, and the Count be unable to devise a method to save their lives or obtain their liberty, the blame was cast at the Count's door, and he was in considerable danger of being deprived of his insignia of authority, which consisted not so much in ornaments or in dress, as in hawks and hounds with which the Senor Count took the diversion of hunting when he thought proper. As the ground which he hunted over was not his own, he incurred some danger of coming in contact with the lord of the soil, attended, perhaps, by his armed followers. There is a tradition (rather apocryphal, it is true), that a Gitano chief, once pursuing this amusement, was encountered by a real Count, who is styled Count Pepe. An engagement ensued between the two parties, which ended in the Gypsies being worsted, and their chief left dying on the field. The slain chief leaves a son, who, at the instigation of his mother, steals the infant heir of his father's enemy, who, reared up amongst the Gypsies, becomes a chief, and, in process of time, hunting over the same ground, slays Count Pepe in the very spot where the blood of the Gypsy had been poured out. This tradition is alluded to in the following stanza:-

'I have a gallant mare in stall;
My mother gave that mare
That I might seek Count Pepe's hall
And steal his son and heir.'

Martin Del Rio, in his TRACTATUS DE MAGIA, speaks of the Gypsies and their Counts to the following effect: 'When, in the year 1584, I was marching in Spain with the regiment, a multitude of these wretches were infesting the fields. It happened that the feast of Corpus Domini was being celebrated, and they requested to be admitted into the town, that they might dance in honour of the sacrifice, as was customary; they did so, but about midday a great tumult arose owing to the many thefts which the women committed, whereupon they fled out of the suburbs, and assembled about St. Mark's, the magnificent mansion and hospital of the knights of St. James, where the ministers of justice attempting to seize them were repulsed by force of arms; nevertheless, all of a sudden, and I know not how, everything was hushed up. At this time they had a Count, a fellow who spoke the Castilian idiom with as much purity as if he had been a native of Toledo; he was acquainted with all the ports of Spain, and all the difficult and broken ground of the provinces. He knew the exact strength of every city, and who were the principal people in each, and the exact amount of their property; there was nothing relating to the state, however secret, that he was not acquainted with; nor did he make a mystery of his knowledge, but publicly boasted of it.'

From the passage quoted above, we learn that the Gitanos in the ancient times were considered as foreigners who prowled about the country; indeed, in many of the laws which at various times have been promulgated against them, they are spoken of as Egyptians, and as such commanded to leave Spain, and return to their native country; at one time they undoubtedly were foreigners in Spain, foreigners by birth, foreigners by language but at the time they are mentioned by the worthy Del Rio, they were certainly not entitled to the appellation. True it is that they spoke a language amongst themselves, unintelligible to the rest of the Spaniards, from whom they differed considerably in feature and complexion, as they still do; but if being born in a country, and being bred there, constitute a right to be considered a native of that country, they had as much claim to the appellation of Spaniards as the worthy author himself. Del Rio mentions, as a remarkable circumstance, the fact of the Gypsy Count speaking Castilian with as much purity as a native of Toledo, whereas it is by no means improbable that the individual in question was a native of that town; but the truth is, at the time we are speaking of, they were generally believed to be not only foreigners, but by means of sorcery to have acquired the power of speaking all languages with equal facility; and Del Rio, who was a believer in magic, and wrote one of the most curious and erudite treatises on the subject ever penned, had perhaps adopted that idea, which possibly originated from their speaking most of the languages and dialects of the Peninsula, which they picked up in their wanderings. That the Gypsy chief was so well acquainted with every town of Spain, and the broken and difficult ground, can cause but little surprise, when we reflect that the life which the Gypsies led was one above all others calculated to afford them that knowledge. They were continually at variance with justice; they were frequently obliged to seek shelter in the inmost recesses of the hills; and when their thievish pursuits led them to the cities, they naturally made themselves acquainted with the names of the principal individuals, in hopes of plundering them. Doubtless the chief possessed all this species of knowledge in a superior degree, as it was his courage, acuteness, and experience alone which placed him at the head of his tribe, though Del Rio from this circumstance wishes to infer that the Gitanos were spies sent by foreign foes, and with some simplicity inquires, 'Quo ant cui rei haec curiosa exploratio? nonne compescenda vagamundorum haec curiositas, etiam si solum peregrini et inculpatae vitae.'

With the Counts rested the management and direction of these remarkable societies; it was they who determined their marches, counter-marches, advances, and retreats; what was to be attempted or avoided; what individuals were to be admitted into the fellowship and privileges of the Gitanos, or who were to be excluded from their society; they settled disputes and sat in judgment over offences. The greatest crimes, according to the Gypsy code, were a quarrelsome disposition, and revealing the secrets of the brotherhood. By this code the members were forbidden to eat, drink, or sleep in the house of a Busno, which signifies any person who is not of the sect of the Gypsies, or to marry out of that sect;

they were likewise not to teach the language of Roma to any but those who, by birth or inauguration, belonged to that sect; they were enjoined to relieve their brethren in distress at any expense or peril; they were to use a peculiar dress, which is frequently alluded to in the Spanish laws, but the particulars of which are not stated; and they were to cultivate the gift of speech to the utmost possible extent, and never to lose anything which might be obtained by a loose and deceiving tongue, to encourage which they had many excellent proverbs, for example -

'The poor fool who closes his mouth never winneth a dollar.'

'The river which runneth with sound bears along with it stones and water.'

CHAPTER III

THE Gitanos not unfrequently made their appearance in considerable numbers, so as to be able to bid defiance to any force which could be assembled against them on a sudden; whole districts thus became a prey to them, and were plundered and devastated.

It is said that, in the year 1618, more than eight hundred of these wretches scoured the country between Castile and Aragon, committing the most enormous crimes. The royal council despatched regular troops against them, who experienced some difficulty in dispersing them.

But we now proceed to touch upon an event which forms an era in the history of the Gitanos of Spain, and which for wildness and singularity throws all other events connected with them and their race, wherever found, entirely into the shade.

THE BOOKSELLER OF LOGRONO

About the middle of the sixteenth century, there resided one Francisco Alvarez in the city of Logrono, the chief town of Rioja, a province which borders on Aragon. He was a man above the middle age, sober, reserved, and in general absorbed in thought; he lived near the great church, and obtained a livelihood by selling printed books and manuscripts in a small shop. He was a very learned man, and was continually reading in the books which he was in the habit of selling, and some of these books were in foreign tongues and characters, so foreign, indeed, that none but himself and some of his friends, the canons, could understand them; he was much visited by the clergy, who were his principal customers, and took much pleasure in listening to his discourse.

He had been a considerable traveller in his youth, and had wandered through all Spain, visiting the various provinces and the most remarkable cities. It was likewise said that he had visited Italy and Barbary. He was, however, invariably silent with respect to his travels, and whenever the subject was mentioned to him, the gloom and melancholy increased which usually clouded his features.

One day, in the commencement of autumn, he was visited by a priest with whom he had long been intimate, and for whom he had always displayed a greater respect and liking than for any other acquaintance. The ecclesiastic found him even more sad than usual, and there was a haggard paleness upon his countenance which alarmed his visitor. The good priest made affectionate inquiries respecting the health of his friend, and whether anything had of late occurred to give him uneasiness; adding at the same time, that he had long suspected that some secret lay heavy upon his mind, which he now conjured him to reveal, as life was uncertain, and it was very possible that he might be quickly summoned from earth into the presence of his Maker.

The bookseller continued for some time in gloomy meditation, till at last he broke silence in these words:- 'It is true I have a secret which weighs heavy upon my mind, and which I am still loth to reveal; but I have a presentiment that my end is approaching, and that a heavy misfortune is about to fall upon this city: I will therefore unburden myself, for it were now a sin to remain silent.

'I am, as you are aware, a native of this town, which I first left when I went to acquire an education at Salamanca; I continued there until I became a licentiate, when I quitted the university and strolled through Spain, supporting myself in general by touching the guitar, according to the practice of penniless students; my adventures were numerous, and I frequently experienced great poverty. Once, whilst making my way from Toledo to Andalusia through the wild mountains, I fell in with and was made captive by a band of the people called Gitanos, or wandering Egyptians; they in general lived amongst these wilds, and plundered or murdered every person whom they met. I should probably have been assassinated by them, but my skill in music perhaps saved my life. I continued with them a considerable time, till at last they persuaded me to become one of them, whereupon I was inaugurated into their society with many strange and horrid ceremonies, and having thus become a Gitano, I went with them to plunder and assassinate upon the roads.

'The Count or head man of these Gitanos had an only daughter, about my own age; she was very beautiful, but, at the same time, exceedingly strong and robust; this Gitana was given to me as a wife or cadjee, and I lived with her several years, and she bore me children.

'My wife was an arrant Gitana, and in her all the wickedness of her race seemed to be concentrated. At last her father was killed in an affray with the troopers of the Hermandad, whereupon my wife and myself succeeded to the authority which he had formerly exercised in the tribe. We had at first loved each other, but at last the Gitano life, with its accompanying wickedness, becoming hateful to my eyes, my wife, who was not slow in perceiving my altered disposition, conceived for me the most deadly hatred; apprehending that I meditated withdrawing myself from the society, and perhaps betraying the secrets of the band, she formed a conspiracy against me, and, at one time, being opposite the Moorish coast, I was seized and bound by the other Gitanos, conveyed across the sea, and delivered as a slave into the hands of the Moors.

'I continued for a long time in slavery in various parts of Morocco and Fez, until I was at length redeemed from my state of bondage by a missionary friar who paid my ransom. With him I shortly after departed for Italy, of which he was a native. In that country I remained some years, until a longing to revisit my native land seized me, when I returned to Spain and established myself here, where I have since lived by vending books, many of which I brought from the strange lands which I visited. I kept my history, however, a profound secret, being afraid of exposing myself to the laws in force against the Gitanos, to which I should instantly become amenable, were it once known that I had at any time been a member of this detestable sect.

'My present wretchedness, of which you have demanded the cause, dates from yesterday; I had been on a short journey to the Augustine convent, which stands on the plain in the direction of Saragossa, carrying with me an Arabian book, which a learned monk was desirous of seeing. Night overtook me ere I could return. I speedily lost my way, and wandered about until I came near a dilapidated edifice with which I was acquainted; I was about to proceed in the direction of the town, when I heard voices within the ruined walls; I listened, and recognised the language of the abhorred Gitanos; I was about to fly, when a word arrested me. It was Drao, which in their tongue signifies the horrid poison with which this race are in the habit of destroying the cattle; they now said that the men of Logrono should rue the Drao which they had been casting. I heard no more, but fled. What increased my fear was, that in the words spoken, I thought I recognised the peculiar jargon of my own tribe; I repeat, that I believe some horrible misfortune is overhanging this city, and that my own days are numbered.'

The priest, having conversed with him for some time upon particular points of the history that he had related, took his leave, advising him to compose his spirits, as he saw no reason why he should indulge in such gloomy forebodings.

The very next day a sickness broke out in the town of Logrono. It was one of a peculiar kind; unlike most others, it did not arise by slow and gradual degrees, but at once appeared in full violence, in the shape of a terrific epidemic. Dizziness in the head was the first symptom: then convulsive retchings, followed by a dreadful struggle between life and death, which generally terminated in favour of the grim destroyer. The bodies, after the spirit which animated them had taken flight, were frightfully swollen, and exhibited a dark blue colour, checkered with crimson spots. Nothing was heard within the houses or the streets, but groans of agony; no remedy was at hand, and the powers of medicine were exhausted in vain upon this terrible pest; so that within a few days the greatest part of the inhabitants of Logrono had perished. The bookseller had not been seen since the commencement of this frightful visitation.

Once, at the dead of night, a knock was heard at the door of the priest, of whom we have already spoken; the priest himself staggered to the door, and opened it, - he was the only one who remained alive in the house, and was himself slowly recovering from the malady which had destroyed all the other inmates; a wild spectral-looking figure presented itself to his eye - it was his friend Alvarez. Both went into the house, when the bookseller, glancing gloomily on the wasted features of the priest, exclaimed, 'You too, I see, amongst others, have cause to rue the Drao which the Gitanos have cast. Know,' he continued, 'that in order to accomplish a detestable plan, the fountains of Logrono have been poisoned by emissaries of the roving bands, who are now assembled in the neighbourhood. On the first appearance of the disorder, from which I happily escaped by tasting the water of a private fountain, which I possess in my own house, I instantly recognised the effects of the poison of the Gitanos, brought by their ancestors from the isles of the Indian sea; and suspecting their intentions, I disguised myself as a Gitano, and went forth in the hope of being able to act as a spy upon their actions. I have been successful, and am at present thoroughly acquainted with their designs. They intended, from the first, to sack the town, as soon as it should have been emptied of its defenders.

'Midday, to-morrow, is the hour in which they have determined to make the attempt. There is no time to be lost; let us, therefore, warn those of our townsmen who still survive, in order that they may make preparations for their defence.'

Whereupon the two friends proceeded to the chief magistrate, who had been but slightly affected by the disorder; he heard the tale of the bookseller with horror and astonishment, and instantly took the best measures possible for frustrating the designs of the Gitanos; all the men capable of bearing arms in Logrono were assembled, and weapons of every description put in their hands. By the advice of the bookseller all the gates of the town were shut, with the exception of the principal one; and the little band of defenders, which barely amounted to sixty men, was stationed in the great square, to which, he said, it was the intention of the Gitanos to penetrate in the first instance, and then, dividing themselves into various parties, to sack the place. The bookseller was, by general desire, constituted leader of the guardians of the town.

It was considerably past noon; the sky was overcast, and tempest clouds, fraught with lightning and thunder, were hanging black and horrid over the town of Logrono. The little troop, resting on their arms, stood awaiting the arrival of their unnatural enemies; rage fired their minds as they thought of the deaths of their fathers, their sons, and their dearest relatives, who had perished, not by the hand of God, but, like infected cattle, by the hellish arts of Egyptian sorcerers. They longed for their appearance, determined to wreak upon them a bloody revenge; not a word was uttered, and profound silence reigned around, only interrupted by the occasional muttering of the thunder-clouds. Suddenly, Alvarez, who had been intently listening, raised his hand with a significant gesture; presently, a sound was heard - a rustling like the waving of trees, or the rushing of distant water; it gradually increased, and seemed to proceed from the narrow street which led from the principal gate into the square. All eyes were turned in that direction…

That night there was repique or ringing of bells in the towers of Logrono, and the few priests who had escaped from the pestilence sang litanies to God and the Virgin for the salvation of the town from the hands of the heathen. The attempt of the Gitanos had been most signally defeated, and the great square and the street were strewn with their corpses. Oh! what frightful objects: there lay grim men more black than mulattos, with fury and rage in their stiffened features; wild women in extraordinary dresses, their hair, black and long as the tail of the horse, spread all dishevelled upon the ground; and gaunt and naked children grasping knives and daggers in their tiny hands. Of the patriotic troop not one appeared to have fallen; and when, after their enemies had retreated with howlings of fiendish despair, they told their numbers, only one man was missing, who was never seen again, and that man was Alvarez.

In the midst of the combat, the tempest, which had for a long time been gathering, burst over Logrono, in lightning, thunder, darkness, and vehement hail.

A man of the town asserted that the last time he had seen Alvarez, the latter was far in advance of his companions, defending himself desperately against three powerful young heathen, who seemed to be acting under the direction of a tall woman who stood nigh, covered with barbaric ornaments, and wearing on her head a rude silver crown.[18]

Such is the tale of the Bookseller of Logrono, and such is the narrative of the attempt of the Gitanos to sack the town in the time of pestilence, which is alluded to by many Spanish authors, but more particularly by the learned Francisco de Cordova, in his DIDASCALIA, one of the most curious and instructive books within the circle of universal literature.

CHAPTER IV

THE Moors, after their subjugation, and previous to their expulsion from Spain, generally resided apart, principally in the suburbs of the towns, where they kept each other in countenance, being hated and despised by the Spaniards, and persecuted on all occasions. By this means they preserved, to a certain extent, the Arabic language, though the use of it was strictly forbidden, and encouraged each other in the secret exercise of the rites of the Mohammedan religion, so that, until the moment of their final expulsion, they continued Moors in almost every sense of the word. Such places were called Morerias, or quarters of the Moors.

In like manner there were Gitanerias, or quarters of the Gitanos, in many of the towns of Spain; and in more than one instance particular barrios or districts are still known by this name, though the Gitanos themselves have long since disappeared. Even in the town of Oviedo, in the heart of the Asturias, a province never famous for Gitanos, there is a place called the Gitaneria, though no Gitano has been known to reside in the town within the memory of man, nor indeed been seen, save, perhaps, as a chance visitor at a fair.

The exact period when the Gitanos first formed these colonies within the towns is not known; the laws, however, which commanded them to abandon their wandering life under penalty of banishment and death, and to become stationary in towns, may have induced them first to take such a step. By the first of these laws, which was made by Ferdinand and Isabella as far back as the year 1499, they are commanded to seek out for themselves masters. This injunction they utterly disregarded. Some of them for fear of the law, or from the hope of bettering their condition, may have settled down in the towns, cities, and villages for a time, but to expect that a people, in whose bosoms was so deeply rooted the love of lawless independence, would subject themselves to the yoke of servitude, from any motive whatever, was going too far; as well might it have been expected, according to the words of the great poet of Persia, THAT THEY WOULD HAVE WASHED THEIR SKINS WHITE.

In these Gitanerias, therefore, many Gypsy families resided, but ever in the Gypsy fashion, in filth and in misery, with little of the fear of man, and nothing of the fear of God before their eyes. Here the swarthy children basked naked in the sun before the doors; here the women prepared love draughts, or told the buena ventura; and here the men plied the trade of the blacksmith, a forbidden occupation, or prepared for sale, by disguising them, animals stolen by themselves or their accomplices. In these places were harboured the strange Gitanos on their arrival, and here were discussed in the Rommany language, which, like the Arabic, was forbidden under severe penalties, plans of fraud and plunder, which were perhaps intended to be carried into effect in a distant province and a distant city.

The great body, however, of the Gypsy race in Spain continued independent wanderers of the plains and the mountains, and indeed the denizens of the Gitanerias were continually sallying forth, either for the purpose of reuniting themselves with the wandering tribes, or of strolling about from town to town, and from fair to fair. Hence the continual complaints in the Spanish laws against the Gitanos who have left their places of domicile, from doing which they were interdicted, even as they were interdicted from speaking their language and following the occupations of the blacksmith and horse-dealer, in which they still persist even at the present day.

The Gitanerias at evening fall were frequently resorted to by individuals widely differing in station from the inmates of these places - we allude to the young and dissolute nobility and hidalgos of Spain. This was generally the time of mirth and festival, and the Gitanos, male and female, danced and sang in the Gypsy fashion beneath the smile of the moon. The Gypsy women and girls were the principal attractions to these visitors; wild and singular as these females are in their appearance, there can be no doubt, for the fact has been frequently proved, that they are capable of exciting passion of the most ardent description, particularly in the bosoms of those who are not of their race, which passion of course becomes the more violent when the almost utter impossibility of gratifying it is known. No females in the world can be more licentious in word and gesture, in dance and in song, than the Gitanas; but there they stop: and so of old, if their titled visitors presumed to seek for more, an unsheathed dagger or gleaming knife speedily repulsed those who expected that the gem most dear amongst the sect of the Roma was within the reach of a Busno.

Such visitors, however, were always encouraged to a certain point, and by this and various other means the Gitanos acquired connections which frequently stood them in good stead in the hour of need. What availed it to the honest labourers of the neighbourhood, or the citizens of the town, to make complaints to the corregidor concerning the thefts and frauds committed by the Gitanos, when perhaps the sons of that very corregidor frequented the nightly dances at the Gitaneria, and were deeply enamoured with some of the dark-eyed singing-girls? What availed making complaints, when perhaps a Gypsy sibyl, the mother of those very girls, had free admission to the house of the corregidor at all times and seasons, and spaed the good fortune to his daughters, promising them counts and dukes, and Andalusian knights in marriage, or prepared philtres for his lady by which she was always to reign supreme in the affections of her husband? And, above all, what availed it to the plundered party to complain that his mule or horse had been stolen, when the Gitano robber, perhaps the husband of the sibyl and the father of the black-eyed Gitanillas, was at that moment actually in treaty with my lord the corregidor himself for supplying him with some splendid thick-maned, long-tailed steed at a small price, to be obtained, as the reader may well suppose, by an infraction of the laws? The favour and protection which the Gitanos experienced from people of high rank is alluded to in the Spanish laws, and can only be accounted for by the motives above detailed.

The Gitanerias were soon considered as public nuisances, on which account the Gitanos were forbidden to live together in particular parts of the town, to hold meetings, and even to intermarry with each other; yet it does not appear that the Gitanerias were ever suppressed by the arm of the law, as many still exist where these singular beings 'marry and are given in marriage,' and meet together to discuss their affairs, which, in their opinion, never flourish unless those of their fellow-creatures suffer. So much for the Gitanerias, or Gypsy colonies in the towns of Spain.

CHAPTER V

'LOS Gitanos son muy malos! - the Gypsies are very bad people,' said the Spaniards of old times. They are cheats; they are highwaymen; they practise sorcery; and, lest the catalogue of their offences should be incomplete, a formal charge of cannibalism was brought against them. Cheats they have always been, and highwaymen, and if not sorcerers, they have always done their best to merit that appellation, by arrogating to themselves supernatural powers; but that they were addicted to cannibalism is a matter not so easily proved.

Their principal accuser was Don Juan de Quinones, who, in the work from which we have already had occasion to quote, gives several anecdotes illustrative of their cannibal propensities. Most of these anecdotes, however, are so highly absurd, that none but the very credulous could ever have vouchsafed them the slightest credit. This author is particularly fond of speaking of a certain juez, or judge, called Don Martin Fajardo, who seems to have been an arrant Gypsy-hunter, and was probably a member of the ancient family of the Fajardos, which still flourishes in Estremadura, and with individuals of which we are acquainted. So it came to pass that this personage was, in the year 1629, at Jaraicejo, in Estremadura, or, as it is written in the little book in question, Zaraizejo, in the capacity of judge; a zealous one he undoubtedly was.

A very strange place is this same Jaraicejo, a small ruinous town or village, situated on a rising ground, with a very wild country all about it. The road from Badajoz to Madrid passes through it; and about two leagues distant, in the direction of Madrid, is the famous mountain pass of Mirabete, from the top of which you enjoy a most picturesque view across the Tagus, which flows below, as far as the huge mountains of Plasencia, the tops of which are generally covered with snow.

So this Don Martin Fajardo, judge, being at Jaraicejo, laid his claw upon four Gitanos, and having nothing, as it appears, to accuse them of, except being Gitanos, put them to the torture, and made them accuse themselves, which they did; for, on the first appeal which was made to the rack, they confessed that they had murdered a female Gypsy in the forest of Las Gamas, and had there eaten her...

I am myself well acquainted with this same forest of Las Gamas, which lies between Jaraicejo and Trujillo; it abounds with chestnut and cork trees, and is a place very well suited either for the purpose of murder or cannibalism. It will be as well to observe that I visited it in company with a band of Gitanos, who bivouacked there, and cooked their supper, which however did not consist of human flesh, but of a puchera, the ingredients of which were beef, bacon, garbanzos, and berdolaga, or field-pease and purslain, - therefore I myself can bear testimony that there is such a forest as Las Gamas, and that it is frequented occasionally by Gypsies, by which two points are established by far the most important to the history in question, or so at least it would be thought in Spain, for being sure of the forest and the Gypsies, few would be incredulous enough to doubt the facts of the murder and cannibalism...

On being put to the rack a second time, the Gitanos confessed that they had likewise murdered and eaten a female pilgrim in the forest aforesaid; and on being tortured yet again, that they had served in the same manner, and in the same forest, a friar of the order of San Francisco, whereupon they were released from the rack and executed. This is one of the anecdotes of Quinones.

And it came to pass, moreover, that the said Fajardo, being in the town of Montijo, was told by the alcalde, that a certain inhabitant of that place had some time previous lost a mare; and wandering about the plains in quest of her, he arrived at a place called Arroyo el Puerco, where stood a ruined house, on entering which he found various Gitanos employed in preparing their dinner, which consisted of a quarter of a human body, which was being roasted before a huge fire: the result, however, we are not told; whether the Gypsies were angry at being disturbed in their cookery, or whether the man of the mare departed unobserved.

Quinones, in continuation, states in his book that he learned (he does not say from whom, but probably from Fajardo) that there was a shepherd of the city of Gaudix, who once lost his way in the wild sierra of Gadol: night came on, and the wind blew cold: he wandered about until he descried a light in the distance, towards which he bent his way, supposing it to be a fire kindled by shepherds: on arriving at the spot, however, he found a whole tribe of Gypsies, who were roasting the half of a man, the other half being hung on a cork-tree: the Gypsies welcomed him very heartily, and requested him to be seated at the fire and to sup with them; but he presently heard them whisper to each other, 'this is a fine fat fellow,' from which he suspected that they were meditating a design upon his body: whereupon, feeling himself sleepy, he made as if he were seeking a spot where to lie, and suddenly darted headlong down the mountain-side, and escaped from their hands without breaking his neck.

These anecdotes scarcely deserve comment; first we have the statement of Fajardo, the fool or knave who tortures wretches, and then puts them to death for the crimes with which they have taxed themselves whilst undergoing the agony of the rack, probably with the hope of obtaining a moment's respite; last comes the tale of the shepherd, who is invited by Gypsies on a mountain at night to partake of a supper of human flesh, and who runs away from them on hearing them talk of the fatness of his own body, as if cannibal robbers detected in their orgies by a single interloper would have afforded him a chance of escaping. Such tales cannot be true.[19]

Cases of cannibalism are said to have occurred in Hungary amongst the Gypsies; indeed, the whole race, in that country, has been accused of cannibalism, to which we have alluded whilst speaking of the Chingany: it is very probable, however, that they were quite innocent of this odious practice, and that the accusation had its origin in popular prejudice, or in the fact of their foul feeding, and their seldom rejecting carrion or offal of any description.

The Gazette of Frankfort for the year 1782, Nos. 157 and 207, states that one hundred and fifty Gypsies were imprisoned charged with this practice; and that the Empress Teresa sent commissioners to inquire into the facts of the accusation, who discovered that they were true; whereupon the empress published a law to oblige all the Gypsies in her dominions to become stationary, which, however, had no effect.

Upon this matter we can state nothing on our own knowledge.

After the above anecdotes, it will perhaps not be amiss to devote a few lines to the subject of Gypsy food and diet. I believe that it has been asserted that the Romas, in all parts of the world, are perfectly indifferent as to what they eat, provided only that they can appease their hunger; and that they have no objection to partake of the carcasses of animals which have died a natural death, and have been left to putrefy by the roadside; moreover, that they use for food all kinds of reptiles and vermin which they can lay their hands upon.

In this there is a vast deal of exaggeration, but at the same time it must be confessed that, in some instances, the habits of the Gypsies in regard to food would seem, at the first glance, to favour the supposition. This observation chiefly holds good with respect to those of the Gypsy race who still continue in a wandering state, and who, doubtless, retain more of the ways and customs of their forefathers than those who have adopted a stationary life. There can be no doubt that the wanderers amongst the Gypsy race are occasionally seen to feast upon carcasses of cattle which have been abandoned to the birds of the air, yet it would be wrong, from this fact, to conclude that the Gypsies were habitual devourers of carrion. Carrion it is true they may occasionally devour, from want of better food, but many of these carcasses are not in reality the carrion which they appear, but are the bodies of animals which the Gypsies have themselves killed by casting drao, in hope that the flesh may eventually be abandoned to them. It is utterly useless to write about the habits of the Gypsies, especially of the wandering tribes, unless you have lived long and intimately with them; and unhappily, up to the present time, all the books which have been published concerning them have been written by those who have introduced themselves into their society for a few hours, and from what they have seen or heard consider themselves competent to give the world an idea of the manners and customs of the mysterious Rommany: thus, because they have been known to beg the carcass of a hog which they themselves have poisoned, it has been asserted that they prefer carrion which has perished of sickness to the meat of the shambles; and because they have been seen to make a ragout of boror (SNAILS), and to roast a hotchiwitchu or hedgehog, it has been supposed that reptiles of every description form a part of their cuisine. It is high time to undeceive the Gentiles on these points. Know, then, O Gentile, whether thou be from the land of the Gorgios [20] or the Busne [21], that the very Gypsies who consider a ragout of snails a delicious dish will not touch an eel, because it bears resemblance to a SNAKE; and that those who will feast on a roasted hedgehog could be induced by no money to taste a squirrel, a delicious and wholesome species of game, living on the purest and most nutritious food which the fields and forests can supply. I myself, while living among the Roms of England, have been regarded almost in the light of a cannibal for cooking the latter animal and preferring it to hotchiwitchu barbecued, or ragout of boror. 'You are but half Rommany, brother,' they would say, 'and you feed gorgiko-nes (LIKE A GENTILE), even as you talk. Tchachipen (IN TRUTH), if we did not know you to be of the Mecralliskoe rat (ROYAL BLOOD) of Pharaoh, we should be justified in driving you forth as a juggel-mush (DOG MAN), one more fitted to keep company with wild beasts and Gorgios than gentle Rommanys.'

No person can read the present volume without perceiving, at a glance, that the Romas are in most points an anomalous people; in their morality there is much of anomaly, and certainly not less in their cuisine.

'Los Gitanos son muy malos; llevan ninos hurtados a Berberia. The Gypsies are very bad people; they steal children and carry them to Barbary, where they sell them to the Moors' - so said the Spaniards in old times. There can be little doubt that even before the fall of the kingdom of Granada, which occurred in the year 1492, the Gitanos had intercourse with the Moors of Spain. Andalusia, which has ever been the province where the Gitano race has most abounded since its arrival, was, until the edict of Philip the Third, which banished more than a million of Moriscos from Spain, principally peopled by Moors, who differed from the Spaniards both in language and religion. By living even as wanderers amongst these people, the Gitanos naturally became acquainted with their tongue, and with many of their customs, which of course much facilitated any connection which they might subsequently form with the Barbaresques. Between the Moors of Barbary and the Spaniards a deadly and continued war raged for centuries, both before and after the expulsion of the Moriscos from Spain. The Gitanos, who cared probably as little for one nation as the other, and who have no sympathy and affection beyond the pale of their own sect, doubtless sided with either as their interest dictated, officiating as spies for both parties and betraying both.

It is likely enough that they frequently passed over to Barbary with stolen children of both sexes, whom they sold to the Moors, who traffic in slaves, whether white or black, even at the present day; and perhaps this kidnapping trade gave occasion to other relations. As they were perfectly acquainted, from their wandering life, with the shores of the Spanish Mediterranean, they must have been of considerable assistance to the Barbary pirates in their marauding trips to the Spanish coasts, both as guides and advisers; and as it was a far easier matter, and afforded a better prospect of gain, to plunder the Spaniards than the Moors, a people almost as wild as themselves, they were, on that account, and that only, more Moors than Christians, and ever willing to assist the former in their forays on the latter.

Quinones observes: 'The Moors, with whom they hold correspondence, let them go and come without any let or obstacle: an instance of this was seen in the year 1627, when two galleys from Spain were carrying assistance to Marmora, which was then besieged by the Moors. These galleys struck on a shoal, when the Moors seized all the people on board, making captives of the Christians and setting at liberty all the Moors, who were chained to the oar; as for the Gypsy galley-slaves whom they found amongst these last, they did not make them slaves, but received them as people friendly to them, and at their devotion; which matter was public and notorious.'

Of the Moors and the Gitanos we shall have occasion to say something in the following chapter.

CHAPTER VI

THERE is no portion of the world so little known as Africa in general; and perhaps of all Africa there is no corner with which Europeans are so little acquainted as Barbary, which nevertheless is only separated from the continent of Europe by a narrow strait of four leagues across.

China itself has, for upwards of a century, ceased to be a land of mystery to the civilised portion of the world; the enterprising children of Loyola having wandered about it in every direction making converts to their doctrine and discipline, whilst the Russians possess better maps of its vast regions than of their own country, and lately, owing to the persevering labour and searching eye of my friend Hyacinth, Archimandrite of Saint John Nefsky, are acquainted with the number of its military force to a man, and also with the names and places of residence of its civil servants. Yet who possesses a map of Fez and Morocco, or would venture to form a conjecture as to how many fiery horsemen Abderrahman, the mulatto emperor, could lead to the field, were his sandy dominions threatened by the Nazarene? Yet Fez is scarcely two hundred leagues distant from Madrid, whilst Maraks, the other great city of the Moors, and which also has given its name to an empire, is scarcely farther removed from Paris, the capital of civilisation: in a word, we scarcely know anything of Barbary, the scanty information which we possess being confined to a few towns on the sea-coast; the zeal of the Jesuit himself being insufficient to induce him to confront the perils of the interior, in the hopeless endeavour of making one single proselyte from amongst the wildest fanatics of the creed of the Prophet Camel-driver.

Are wanderers of the Gypsy race to be found in Barbary? This is a question which I have frequently asked myself. Several respectable authors have, I believe, asserted the fact, amongst whom Adelung, who, speaking of the Gypsies, says: 'Four hundred years have passed away since they departed from their native land. During this time, they have spread themselves through the whole of Western Asia, Europe, and Northern Africa.' [22] But it is one thing to make an assertion, and another to produce the grounds for making it. I believe it would require a far greater stock of information than has hitherto been possessed by any one who has written on the subject of the Gypsies, to justify him in asserting positively that after traversing the west of Europe, they spread themselves over Northern Africa, though true it is that to those who take a superficial view of the matter, nothing appears easier and more natural than to come to such a conclusion.

Tarifa, they will say, the most western part of Spain, is opposite to Tangier, in Africa, a narrow sea only running between, less wide than many rivers. Bands, therefore, of these wanderers, of course, on reaching Tarifa, passed over into Africa, even as thousands crossed the channel from France to England. They have at all times shown themselves extravagantly fond of a roving life. What land is better adapted for such a life than Africa and its wilds? What land, therefore, more likely to entice them?

All this is very plausible. It was easy enough for the Gitanos to pass over to Tangier and Tetuan from the Spanish towns of Tarifa and Algeziras. In the last chapter I have stated my belief of the fact, and that moreover they formed certain connections with the Moors of the coast, to whom it is likely that they occasionally sold children stolen in Spain; yet such connection would by no means have opened them a passage into the interior of Barbary, which is inhabited by wild and fierce people, in comparison with whom the Moors of the coast, bad as they always have been, are gentle and civilised.

To penetrate into Africa, the Gitanos would have been compelled to pass through the tribes who speak the Shilha language, and who are the descendants of the ancient Numidians. These tribes are the most untamable and warlike of mankind, and at the same time the most suspicious, and those who entertain the greatest aversion to foreigners. They are dreaded by the Moors themselves, and have always remained, to a certain degree, independent of the emperors of Morocco. They are the most terrible of robbers and murderers, and entertain far more reluctance to spill water than the blood of their fellow-creatures: the Bedouins, also, of the Arabian race, are warlike, suspicious, and cruel; and would not have failed instantly to attack bands of foreign wanderers, wherever they found them, and in all probability would have exterminated them. Now the Gitanos, such as they arrived in Barbary, could not have defended themselves against such enemies, had they even arrived in large divisions, instead of bands of twenties and thirties, as is their custom to travel. They are not by nature nor by habit a warlike race, and would have quailed before the Africans, who, unlike most other people, engage in wars from what appears to be an innate love of the cruel and bloody scenes attendant on war.

It may be said, that if the Gitanos were able to make their way from the north of India, from Multan, for example, the province which the learned consider to be the original dwelling-place of the race, to such an immense distance as the western part of Spain, passing necessarily through many wild lands and tribes, why might they not have penetrated into the heart of Barbary, and wherefore may not their descendants be still there, following the same kind of life as the European Gypsies, that is, wandering about from place to place, and maintaining themselves by deceit and robbery?

But those who are acquainted but slightly with the condition of Barbary are aware that it would be less difficult and dangerous for a company of foreigners to proceed from Spain to Multan, than from the nearest seaport in Barbary to Fez, an insignificant distance. True it is, that, from their intercourse with the Moors of Spain, the Gypsies might have become acquainted with the Arabic language, and might even have adopted the Moorish dress, ere entering Barbary; and, moreover, might have professed belief in the religion of Mahomet; still they would have been known as foreigners, and, on that account, would have been assuredly attacked by the people of the interior, had they gone amongst them, who, according to the usual practice, would either have massacred them or made them slaves; and as slaves, they would have been separated. The mulatto hue of their countenances would probably have insured them the latter fate, as all blacks and mulattos in the dominions of the Moor are properly slaves, and can be bought and sold, unless by some means or other they become free, in which event their colour is no obstacle to their elevation to the highest employments and dignities, to their becoming pashas of cities and provinces, or even to their ascending the throne. Several emperors of Morocco have been mulattos.

Above I have pointed out all the difficulties and dangers which must have attended the path of the Gitanos, had they passed from Spain into Barbary, and attempted to spread themselves over that region, as over Europe and many parts of Asia. To these observations I have been led by the assertion that they accomplished this, and no proof of the fact having, as I am aware, ever been adduced; for who amongst those who have made such a statement has seen or conversed with the Egyptians of Barbary, or had sufficient intercourse with them to justify him in the assertion that they are one and the same people as those of Europe, from whom they differ about as much as the various tribes which inhabit various European countries differ from each other? At the same time, I wish it to be distinctly understood that I am far from denying the existence of Gypsies in various parts of the interior of Barbary. Indeed, I almost believe the fact, though the information which I possess is by no means of a description which would justify me in speaking with full certainty; I having myself never come in contact with any sect or caste of people amongst the Moors, who not only tallied in their pursuits with the Rommany, but who likewise spoke amongst themselves a dialect of the language of Roma; nor am I aware that any individual worthy of credit has ever presumed to say that he has been more fortunate in these respects.

Nevertheless, I repeat that I am inclined to believe that Gypsies virtually exist in Barbary, and my reasons I shall presently adduce; but I will here observe, that if these strange outcasts did indeed contrive to penetrate into the heart of that savage and inhospitable region, they could only have succeeded after having become well acquainted with the Moorish language, and when, after a considerable sojourn on the coast, they had raised for themselves a name, and were regarded with superstitious fear; in a word, if they walked this land of peril untouched and unscathed, it was not that they were considered as harmless and inoffensive people, which, indeed, would not have protected them, and which assuredly they were not; it was not that they were mistaken for wandering Moors and Bedouins, from whom they differed in feature and complexion, but because, wherever they went, they were dreaded as the possessors of supernatural powers, and as mighty sorcerers.

There is in Barbary more than one sect of wanderers, which, to the cursory observer, might easily appear, and perhaps have appeared, in the right of legitimate Gypsies. For example, there are the Beni Aros. The proper home of these people is in certain high mountains in the neighbourhood of Tetuan, but they are to be found roving about the whole kingdom of Fez. Perhaps it would be impossible to find, in the whole of Northern Africa, a more detestable caste. They are beggars by profession, but are exceedingly addicted to robbery and murder; they are notorious drunkards, and are infamous, even in Barbary, for their unnatural lusts. They are, for the most part, well made and of comely features. I have occasionally spoken with them; they are Moors, and speak no language but the Arabic.

Then there is the sect of Sidi Hamed au Muza, a very roving people, companies of whom are generally to be found in all the principal towns of Barbary. The men are expert vaulters and tumblers, and perform wonderful feats of address with swords and daggers, to the sound of wild music, which the women, seated on the ground, produce from uncouth instruments; by these means they obtain a livelihood. Their dress is picturesque, scarlet vest and white drawers. In many respects they not a little resemble the Gypsies; but they are not an evil people, and are looked upon with much respect by the Moors, who call them Santons. Their patron saint is Hamed au Muza, and from him they derive their name. Their country is on the confines of the Sahara, or great desert, and their language is the Shilhah, or a dialect thereof. They speak but little Arabic. When I saw them for the first time, I believed them to be of the Gypsy caste, but was soon undeceived. A more wandering race does not exist than the children of Sidi Hamed au Muza. They have even visited France, and exhibited their dexterity and agility at Paris and Marseilles.

I will now say a few words concerning another sect which exists in Barbary, and will here premise, that if those who compose it are not Gypsies, such people are not to be found in North Africa, and the assertion, hitherto believed, that they abound there, is devoid of foundation. I allude to certain men and women, generally termed by the Moors 'Those of the Dar-bushi-fal,' which word is equivalent to prophesying or fortune-telling. They are great wanderers, but have also their fixed dwellings or villages, and such a place is called 'Char Seharra,' or witch-hamlet. Their manner of life, in every respect, resembles that of the Gypsies of other countries; they are wanderers during the greatest part of the year, and subsist principally by pilfering and fortune-telling. They deal much in mules and donkeys, and it is believed, in Barbary, that they can change the colour of any animal by means of sorcery, and so disguise him as to sell him to his very proprietor, without fear of his being recognised. This latter trait is quite characteristic of the Gypsy race, by whom the same thing is practised in most parts of the world. But the Moors assert, that the children of the Dar-bushi-fal can not only change the colour of a horse or a mule, but likewise of a human being, in one night, transforming a white into a black, after which they sell him for a slave; on which account the superstitious Moors regard them with the utmost dread, and in general prefer passing the night in the open fields to sleeping in their hamlets. They are said to possess a particular language, which is neither Shilhah nor Arabic, and which none but themselves understand; from all which circumstances I am led to believe, that the children of the Dar-bushi-fal are legitimate Gypsies, descendants of those who passed over to Barbary from Spain. Nevertheless, as it has never been my fortune to meet or to converse with any of this caste, though they are tolerably numerous in Barbary, I am far from asserting that they are of Gypsy race. More enterprising individuals than myself may, perhaps, establish the fact. Any particular language or jargon which they speak amongst themselves will be the best criterion. The word which they employ for 'water' would decide the point; for the Dar-bushi-fal are not Gypsies, if, in their peculiar speech, they designate that blessed element and article most necessary to human existence by aught else than the Sanscrit term 'Pani,' a word brought by the race from sunny Ind, and esteemed so holy that they have never even presumed to modify it.

The following is an account of the Dar-bushi-fal, given me by a Jew of Fez, who had travelled much in Barbary, and which I insert almost literally as I heard it from his mouth. Various other individuals, Moors, have spoken of them in much the same manner.

'In one of my journeys I passed the night in a place called Mulai- Jacub Munsur.

'Not far from this place is a Char Seharra, or witch-hamlet, where dwell those of the Dar-bushi-fal. These are very evil people, and powerful enchanters; for it is well known that if any traveller stop to sleep in their Char, they will with their sorceries, if he be a white man, turn him as black as a coal, and will afterwards sell him as a negro. Horses and mules they serve in the same manner, for if they are black, they will turn them red, or any other colour which best may please them; and although the owners demand justice of the authorities, the sorcerers always come off best. They have a language which they use among themselves, very different from all other languages, so much so that it is impossible to understand them. They are very swarthy, quite as much so as mulattos, and their faces are exceedingly lean. As for their legs, they are like reeds; and when they run, the devil himself cannot overtake them. They tell Dar-bushi-fal with flour; they fill a plate, and then they are able to tell you anything you ask them. They likewise tell it with a shoe; they put it in their mouth, and then they will recall to your memory every action of your life. They likewise tell Dar-bushi-fal with oil; and indeed are, in every respect, most powerful sorcerers.

'Two women, once on a time, came to Fez, bringing with them an exceedingly white donkey, which they placed in the middle of the square called Faz el Bali; they then killed it, and cut it into upwards of thirty pieces. Upon the ground there was much of the donkey's filth and dung; some of this they took in their hands, when it straight assumed the appearance of fresh dates. There were some people who were greedy enough to put these dates into their mouths, and then they found that it was dung. These women deceived me amongst the rest with a date; when I put it into my mouth, lo and behold it was the donkey's dung. After they had collected much money from the spectators, one of them took a needle, and ran it into the tail of the donkey, crying "Arrhe li dar" (Get home), whereupon the donkey instantly rose up, and set off running, kicking every now and then most furiously; and it was remarked, that not one single trace of blood remained upon the ground, just as if they had done nothing to it. Both these women were of the very same Char Seharra which I have already mentioned. They likewise took paper, and cut it into the shape of a peseta, and a dollar, and a half-dollar, until they had made many pesetas and dollars, and then they put them into an earthen pan over a fire, and when they took them out, they appeared just fresh from the stamp, and with such money these people buy all they want.

'There was a friend of my grandfather, who came frequently to our house, who was in the habit of making this money. One day he took me with him to buy white silk; and when they had shown him some, he took the silk in his hand, and pressed it to his mouth, and then I saw that the silk, which was before white, had become green, even as grass. The master of the shop said, "Pay me for my silk." "Of what colour was your silk?" he demanded. "White," said the man; whereupon, turning round, he cried, "Good people, behold, the white silk is green"; and so he got a pound of silk for nothing; and he also was of the Char Seharra.

'They are very evil people indeed, and the emperor himself is afraid of them. The poor wretch who falls into their hands has cause to rue; they always go badly dressed, and exhibit every appearance of misery, though they are far from being miserable. Such is the life they lead.'

There is, of course, some exaggeration in the above account of the Dar-bushi-fal; yet there is little reason to doubt that there is a foundation of truth in all the facts stated. The belief that they are enabled, by sorcery, to change a white into a black man had its origin in the great skill which they possess in altering the appearance of a horse or a mule, and giving it another colour. Their changing white into green silk is a very simple trick, and is accomplished by dexterously substituting one thing for another. Had the man of the Dar-bushi-fal been searched, the white silk would have been found upon him. The Gypsies, wherever they are found, are fond of this species of fraud. In Germany, for example, they go to the wine-shop with two pitchers exactly similar, one in their hand empty, and the other beneath their cloaks filled with water; when the empty pitcher is filled with wine they pretend to be dissatisfied with the quality, or to have no money, but contrive to substitute the pitcher of water in its stead, which the wine- seller generally snatches up in anger, and pours the contents back, as he thinks, into the butt - but it is not wine but water which he pours. With respect to the donkey, which APPEARED to be cut in pieces, but which afterwards, being pricked in the tail, got up and ran home, I have little to say, but that I have myself seen almost as strange things without believing in sorcery.

As for the dates of dung, and the paper money, they are mere feats of legerdemain.

I repeat, that if legitimate Gypsies really exist in Barbary, they are the men and women of the Dar-bushi-fal.

CHAPTER VII

CHIROMANCY, or the divination of the hand, is, according to the orthodox theory, the determining from certain lines upon the hand the quality of the physical and intellectual powers of the possessor.

The whole science is based upon the five principal lines in the hand, and the triangle which they form in the palm. These lines, which have all their particular and appropriate names, and the principal of which is called 'the line of life,' are, if we may believe those who have written on the subject, connected with the heart, with the genitals, with the brain, with the liver or stomach, and the head. Torreblanca, [23] in his curious and learned book on magic, observes: 'In judging these lines you must pay attention to their substance, colour, and continuance, together with the disposition of the correspondent member; for, if the line be well and clearly described, and is of a vivid colour, without being intermitted or PUNCTURIS INFECTA, it denotes the good complexion and virtue of its member, according to Aristotle.

'So that if the line of the heart be found sufficiently long and reasonably deep, and not crossed by other accidental lines, it is an infallible sign of the health of the heart and the great virtue of the heart, and the abundance of spirits and good blood in the heart, and accordingly denotes boldness and liberal genius for every work.'

In like manner, by means of the hepatal line, it is easy to form an accurate judgment as to the state of a person's liver, and of his powers of digestion, and so on with respect to all the other organs of the body.

After having laid down all the rules of chiromancy with the utmost possible clearness, the sage Torreblanca exclaims: 'And with these terminate the canons of true and catholic chiromancy; for as for the other species by which people pretend to divine concerning the affairs of life, either past or to come, dignities, fortunes, children, events, chances, dangers, etc., such chiromancy is not only reprobated by theologians, but by men of law and physic, as a foolish, false, vain, scandalous, futile, superstitious practice, smelling much of divinery and a pact with the devil.'

Then, after mentioning a number of erudite and enlightened men of the three learned professions, who have written against such absurd superstitions, amongst whom he cites Martin Del Rio, he falls foul of the Gypsy wives in this manner: 'A practice turned to profit by the wives of that rabble of abandoned miscreants whom the Italians call Cingari, the Latins Egyptians, and we Gitanos, who, notwithstanding that they are sent by the Turks into Spain for the purpose of acting as spies upon the Christian religion, pretend that they are wandering over the world in fulfilment of a penance enjoined upon them, part of which penance seems to be the living by fraud and imposition.' And shortly afterwards he remarks: 'Nor do they derive any authority for such a practice from those words in Exodus, [24] "et quasi signum in manu tua," as that passage does not treat of chiromancy, but of the festival of unleavened bread; the observance of which, in order that it might be memorable to the Hebrews, the sacred historian said should be as a sign upon the hand; a metaphor derived from those who, when they wish to remember anything, tie a thread round their finger, or put a ring upon it; and still less I ween does that chapter of Job [25] speak in their favour, where is written, "Qui in manu hominis signat, ut norint omnes opera sua," because the divine power is meant thereby which is preached to those here below: for the hand is intended for power and magnitude, Exod. chap. xiv., [26] or stands for free will, which is placed in a man's hand, that is, 7in his power. Wisdom, chap. xxxvi. "In manibus abscondit lucem," [27] etc. etc. etc.

No, no, good Torreblanca, we know perfectly well that the witch- wives of Multan, who for the last four hundred years have been running about Spain and other countries, telling fortunes by the hand, and deriving good profit from the same, are not countenanced in such a practice by the sacred volume; we yield as little credit to their chiromancy as we do to that which you call the true and catholic, and believe that the lines of the hand have as little connection with the events of life as with the liver and stomach, notwithstanding Aristotle, who you forget was a heathen, and knew as little and cared as little for the Scriptures as the Gitanos, whether male or female, who little reck what sanction any of their practices may receive from authority, whether divine or human, if the pursuit enable them to provide sufficient for the existence, however poor and miserable, of their families and themselves.

A very singular kind of women are the Gitanas, far more remarkable in most points than their husbands, in whose pursuits of low cheating and petty robbery there is little capable of exciting much interest; but if there be one being in the world who, more than another, deserves the title of sorceress (and where do you find a word of greater romance and more thrilling interest?), it is the Gypsy female in the prime and vigour of her age and ripeness of her understanding - the Gypsy wife, the mother of two or three children. Mention to me a point of devilry with which that woman is not acquainted. She can at any time, when it suits her, show herself as expert a jockey as her husband, and he appears to advantage in no other character, and is only eloquent when descanting on the merits of some particular animal; but she can do much more: she is a prophetess, though she believes not in prophecy; she is a physician, though she will not taste her own philtres; she is a procuress, though she is not to be procured; she is a singer of obscene songs, though she will suffer no obscene hand to touch her; and though no one is more tenacious of the little she possesses, she is a cutpurse and a shop-lifter whenever opportunity shall offer.

In all times, since we have known anything of these women, they have been addicted to and famous for fortune-telling; indeed, it is their only ostensible means of livelihood, though they have various others which they pursue more secretly. Where and how they first learned the practice we know not; they may have brought it with them from the East, or they may have adopted it, which is less likely, after their arrival in Europe. Chiromancy, from the most remote periods, has been practised in all countries. Neither do we know, whether in this practice they were ever guided by fixed and certain rules; the probability, however, is, that they were not, and that they never followed it but as a means of fraud and robbery; certainly, amongst all the professors of this art that ever existed, no people are more adapted by nature to turn it to account than these females, call them by whatever name you will, Gitanas, Ziganas, Gypsies, or Bohemians; their forms, their features, the expression of their countenances are ever wild and Sibylline, frequently beautiful, but never vulgar. Observe, for example, the Gitana, even her of Seville. She is standing before the portal of a large house in one of the narrow Moorish streets of the capital of Andalusia; through the grated iron door, she looks in upon the court; it is paved with small marble slabs of almost snowy whiteness; in the middle is a fountain distilling limpid water, and all around there is a profusion of macetas, in which flowering plants and aromatic shrubs are growing, and at each corner there is an orange tree, and the perfume of the azahar may be distinguished; you hear the melody of birds from a small aviary beneath the piazza which surrounds the court, which is surmounted by a toldo or linen awning, for it is the commencement of May, and the glorious sun of Andalusia is burning with a splendour too intense for his rays to be borne with impunity. It is a fairy scene such as nowhere meets the eye but at Seville, or perhaps at Fez and Shiraz, in the palaces of the Sultan and the Shah. The Gypsy looks through the iron-grated door, and beholds, seated near the fountain, a richly dressed dame and two lovely delicate maidens; they are busied at their morning's occupation, intertwining with their sharp needles the gold and silk on the tambour; several female attendants are seated behind. The Gypsy pulls the bell, when is heard the soft cry of 'Quien es'; the door, unlocked by means of a string, recedes upon its hinges, when in walks the Gitana, the witch-wife of Multan, with a look such as the tiger-cat casts when she stealeth from her jungle into the plain.

Yes, well may you exclaim 'Ave Maria purissima,' ye dames and maidens of Seville, as she advances towards you; she is not of yourselves, she is not of your blood, she or her fathers have walked to your climate from a distance of three thousand leagues. She has come from the far East, like the three enchanted kings, to Cologne; but, unlike them, she and her race have come with hate and not with love. She comes to flatter, and to deceive, and to rob, for she is a lying prophetess, and a she-Thug; she will greet you with blessings which will make your hearts rejoice, but your hearts' blood would freeze, could you hear the curses which to herself she murmurs against you; for she says, that in her children's veins flows the dark blood of the 'husbands,' whilst in those of yours flows the pale tide of the 'savages,' and therefore she would gladly set her foot on all your corses first poisoned by her hands. For all her love

- and she can love - is for the Romas; and all her hate - and who can hate like her? - is for the Busnees; for she says that the world would be a fair world if there were no Busnees, and if the Romamiks could heat their kettles undisturbed at the foot of the olive-trees; and therefore she would kill them all if she could and if she dared. She never seeks the houses of the Busnees but for the purpose of prey; for the wild animals of the sierra do not more abhor the sight of man than she abhors the countenances of the Busnees. She now comes to prey upon you and to scoff at you. Will you believe her words? Fools! do you think that the being before ye has any sympathy for the like of you?

She is of the middle stature, neither strongly nor slightly built, and yet her every movement denotes agility and vigour. As she stands erect before you, she appears like a falcon about to soar, and you are almost tempted to believe that the power of volition is hers; and were you to stretch forth your hand to seize her, she would spring above the house-tops like a bird. Her face is oval, and her features are regular but somewhat hard and coarse, for she was born amongst rocks in a thicket, and she has been wind-beaten and sun-scorched for many a year, even like her parents before her; there is many a speck upon her cheek, and perhaps a scar, but no dimples of love; and her brow is wrinkled over, though she is yet young. Her complexion is more than dark, for it is almost that of a mulatto; and her hair, which hangs in long locks on either side of her face, is black as coal, and coarse as the tail of a horse, from which it seems to have been gathered.

There is no female eye in Seville can support the glance of hers, - so fierce and penetrating, and yet so artful and sly, is the expression of their dark orbs; her mouth is fine and almost delicate, and there is not a queen on the proudest throne between Madrid and Moscow who might not and would not envy the white and even rows of teeth which adorn it, which seem not of pearl but of the purest elephant's bone of Multan. She comes not alone; a swarthy two-year-old bantling clasps her neck with one arm, its naked body half extant from the coarse blanket which, drawn round her shoulders, is secured at her bosom by a skewer. Though tender of age, it looks wicked and sly, like a veritable imp of Roma. Huge rings of false gold dangle from wide slits in the lobes of her ears; her nether garments are rags, and her feet are cased in hempen sandals. Such is the wandering Gitana, such is the witch- wife of Multan, who has come to spae the fortune of the Sevillian countess and her daughters.

'O may the blessing of Egypt light upon your head, you high-born lady! (May an evil end overtake your body, daughter of a Busnee harlot!) and may the same blessing await the two fair roses of the Nile here flowering by your side! (May evil Moors seize them and carry them across the water!) O listen to the words of the poor woman who is come from a distant country; she is of a wise people, though it has pleased the God of the sky to punish them for their sins by sending them to wander through the world. They denied shelter to the Majari, whom you call the queen of heaven, and to the Son of God, when they flew to the land of Egypt before the wrath of the wicked king; it is said that they even refused them a draught of the sweet waters of the great river when the blessed two were athirst. O you will say that it was a heavy crime; and truly so it was, and heavily has the Lord punished the Egyptians. He has sent us a-wandering, poor as you see, with scarcely a blanket to cover us. O blessed lady, (Accursed be thy dead, as many as thou mayest have,) we have no money to buy us bread; we have only our wisdom with which to support ourselves and our poor hungry babes; when God took away their silks from the Egyptians, and their gold from the Egyptians, he left them their wisdom as a resource that they might not starve. O who can read the stars like the Egyptians? and who can read the lines of the palm like the Egyptians? The poor woman read in the stars that there was a rich ventura for all of this goodly house, so she followed the bidding of the stars and came to declare it. O blessed lady, (I defile thy dead corse,) your husband is at Granada, fighting with king Ferdinand against the wild Corahai! (May an evil ball smite him and split his head!) Within three months he shall return with twenty captive Moors, round the neck of each a chain of gold. (God grant that when he enter the house a beam may fall upon him and crush him!) And within nine months after his return God shall bless you with a fair chabo, the pledge for which you have sighed so long. (Accursed be the salt placed in its mouth in the church when it is baptized!) Your palm, blessed lady, your palm, and the palms of all I see here, that I may tell you all the rich ventura which is hanging over this good house; (May evil lightning fall upon it and consume it!) but first let me sing you a song of Egypt, that the spirit of the Chowahanee may descend more plenteously upon the poor woman.'

Her demeanour now instantly undergoes a change. Hitherto she has been pouring forth a lying and wild harangue without much flurry or agitation of manner. Her speech, it is true, has been rapid, but her voice has never been raised to a very high key; but she now stamps on the ground, and placing her hands on her hips, she moves quickly to the right and left, advancing and retreating in a sidelong direction. Her glances become more fierce and fiery, and her coarse hair stands erect on her head, stiff as the prickles of the hedgehog; and now she commences clapping her hands, and uttering words of an unknown tongue, to a strange and uncouth tune. The tawny bantling seems inspired with the same fiend, and, foaming at the mouth, utters wild sounds, in imitation of its dam. Still more rapid become the sidelong movements of the Gitana. Movement! she springs, she bounds, and at every bound she is a yard above the ground. She no longer bears the child in her bosom; she plucks it from thence, and fiercely brandishes it aloft, till at last, with a yell she tosses it high into the air, like a ball, and then, with neck and head thrown back, receives it, as it falls, on her hands and breast, extracting a cry from the terrified beholders. Is it possible she can be singing? Yes, in the wildest style of her people; and here is a snatch of the song, in the language of Roma, which she occasionally screams -

'En los sastos de yesque plai me diquelo,
Doscusanas de sonacai terelo, -
Corojai diquelo abillar,
Y ne asislo chapescar, chapescar.'

'On the top of a mountain I stand,
With a crown of red gold in my hand, -
Wild Moors came trooping o'er the lea,
O how from their fury shall I flee, flee, flee?
O how from their fury shall I flee?'

Such was the Gitana in the days of Ferdinand and Isabella, and much the same is she now in the days of Isabel and Christina.

Of the Gitanas and their practices I shall have much to say on a future occasion, when speaking of those of the present time, with many of whom I have had no little intercourse. All the ancient Spanish authors who mention these women speak of them in unmeasured terms of abhorrence, employing against them every abusive word contained in the language in which they wrote. Amongst other vile names, they have been called harlots, though perhaps no females on earth are, and have ever been, more chaste in their own persons, though at all times willing to encourage licentiousness in others, from a hope of gain. It is one thing to be a procuress, and another to be a harlot, though the former has assuredly no reason to complain if she be confounded with the latter. 'The Gitanas,' says Doctor Sancho de Moncada, in his discourse concerning the Gypsies, which I shall presently lay before the reader, 'are public harlots, common, as it is said, to all the Gitanos, and with dances, demeanour, and filthy songs, are the cause of infinite harm to the souls of the vassals of your Majesty (Philip III.), as it is notorious what infinite harm they have caused in many honourable houses. The married women whom they have separated from their husbands, and the maidens whom they have perverted; and finally, in the best of these Gitanas, any one may recognise all the signs of a harlot given by the wise king: "they are gadders about, whisperers, always unquiet in the places and corners."' [28]

The author of Alonso, [29] he who of all the old Spanish writers has written most graphically concerning the Gitanos, and I believe with most correctness, puts the following account of the Gitanas, and their fortune-telling practices, into the entertaining mouth of his hero:-

'O how many times did these Gitanas carry me along with them, for being, after all, women, even they have their fears, and were glad of me as a protector: and so they went through the neighbouring villages, and entered the houses a-begging, giving to understand thereby their poverty and necessity, and then they would call aside the girls, in order to tell them the buena ventura, and the young fellows the good luck which they were to enjoy, never failing in the first place to ask for a cuarto or real, in order to make the sign of the cross; and with these flattering words, they got as much as they could, although, it is true, not much in money, as their harvest in that article was generally slight; but enough in bacon to afford subsistence to their husbands and bantlings. I looked on and laughed at the simplicity of those foolish people, who, especially such as wished to be married, were as satisfied and content with what the Gitana told them, as if an apostle had spoken it.'

The above description of Gitanas telling fortunes amongst the villages of Navarre, and which was written by a Spanish author at the commencement of the seventeenth century, is, in every respect, applicable, as the reader will not fail to have observed, to the English Gypsy women of the present day, engaged in the same occupation in the rural districts of England, where the first demand of the sibyls is invariably a sixpence, in order that they may cross their hands with silver, and where the same promises are made, and as easily believed; all which, if it serves to confirm the opinion that in all times the practices and habits of the Egyptian race have been, in almost all respects, the same as at the present day, brings us also to the following mortifying conclusion, - that mental illumination, amongst the generality of mankind, has made no progress at all; as we observe in the nineteenth century the same gross credulity manifested as in the seventeenth, and the inhabitants of one of the countries most celebrated for the arts of civilisation, imposed upon by the same stale tricks which served to deceive two centuries before in Spain, a country whose name has long and justly been considered as synonymous with every species of ignorance and barbarism.

The same author, whilst speaking of these female Thugs, relates an anecdote very characteristic of them; a device at which they are adepts, which they love to employ, and which is generally attended with success. It is the more deserving attention, as an instance of the same description, attended with very similar circumstances, occurred within the sphere of my own knowledge in my own country. This species of deceit is styled, in the peculiar language of the Rommany, HOKKANO BARO, or the 'great trick'; it being considered by the women as their most fruitful source of plunder. The story, as related by Alonso, runs as follows:-

'A band of Gitanos being in the neighbourhood of a village, one of the women went to a house where lived a lady alone. This lady was a young widow, rich, without children, and of very handsome person. After having saluted her, the Gypsy repeated the harangue which she had already studied, to the effect that there was neither bachelor, widower, nor married man, nobleman, nor gallant, endowed with a thousand graces, who was not dying for love of her; and then continued: "Lady, I have contracted a great affection for you, and since I know that you well merit the riches you possess, notwithstanding you live heedless of your good fortune, I wish to reveal to you a secret. You must know, then, that in your cellar you have a vast treasure; nevertheless you will experience great difficulty in arriving at it, as it is enchanted, and to remove it is impossible, save alone on the eve of Saint John. We are now at the eighteenth of June, and it wants five days to the twenty-third; therefore, in the meanwhile, collect some jewels of gold and silver, and likewise some money, whatever you please, provided it be not copper, and provide six tapers, of white or yellow wax, for at the time appointed I will come with a sister of mine, when we will extract from the cellar such abundance of riches, that you will be able to live in a style which will excite the envy of the whole country." The ignorant widow, hearing these words, put implicit confidence in the deceiver, and imagined that she already possessed all the gold of Arabia and the silver of Potosi.

'The appointed day arrived, and not more punctual were the two Gypsies, than anxiously expected by the lady. Being asked whether she had prepared all as she had been desired, she replied in the affirmative, when the Gypsy thus addressed her: "You must know, good lady, that gold calls forth gold, and silver calls forth silver; let us light these tapers, and descend to the cellar before it grows late, in order that we may have time for our conjurations." Thereupon the trio, the widow and the two Gypsies, went down, and having lighted the tapers and placed them in candlesticks in the shape of a circle, they deposited in the midst a silver tankard, with some pieces of eight, and some corals tipped with gold, and other jewels of small value. They then told the lady, that it was necessary for them all to return to the staircase by which they had descended to the cellar, and there they uplifted their hands, and remained for a short time as if engaged in prayer.

'The two Gypsies then bade the widow wait for them, and descended again, when they commenced holding a conversation, speaking and answering alternately, and altering their voices in such a manner that five or six people appeared to be in the cellar. "Blessed little Saint John," said one, "will it be possible to remove the treasure which you keep hidden here?" "O yes, and with a little more trouble it will be yours," replied the Gypsy sister, altering her voice to a thin treble, as if it proceeded from a child four or five years old. In the meantime, the lady remained astonished, expecting the promised riches, and the two Gitanas presently coming to her, said, "Come up, lady, for our desire is upon the point of being gratified. Bring down the best petticoat, gown, and mantle which you have in your chest, that I may dress myself, and appear in other guise to what I do now." The simple woman, not perceiving the trick they were playing upon her, ascended with them to the doorway, and leaving them alone, went to fetch the things which they demanded. Thereupon the two Gypsies, seeing themselves at liberty, and having already pocketed the gold and silver which had been deposited for their conjuration, opened the street door, and escaped with all the speed they could.

'The beguiled widow returned laden with the clothes, and not finding those whom she had left waiting, descended into the cellar, when, perceiving the trick which they had played her, and the robbery which they had committed in stealing her jewels, she began to cry and weep, but all in vain. All the neighbours hastened to her, and to them she related her misfortune, which served more to raise laughter and jeers at her expense than to excite pity; though the subtlety of the two she-thieves was universally praised. These latter, as soon as they had got out of the door, knew well how to conceal themselves, for having once reached the mountain it was not possible to find them. So much for their divination, their foreseeing things to come, their power over the secrets of nature, and their knowledge of the stars.'

The Gitanas in the olden time appear to have not unfrequently been subjected to punishment as sorceresses, and with great justice, as the abominable trade which they drove in philtres and decoctions certainly entitled them to that appellation, and to the pains and penalties reserved for those who practised what was termed 'witchcraft.'

Amongst the crimes laid to their charge, connected with the exercise of occult powers, there is one, however, of which they were certainly not capable, as it is a purely imaginary one, though if they were punished for it, they had assuredly little right to complain, as the chastisement they met was fully merited by practices equally malefic as the crime imputed to them, provided that were possible. IT WAS CASTING THE EVIL EYE.

CHAPTER VIII

IN the Gitano language, casting the evil eye is called QUERELAR NASULA, which simply means making sick, and which, according to the common superstition, is accomplished by casting an evil look at people, especially children, who, from the tenderness of their constitution, are supposed to be more easily blighted than those of a more mature age. After receiving the evil glance, they fall sick, and die in a few hours.

The Spaniards have very little to say respecting the evil eye, though the belief in it is very prevalent, especially in Andalusia amongst the lower orders. A stag's horn is considered a good safeguard, and on that account a small horn, tipped with silver, is frequently attached to the children's necks by means of a cord braided from the hair of a black mare's tail. Should the evil glance be cast, it is imagined that the horn receives it, and instantly snaps asunder. Such horns may be purchased in some of the silversmiths' shops at Seville.

The Gitanos have nothing more to say on this species of sorcery than the Spaniards, which can cause but little surprise, when we consider that they have no traditions, and can give no rational account of themselves, nor of the country from which they come.

Some of the women, however, pretend to have the power of casting it, though if questioned how they accomplish it, they can return no answer. They will likewise sell remedies for the evil eye, which need not be particularised, as they consist of any drugs which they happen to possess or be acquainted with; the prescribers being perfectly reckless as to the effect produced on the patient, provided they receive their paltry reward.

I have known these beings offer to cure the glanders in a horse (an incurable disorder) with the very same powders which they offer as a specific for the evil eye.

Leaving, therefore, for a time, the Spaniards and Gitanos, whose ideas on this subject are very scanty and indistinct, let us turn to other nations amongst whom this superstition exists, and endeavour to ascertain on what it is founded, and in what it consists. The fear of the evil eye is common amongst all oriental people, whether Turks, Arabs, or Hindoos. It is dangerous in some parts to survey a person with a fixed glance, as he instantly concludes that you are casting the evil eye upon him. Children, particularly, are afraid of the evil eye from the superstitious fear inculcated in their minds in the nursery. Parents in the East feel no delight when strangers look at their children in admiration of their loveliness; they consider that you merely look at them in order to blight them. The attendants on the children of the great are enjoined never to permit strangers to fix their glance upon them. I was once in the shop of an Armenian at Constantinople, waiting to see a procession which was expected to pass by; there was a Janisary there, holding by the hand a little boy about six years of age, the son of some Bey; they also had come to see the procession. I was struck with the remarkable loveliness of the child, and fixed my glance upon it: presently it became uneasy, and turning to the Janisary, said: 'There are evil eyes upon me; drive them away.' 'Take your eyes off the child, Frank,' said the Janisary, who had a long white beard, and wore a hanjar. 'What harm can they do to the child, efendijem?' said I. 'Are they not the eyes of a Frank?' replied the Janisary; 'but were they the eyes of Omar, they should not rest on the child.' 'Omar,' said I, 'and why not Ali? Don't you love Ali?' 'What matters it to you whom I love,' said the Turk in a rage; 'look at the child again with your chesm fanar and I will smite you.' 'Bad as my eyes are,' said I, 'they can see that you do not love Ali.' 'Ya Ali, ya Mahoma, Alahhu!' [30] said the Turk, drawing his hanjar. All Franks, by which are meant Christians, are considered as casters of the evil eye. I was lately at Janina in Albania, where a friend of mine, a Greek gentleman, is established as physician. 'I have been visiting the child of a Jew that is sick,' said he to me one day; 'scarcely, however, had I left the house, when the father came running after me. "You have cast the evil eye on my child," said he; "come back and spit in its face." And I assure you,' continued my friend, 'that notwithstanding all I could say, he compelled me to go back and spit in the face of his child.'

Perhaps there is no nation in the world amongst whom this belief is so firmly rooted and from so ancient a period as the Jews; it being a subject treated of, and in the gravest manner, by the old Rabbinical writers themselves, which induces the conclusion that the superstition of the evil eye is of an antiquity almost as remote as the origin of the Hebrew race; (and can we go farther back?) as the oral traditions of the Jews, contained and commented upon in what is called the Talmud, are certainly not less ancient than the inspired writings of the Old Testament, and have unhappily been at all times regarded by them with equal if not greater reverence.

The evil eye is mentioned in Scripture, but of course not in the false and superstitious sense; evil in the eye, which occurs in Prov. xxiii. v. 6, merely denoting niggardness and illiberality. The Hebrew words are AIN RA, and stand in contradistinction to AIN TOUB, or the benignant in eye, which denotes an inclination to bounty and liberality.

It is imagined that this blight is most easily inflicted when a person is enjoying himself with little or no care for the future, when he is reclining in the sun before the door, or when he is full of health and spirits: it may be cast designedly or not; and the same effect may be produced by an inadvertent word. It is deemed partially unlucky to say to any person, 'How well you look'; as the probabilities are that such an individual will receive a sudden blight and pine away. We have however no occasion to go to Hindoos, Turks, and Jews for this idea; we shall find it nearer home, or something akin to it. Is there one of ourselves, however enlightened and free from prejudice, who would not shrink, even in the midst of his highest glee and enjoyment, from saying, 'How happy I am!' or if the words inadvertently escaped him, would he not consider them as ominous of approaching evil, and would he not endeavour to qualify them by saying, 'God preserve me!' - Ay, God preserve you, brother! Who knows what the morrow will bring forth?

The common remedy for the evil eye, in the East, is the spittle of the person who has cast it, provided it can be obtained. 'Spit in the face of my child,' said the Jew of Janina to the Greek physician: recourse is had to the same means in Barbary, where the superstition is universal. In that country both Jews and Moors carry papers about with them scrawled with hieroglyphics, which are prepared by their respective priests, and sold. These papers, placed in a little bag, and hung about the person, are deemed infallible preservatives from the 'evil eye.'

Let us now see what the TALMUD itself says about the evil eye. The passage which we are about to quote is curious, not so much from the subject which it treats of, as in affording an example of the manner in which the Rabbins are wont to interpret the Scripture, and the strange and wonderful deductions which they draw from words and phrases apparently of the greatest simplicity.

'Whosoever when about to enter into a city is afraid of evil eyes, let him grasp the thumb of his right hand with his left hand, and his left-hand thumb with his right hand, and let him cry in this manner: "I am such a one, son of such a one, sprung from the seed of Joseph"; and the evil eyes shall not prevail against him. JOSEPH IS A FRUITFUL BOUGH, A FRUITFUL BOUGH BY A WELL, [31] etc. Now you should not say BY A WELL, but OVER AN EYE. [32] Rabbi Joseph Bar Henina makes the following deduction: AND THEY SHALL BECOME (the seed of Joseph) LIKE FISHES IN MULTITUDE IN THE MIDST OF THE EARTH. [33] Now the fishes of the sea are covered by the waters, and the evil eye has no power over them; and so over those of the seed of Joseph the evil eye has no power.'

I have been thus diffuse upon the evil eye, because of late years it has been a common practice of writers to speak of it without apparently possessing any farther knowledge of the subject than what may be gathered from the words themselves.

Like most other superstitions, it is, perhaps, founded on a physical reality.

I have observed, that only in hot countries, where the sun and moon are particularly dazzling, the belief in the evil eye is prevalent. If we turn to Scripture, the wonderful book which is capable of resolving every mystery, I believe that we shall presently come to the solution of the evil eye. 'The sun shall not smite thee by day, nor the moon by night.' Ps. cxxi. v. 6.

Those who wish to avoid the evil eye, instead of trusting in charms, scrawls, and Rabbinical antidotes, let them never loiter in the sunshine before the king of day has nearly reached his bourn in the west; for the sun has an evil eye, and his glance produces brain fevers; and let them not sleep uncovered beneath the smile of the moon, for her glance is poisonous, and produces insupportable itching in the eye, and not unfrequently blindness.

The northern nations have a superstition which bears some resemblance to the evil eye, when allowance is made for circumstances. They have no brilliant sun and moon to addle the brain and poison the eye, but the grey north has its marshes, and fenny ground, and fetid mists, which produce agues, low fevers, and moping madness, and are as fatal to cattle as to man. Such disorders are attributed to elves and fairies. This superstition still lingers in some parts of England under the name of elf-shot, whilst, throughout the north, it is called elle-skiod, and elle- vild (fairy wild). It is particularly prevalent amongst shepherds and cow-herds, the people who, from their manner of life, are most exposed to the effects of the elf-shot. Those who wish to know more of this superstition are referred to Thiele's - DANSKE FOLKESAGN, and to the notes of the KOEMPE-VISER, or popular Danish Ballads.

CHAPTER IX

WHEN the six hundred thousand men, [34] and the mixed multitude of women and children, went forth from the land of Egypt, the God whom they worshipped, the only true God, went before them by day in a pillar of cloud, to lead them the way, and by night in a pillar of fire to give them light; this God who rescued them from slavery, who guided them through the wilderness, who was their captain in battle, and who cast down before them the strong walls which encompassed the towns of their enemies, this God they still remember, after the lapse of more than three thousand years, and still worship with adoration the most unbounded. If there be one event in the eventful history of the Hebrews which awakens in their minds deeper feelings of gratitude than another, it is the exodus; and that wonderful manifestation of olden mercy still serves them as an assurance that the Lord will yet one day redeem and gather together his scattered and oppressed people. 'Art thou not the God who brought us out of the land of bondage?' they exclaim in the days of their heaviest trouble and affliction. He who redeemed Israel from the hand of Pharaoh is yet capable of restoring the kingdom and sceptre to Israel.

If the Rommany trusted in any God at the period of THEIR exodus, they must speedily have forgotten him. Coming from Ind, as they most assuredly did, it was impossible for them to have known the true, and they must have been followers (if they followed any) either of Buddh, or Brahmah, those tremendous phantoms which have led, and are likely still to lead, the souls of hundreds of millions to destruction; yet they are now ignorant of such names, nor does it appear that such were ever current amongst them subsequent to their arrival in Europe, if indeed they ever were. They brought with them no Indian idols, as far as we are able to judge at the present time, nor indeed Indian rites or observances, for no traces of such are to be discovered amongst them.

All, therefore, which relates to their original religion is shrouded in mystery, and is likely so to remain. They may have been idolaters, or atheists, or what they now are, totally neglectful of worship of any kind; and though not exactly prepared to deny the existence of a Supreme Being, as regardless of him as if he existed not, and never mentioning his name, save in oaths and blasphemy, or in moments of pain or sudden surprise, as they have heard other people do, but always without any fixed belief, trust, or hope.

There are certainly some points of resemblance between the children of Roma and those of Israel. Both have had an exodus, both are exiles and dispersed amongst the Gentiles, by whom they are hated and despised, and whom they hate and despise, under the names of Busnees and Goyim; both, though speaking the language of the Gentiles, possess a peculiar tongue, which the latter do not understand, and both possess a peculiar cast of countenance, by which they may, without difficulty, be distinguished from all other nations; but with these points the similarity terminates. The Israelites have a peculiar religion, to which they are fanatically attached; the Romas have none, as they invariably adopt, though only in appearance, that of the people with whom they chance to sojourn; the Israelites possess the most authentic history of any people in the world, and are acquainted with and delight to recapitulate all that has befallen their race, from ages the most remote; the Romas have no history, they do not even know the name of their original country; and the only tradition which they possess, that of their Egyptian origin, is a false one, whether invented by themselves or others; the Israelites are of all people the most wealthy, the Romas the most poor - poor as a Gypsy being proverbial amongst some nations, though both are equally greedy of gain; and finally, though both are noted for peculiar craft and cunning, no people are more ignorant than the Romas, whilst the Jews have always been a learned people, being in possession of the oldest literature in the world, and certainly the most important and interesting.

Sad and weary must have been the path of the mixed rabble of the Romas, when they left India's sunny land and wended their way to the West, in comparison with the glorious exodus of the

Israelites from Egypt, whose God went before them in cloud and in fire, working miracles and astonishing the hearts of their foes.

Even supposing that they worshipped Buddh or Brahmah, neither of these false deities could have accomplished for them what God effected for his chosen people, although it is true that the idea that a Supreme Being was watching over them, in return for the reverence paid to his image, might have cheered them 'midst storm and lightning, 'midst mountains and wildernesses, 'midst hunger and drought; for it is assuredly better to trust even in an idol, in a tree, or a stone, than to be entirely godless; and the most superstitious hind of the Himalayan hills, who trusts in the Grand Foutsa in the hour of peril and danger, is more wise than the most enlightened atheist, who cherishes no consoling delusion to relieve his mind, oppressed by the terrible ideas of reality.

But it is evident that they arrived at the confines of Europe without any certain or rooted faith. Knowing, as we do, with what tenacity they retain their primitive habits and customs, their sect being, in all points, the same as it was four hundred years ago, it appears impossible that they should have forgotten their peculiar god, if in any peculiar god they trusted.

Though cloudy ideas of the Indian deities might be occasionally floating in their minds, these ideas, doubtless, quickly passed away when they ceased to behold the pagodas and temples of Indian worship, and were no longer in contact with the enthusiastic adorers of the idols of the East; they passed away even as the dim and cloudy ideas which they subsequently adopted of the Eternal and His Son, Mary and the saints, would pass away when they ceased to be nourished by the sight of churches and crosses; for should it please the Almighty to reconduct the Romas to Indian climes, who can doubt that within half a century they would entirely forget all connected with the religion of the West! Any poor shreds of that faith which they bore with them they would drop by degrees as they would relinquish their European garments when they became old, and as they relinquished their Asiatic ones to adopt those of Europe; no particular dress makes a part of the things essential to the sect of Roma, so likewise no particular god and no particular religion.

Where these people first assumed the name of Egyptians, or where that title was first bestowed upon them, it is difficult to determine; perhaps, however, in the eastern parts of Europe, where it should seem the grand body of this nation of wanderers made a halt for a considerable time, and where they are still to be found in greater numbers than in any other part. One thing is certain, that when they first entered Germany, which they speedily overran, they appeared under the character of Egyptians, doing penance for the sin of having refused hospitality to the Virgin and her Son, and, of course, as believers in the Christian faith, notwithstanding that they subsisted by the perpetration of every kind of robbery and imposition; Aventinus (ANNALES BOIORUM, 826) speaking of them says: 'Adeo tamen vana superstitio hominum mentes, velut lethargus invasit, ut eos violari nefas putet, atque grassari, furari, imponere passim sinant.'

This singular story of banishment from Egypt, and Wandering through the world for a period of seven years, for inhospitality displayed to the Virgin, and which I find much difficulty in attributing to the invention of people so ignorant as the Romas, tallies strangely with the fate foretold to the ancient Egyptians in certain chapters of Ezekiel, so much so, indeed, that it seems to be derived from that source. The Lord is angry with Egypt because its inhabitants have been a staff of reed to the house of Israel, and thus he threatens them by the mouth of his prophet.

'I will make the land of Egypt desolate in the midst of the countries that are desolate, and her cities among the cities that are laid waste shall be desolate forty years: and I will scatter the Egyptians among the nations, and will disperse them through the countries.' Ezek., chap. xxix. v. 12. 'Yet thus saith the Lord God; at the end of forty years will I gather the Egyptians from the people whither they were scattered.' v. 13.

'Thus saith the Lord; I will make the multitude of Egypt to cease, by the hand of Nebuchadnezzar, king of Babylon.' Chap. xxx. v. 10.

'And I will scatter the Egyptians among the nations, and disperse them among the countries; and they shall know that I am the Lord.' Chap. xxx. v. 26.

The reader will at once observe that the apocryphal tale which the Romas brought into Germany, concerning their origin and wanderings, agrees in every material point with the sacred prophecy. The ancient Egyptians were to be driven from their country and dispersed amongst the nations, for a period of forty years, for having been the cause of Israel's backsliding, and for not having known the Lord, - the modern pseudo-Egyptians are to be dispersed among the nations for seven years, for having denied hospitality to the Virgin and her child. The prophecy seems only to have been remodelled for the purpose of suiting the taste of the time; as no legend possessed much interest in which the Virgin did not figure, she and her child are here introduced instead of the Israelites, and the Lord of Heaven offended with the Egyptians; and this legend appears to have been very well received in Germany, for a time at least, for, as Aventinus observes, it was esteemed a crime of the first magnitude to offer any violence to the Egyptian pilgrims, who were permitted to rob on the highway, to commit larceny, and to practise every species of imposition with impunity.

The tale, however, of the Romas could hardly have been invented by themselves, as they were, and still are, utterly unacquainted with the Scripture; it probably originated amongst the priests and learned men of the east of Europe, who, startled by the sudden apparition of bands of people foreign in appearance and language, skilled in divination and the occult arts, endeavoured to find in Scripture a clue to such a phenomenon; the result of which was, that the Romas of Hindustan were suddenly transformed into Egyptian penitents, a title which they have ever since borne in various parts of Europe. There are no means of ascertaining whether they themselves believed from the first in this story; they most probably took it on credit, more especially as they could give no account of themselves, there being every reason for supposing that from time immemorial they had existed in the East as a thievish wandering sect, as they at present do in Europe, without history or traditions, and unable to look back for a period of eighty years. The tale moreover answered their purpose, as beneath the garb of penitence they could rob and cheat with impunity, for a time at least. One thing is certain, that in whatever manner the tale of their Egyptian descent originated, many branches of the sect place implicit confidence in it at the present day, more especially those of England and Spain.

Even at the present time there are writers who contend that the Romas are the descendants of the ancient Egyptians, who were scattered amongst the nations by the Assyrians. This belief they principally found upon particular parts of the prophecy from which we have already quoted, and there is no lack of plausibility in the arguments which they deduce therefrom. The Egyptians, say they, were to fall upon the open fields, they were not to be brought together nor gathered; they were to be dispersed through the countries, their idols were to be destroyed, and their images were to cease out of Noph! In what people in the world do these denunciations appear to be verified save the Gypsies? - a people who pass their lives in the open fields, who are not gathered together, who are dispersed through the countries, who have no idols, no images, nor any fixed or certain religion.

In Spain, the want of religion amongst the Gitanos was speedily observed, and became quite as notorious as their want of honesty; they have been styled atheists, heathen idolaters, and Moors. In the little book of Quinones', we find the subject noticed in the following manner:-

'They do not understand what kind of thing the church is, and never enter it but for the purpose of committing sacrilege. They do not know the prayers; for I examined them myself, males and females, and they knew them not, or if any, very imperfectly. They never partake of the Holy Sacraments, and though they marry relations they procure no dispensations. [35] No one knows whether they are baptized. One of the five whom I caused to be hung a few days ago was baptized in the prison, being at the time upwards of thirty years of age. Don Martin Fajardo says that two Gitanos and a Gitana, whom he hanged in the village of Torre Perojil, were baptized at the foot of the gallows, and declared themselves Moors.

'They invariably look out, when they marry, if we can call theirs marrying, for the woman most dexterous in pilfering and deceiving, caring nothing whether she is akin to them or married already, [36] for it is only necessary to keep her company and to call her wife. Sometimes they purchase them from their husbands, or receive them as pledges: so says, at least, Doctor Salazar de Mendoza.

'Friar Melchior of Guelama states that he heard asserted of two Gitanos what was never yet heard of any barbarous nation, namely, that they exchanged their wives, and that as one was more comely looking than the other, he who took the handsome woman gave a certain sum of money to him who took the ugly one. The licentiate Alonzo Duran has certified to me, that in the year 1623-4, one Simon Ramirez, captain of a band of Gitanos, repudiated Teresa because she was old, and married one called Melchora, who was young and handsome, and that on the day when the repudiation took place and the bridal was celebrated he was journeying along the road, and perceived a company feasting and revelling beneath some trees in a plain within the jurisdiction of the village of Deleitosa, and that on demanding the cause he was told that it was on account of Simon Ramirez marrying one Gitana and casting off another; and that the repudiated woman told him, with an agony of tears, that he abandoned her because she was old, and married another because she was young. Certainly Gitanos and Gitanas confessed before Don Martin Fajardo that they did not really marry, but that in their banquets and festivals they selected the woman whom they liked, and that it was lawful for them to have as many as three mistresses, and on that account they begat so many children. They never keep fasts nor any ecclesiastical command. They always eat meat, Friday and Lent not excepted; the morning when I seized those whom I afterwards executed, which was in Lent, they had three lambs which they intended to eat for their dinner that day. - Quinones, page 13.

Although what is stated in the above extracts, respecting the marriages of the Gitanos and their licentious manner of living, is, for the most part, incorrect, there is no reason to conclude the same with respect to their want of religion in the olden time, and their slight regard for the forms and observances of the church, as their behaviour at the present day serves to confirm what is said on those points. From the whole, we may form a tolerably correct idea of the opinions of the time respecting the Gitanos in matters of morality and religion. A very natural question now seems to present itself, namely, what steps did the government of Spain, civil and ecclesiastical, which has so often trumpeted its zeal in the cause of what it calls the Christian religion, which has so often been the scourge of the Jew, of the Mahometan, and of the professors of the reformed faith; what steps did it take towards converting, punishing, and rooting out from Spain, a sect of demi- atheists, who, besides being cheats and robbers, displayed the most marked indifference for the forms of the Catholic religion, and presumed to eat flesh every day, and to intermarry with their relations, without paying the vicegerent of Christ here on earth for permission so to do?

The Gitanos have at all times, since their first appearance in Spain, been notorious for their contempt of religious observances; yet there is no proof that they were subjected to persecution on that account. The men have been punished as robbers and murderers, with the gallows and the galleys; the women, as thieves and sorceresses, with imprisonment, flagellation, and sometimes death; but as a rabble, living without fear of God, and, by so doing, affording an evil example to the nation at large, few people gave themselves much trouble about them, though they may have occasionally been designated as such in a royal edict, intended to check their robberies, or by some priest from the pulpit, from whose stable they had perhaps contrived to extract the mule which previously had the honour of ambling beneath his portly person.

The Inquisition, which burnt so many Jews and Moors, and conscientious Christians, at Seville and Madrid, and in other parts of Spain, seems to have exhibited the greatest clemency and forbearance to the Gitanos. Indeed, we cannot find one instance of its having interfered with them. The charge of restraining the excesses of the Gitanos was abandoned entirely to the secular authorities, and more particularly to the Santa Hermandad, a kind of police instituted for the purpose of clearing the roads of robbers. Whilst I resided at Cordova, I was acquainted with an aged ecclesiastic, who was priest of a village called Puente, at about two leagues' distance from the city. He was detained in Cordova on account of his political opinions, though he was otherwise at liberty. We lived together at the same house; and he frequently visited me in my apartment.

This person, who was upwards of eighty years of age, had formerly been inquisitor at Cordova. One night, whilst we were seated together, three Gitanos entered to pay me a visit, and on observing the old ecclesiastic, exhibited every mark of dissatisfaction, and speaking in their own idiom, called him a BALICHOW, and abused priests in general in most unmeasured terms. On their departing, I inquired of the old man whether he, who having been an inquisitor, was doubtless versed in the annals of the holy office, could inform me whether the Inquisition had ever taken any active measures for the suppression and punishment of the sect of the Gitanos: whereupon he replied, 'that he was not aware of one case of a Gitano having been tried or punished by the Inquisition'; adding these remarkable words: 'The Inquisition always looked upon them with too much contempt to give itself the slightest trouble concerning them; for as no danger either to the state, or the church of Rome, could proceed from the Gitanos, it was a matter of perfect indifference to the holy office whether they lived without religion or not. The holy office has always reserved its anger for people very different; the Gitanos having at all times been GENTE BARATA Y DESPRECIABLE.

Indeed, most of the persecutions which have arisen in Spain against Jews, Moors, and Protestants, sprang from motives with which fanaticism and bigotry, of which it is true the Spaniards have their full share, had very little connection. Religion was assumed as a mask to conceal the vilest and most detestable motives which ever yet led to the commission of crying injustice; the Jews were doomed to persecution and destruction on two accounts, - their great riches, and their high superiority over the Spaniards in learning and intellect. Avarice has always been the dominant passion in Spanish minds, their rage for money being only to be compared to the wild hunger of wolves for horse-flesh in the time of winter: next to avarice, envy of superior talent and accomplishment is the prevailing passion. These two detestable feelings united, proved the ruin of the Jews in Spain, who were, for a long time, an eyesore, both to the clergy and laity, for their great riches and learning. Much the same causes insured the expulsion of the Moriscos, who were abhorred for their superior industry, which the Spaniards would not imitate; whilst the reformation was kept down by the gaunt arm of the Inquisition, lest the property of the church should pass into other and more deserving hands. The faggot piles in the squares of Seville and Madrid, which consumed the bodies of the Hebrew, the Morisco, and the Protestant, were lighted by avarice and envy, and those same piles would likewise have consumed the mulatto carcass of the Gitano, had he been learned and wealthy enough to become obnoxious to the two master passions of the Spaniards.

Of all the Spanish writers who have written concerning the Gitanos, the one who appears to have been most scandalised at the want of religion observable amongst them, and their contempt for things sacred, was a certain Doctor Sancho De Moncada.

This worthy, whom we have already had occasion to mention, was Professor of Theology at the University of Toledo, and shortly after the expulsion of the Moriscos had been brought about by the intrigues of the monks and robbers who thronged the court of Philip the Third, he endeavoured to get up a cry against the Gitanos similar to that with which for the last half-century Spain had resounded against the unfortunate and oppressed Africans, and to effect this he published a discourse, entitled 'The Expulsion of the Gitanos,' addressed to Philip the Third, in which he conjures that monarch, for the sake of morality and everything sacred, to complete the good work he had commenced, and to send the Gitanos packing after the Moriscos.

Whether this discourse produced any benefit to the author, we have no means of ascertaining. One thing is certain, that it did no harm to the Gitanos, who still continue in Spain.

If he had other expectations, he must have understood very little of the genius of his countrymen, or of King Philip and his court. It would have been easier to get up a crusade against the wild cats of the sierra, than against the Gitanos, as the former have skins to reward those who slay them. His discourse, however, is well worthy of perusal, as it exhibits some learning, and comprises many curious details respecting the Gitanos, their habits, and their practices. As it is not very lengthy, we here subjoin it, hoping that the reader will excuse its many absurdities, for the sake of its many valuable facts.

CHAPTER X

'SIRE,

'The people of God were always afflicted by the Egyptians, but the Supreme King delivered them from their hands by means of many miracles, which are related in the Holy Scriptures; and now, without having recourse to so many, but only by means of the miraculous talent which your Majesty possesses for expelling such reprobates, he will, doubtless, free this kingdom from them, which is what is supplicated in this discourse, and it behoves us, in the first place, to consider

'WHO ARE THE GITANOS?

'Writers generally agree that the first time the Gitanos were seen in Europe was the year 1417, which was in the time of Pope Martinus the Fifth and King Don John the Second; others say that Tamerlane had them in his camp in 1401, and that their captain was Cingo, from whence it is said that they call themselves Cingary. But the opinions concerning their origin are infinite.

'The first is that they are foreigners, though authors differ much with respect to the country from whence they came. The majority say that they are from Africa, and that they came with the Moors when Spain was lost; others that they are Tartars, Persians, Cilicians, Nubians, from Lower Egypt, from Syria, or from other parts of Asia and Africa, and others consider them to be descendants of Chus, son of Cain; others say that they are of European origin, Bohemians, Germans, or outcasts from other nations of this quarter of the world.

'The second and sure opinion is, that those who prowl about Spain are not Egyptians, but swarms of wasps and atheistical wretches, without any kind of law or religion, Spaniards, who have introduced this Gypsy life or sect, and who admit into it every day all the idle and broken people of Spain. There are some foreigners who would make Spain the origin and fountain of all the Gypsies of Europe, as they say that they proceeded from a river in Spain called Cija, of which Lucan makes mention; an opinion, however, not much adopted amongst the learned. In the opinion of respectable authors, they are called Cingary or Cinli, because they in every respect resemble the bird cinclo, which we call in Spanish Motacilla, or aguzanieve (wagtail), which is a vagrant bird and builds no nest, [37] but broods in those of other birds, a bird restless and poor of plumage, as AElian writes.

'THE GITANOS ARE VERY HURTFUL TO SPAIN

'There is not a nation which does not consider them as a most pernicious rabble; even the Turks and Moors abominate them, amongst whom this sect is found under the names of Torlaquis, [38] Hugiemalars, and Dervislars, of whom some historians make mention, and all agree that they are most evil people, and highly detrimental to the country where they are found.

'In the first place, because in all parts they are considered as enemies of the states where they wander, and as spies and traitors to the crown; which was proven by the emperors Maximilian and Albert, who declared them to be such in public edicts; a fact easy to be believed, when we consider that they enter with ease into the enemies' country, and know the languages of all nations.

'Secondly, because they are idle vagabond people, who are in no respect useful to the kingdom; without commerce, occupation, or trade of any description; and if they have any it is making picklocks and pothooks for appearance sake, being wasps, who only live by sucking and impoverishing the country, sustaining themselves by the sweat of the miserable labourers, as a German poet has said of them:-

> "Quos aliena juvant, propriis habitare molestum,
> Fastidit patrium non nisi nosse solum."

They are much more useless than the Moriscos, as these last were of some service to the state and the royal revenues, but the

Gitanos are neither labourers, gardeners, mechanics, nor merchants, and only serve, like the wolves, to plunder and to flee.

'Thirdly, because the Gitanas are public harlots, common, as it is said, to all the Gitanos, and with dances, demeanour, and filthy songs, are the cause of continual detriment to the souls of the vassals of your Majesty, it being notorious that they have done infinite harm in many honourable houses by separating the married women from their husbands, and perverting the maidens: and finally, in the best of these Gitanas any one may recognise all the signs of a harlot given by the wise king; they are gadders about, whisperers, always unquiet in places and corners.

'Fourthly, because in all parts they are accounted famous thieves, about which authors write wonderful things; we ourselves have continual experience of this fact in Spain, where there is scarcely a corner where they have not committed some heavy offence.

'Father Martin Del Rio says they were notorious when he was in Leon in the year 1584; as they even attempted to sack the town of Logrono in the time of the pest, as Don Francisco De Cordoba writes in his DIDASCALIA. Enormous cases of their excesses we see in infinite processes in all the tribunals, and particularly in that of the Holy Brotherhood; their wickedness ascending to such a pitch, that they steal children, and carry them for sale to Barbary; the reason why the Moors call them in Arabic, RASO CHERANY, [39] which, as Andreas Tebetus writes, means MASTER THIEVES. Although they are addicted to every species of robbery, they mostly practise horse and cattle stealing, on which account they are called in law ABIGEOS, and in Spanish QUATREROS, from which practice great evils result to the poor labourers. When they cannot steal cattle, they endeavour to deceive by means of them, acting as TERCEROS, in fairs and markets.

'Fifthly, because they are enchanters, diviners, magicians, chiromancers, who tell the future by the lines of the hand, which is what they call BUENA VENTURA, and are in general addicted to all kind of superstition.

'This is the opinion entertained of them universally, and which is confirmed every day by experience; and some think that they are caller Cingary, from the great Magian Cineus, from whom it is said they learned their sorceries, and from which result in

Spain (especially amongst the vulgar) great errors, and superstitious credulity, mighty witchcrafts, and heavy evils, both spiritual and corporeal.

'Sixthly, because very devout men consider them as heretics, and many as Gentile idolaters, or atheists, without any religion, although they exteriorly accommodate themselves to the religion of the country in which they wander, being Turks with the Turks, heretics with the heretics, and, amongst the Christians, baptizing now and then a child for form's sake. Friar Jayme Bleda produces a hundred signs, from which he concludes that the Moriscos were not Christians, all which are visible in the Gitanos; very few are known to baptize their children; they are not married, but it is believed that they keep the women in common; they do not use dispensations, nor receive the sacraments; they pay no respect to images, rosaries, bulls, neither do they hear mass, nor divine services; they never enter the churches, nor observe fasts, Lent, nor any ecclesiastical precept; which enormities have been attested by long experience, as every person says.

'Finally, they practise every kind of wickedness in safety, by discoursing amongst themselves in a language with which they understand each other without being understood, which in Spain is called Gerigonza, which, as some think, ought to be called Cingerionza, or language of Cingary. The king our lord saw the evil of such a practice in the law which he enacted at Madrid, in the year 1566, in which he forbade the Arabic to the Moriscos, as the use of different languages amongst the natives of one kingdom opens a door to treason, and is a source of heavy inconvenience; and this is exemplified more in the case of the Gitanos than of any other people.

'THE GITANOS OUGHT TO BE SEIZED WHEREVER FOUND

'The civil law ordains that vagrants be seized wherever they are found, without any favour being shown to them; in conformity with which, the Gitanos in the Greek empire were given as slaves to those who should capture them; as respectable authors write. Moreover, the emperor, our lord, has decreed by a law made in Toledo, in the year 1525, THAT THE THIRD TIME THEY BE FOUND WANDERING THEY SHALL SERVE AS SLAVES DURING THEIR WHOLE LIFE TO THOSE WHO CAPTURE

THEM. Which can be easily justified, inasmuch as there is no shepherd who does not place barriers against the wolves, and does not endeavour to save his flock, and I have already exposed to your Majesty the damage which the Gitanos perpetrate in Spain.

'THE GITANOS OUGHT TO BE CONDEMNED TO DEATH

'The reasons are many. The first, for being spies, and traitors to the crown; the second as idlers and vagabonds.

'It ought always to be considered, that no sooner did the race of man begin, after the creation of the world, than the important point of civil policy arose of condemning vagrants to death; for Cain was certain that he should meet his destruction in wandering as a vagabond for the murder of Abel. ERO VAGUS ET PROFUGUS IN TERRA: OMNIS IGITUR QUI INVENERIT ME, OCCIDET ME. Now, the IGITUR stands here as the natural consequence of VAGUS ERO; as it is evident, that whoever shall see me must kill me, because he sees me a wanderer. And it must always be remembered, that at that time there were no people in the world but the parents and brothers of Cain, as St. Ambrose has remarked. Moreover, God, by the mouth of Jeremias, menaced his people, that all should devour them whilst they went wandering amongst the mountains. And it is a doctrine entertained by theologians, that the mere act of wandering, without anything else, carries with it a vehement suspicion of capital crime. Nature herself demonstrates it in the curious political system of the bees, in whose well-governed republic the drones are killed in April, when they commence working.

'The third, because they are stealers of four-footed beasts, who are condemned to death by the laws of Spain, in the wise code of the famous King Don Alonso; which enactment became a part of the common law.

'The fourth, for wizards, diviners, and for practising arts which are prohibited under pain of death by the divine law itself. And Saul is praised for having caused this law to be put in execution in the beginning of his reign; and the Holy Scripture attributes to the breach of it (namely, his consulting the witch) his disastrous death, and the transfer of the kingdom to David. The Emperor Constantine the Great, and other emperors who founded the civil law, condemned to death those who should practise such facinorousness, - as the President of Tolosa has written.

'The last and most urgent cause is, that they are heretics, if what is said be truth; and it is the practice of the law in Spain to burn such.

'THE GITANOS ARE EXPELLED FROM THE COUNTRY BY THE LAWS OF SPAIN

'Firstly, they are comprehended as hale beggars in the law of the wise king, Don Alonso, by which he expelled all sturdy beggars, as being idle and useless.

'Secondly, the law expels public harlots from the city; and of this matter I have already said something in my second chapter.

'Thirdly, as people who cause scandal, and who, as is visible at the first glance, are prejudicial to morals and common decency. Now, it is established by the statute law of these kingdoms, that such people be expelled therefrom; it is said so in the well- pondered words of the edict for the expulsion of the Moors: "And forasmuch as the sense of good and Christian government makes it a matter of conscience to expel from the kingdoms the things which cause scandal, injury to honest subjects, danger to the state, and above all, disloyalty to the Lord our God." Therefore, considering the incorrigibility of the Gitanos, the Spanish kings made many holy laws in order to deliver their subjects from such pernicious people.

'Fourthly, the Catholic princes, Ferdinand and Isabella, by a law which they made in Medina del Campo, in the year 1494, and which the emperor our lord renewed in Toledo in 1523, and in Madrid in 1528 and 1534, and the late king our lord, in 1560, banished them perpetually from Spain, and gave them as slaves to whomsoever should find them, after the expiration of the term specified in the edict - laws which are notorious even amongst strangers. The words are:- "We declare to be vagabonds, and subject to the aforesaid penalty, the Egyptians and foreign tinkers, who by laws and statutes of these kingdoms are commanded to depart therefrom; and the poor sturdy beggars, who contrary to the order given in the new edict, beg for alms and wander about."

'THE LAWS ARE VERY JUST WHICH EXPEL THE GITANOS FROM THE STATES

All the doctors, who are of opinion that the Gitanos may be condemned to death, would consider it as an act of mercy in your Majesty to banish them perpetually from Spain, and at the same time as exceedingly just. Many and learned men not only consider that it is just to expel them, but cannot sufficiently wonder that they are tolerated in Christian states, and even consider that such toleration is an insult to the kingdoms.

'Whilst engaged in writing this, I have seen a very learned memorial, in which Doctor Salazar de Mendoza makes the same supplication to your Majesty which is made in this discourse, holding it to be the imperious duty of every good government.

'It stands in reason that the prince is bound to watch for the welfare of his subjects, and the wrongs which those of your Majesty receive from the Gitanos I have already exposed in my second chapter; it being a point worthy of great consideration that the wrongs caused by the Moriscos moved your royal and merciful bosom to drive them out, although they were many, and their departure would be felt as a loss to the population, the commerce, the royal revenues, and agriculture. Now, with respect to the Gitanos, as they are few, and perfectly useless for everything, it appears more necessary to drive them forth, the injuries which they cause being so numerous.

'Secondly, because the Gitanos, as I have already said, are Spaniards; and as others profess the sacred orders of religion, even so do these fellows profess gypsying, which is robbery and all the other vices enumerated in chapter the second. And whereas it is just to banish from the kingdom those who have committed any heavy delinquency, it is still more so to banish those who profess to be injurious to all.

'Thirdly, because all the kings and rulers have always endeavoured to eject from their kingdoms the idle and useless. And it is very remarkable, that the law invariably commands them to be expelled, and the republics of Athens and Corinth were accustomed to do so - casting them forth like dung, even as Athenaeus writes: NOS GENUS HOC MORTALIUM EJICIMUS EX HAC URBE VELUT PURGAMINA. Now the profession of the Gypsy is idleness.

'Fourthly, because the Gitanos are diviners, enchanters, and mischievous wretches, and the law commands us to expel such from the state.

'In the fifth place, because your Majesty, in the Cortes at present assembled, has obliged your royal conscience to fulfil all the articles voted for the public service, and the forty-ninth says: "One of the things at present most necessary to be done in these kingdoms, is to afford a remedy for the robberies, plundering and murders committed by the Gitanos, who go wandering about the country, stealing the cattle of the poor, and committing a thousand outrages, living without any fear of God, and being Christians only in name. It is therefore deemed expedient, that your Majesty command them to quit these kingdoms within six months, to be reckoned from the day of the ratification of these presents, and that they do not return to the same under pain of death."

'Against this, two things may possibly be urged:-

'The first, that the laws of Spain give unto the Gitanos the alternative of residing in large towns, which, it appears, would be better than expelling them. But experience, recognised by grave and respectable men, has shown that it is not well to harbour these people; for their houses are dens of thieves, from whence they prowl abroad to rob the land.

'The second, that it appears a pity to banish the women and children. But to this can be opposed that holy act of your Majesty which expelled the Moriscos, and the children of the Moriscos, for the reason given in the royal edict. WHENEVER ANY DETESTABLE CRIME IS COMMITTED BY ANY UNIVERSITY, IT IS WELL TO PUNISH ALL. And the most detestable crimes of all are those which the Gitanos commit, since it is notorious that they subsist on what they steal; and as to the children, there is no law which obliges us to bring up wolf- whelps, to cause here-after certain damage to the flock.

'IT HAS EVER BEEN THE PRACTICE OF PRINCES TO EXPEL THE GITANOS

'Every one who considers the manner of your Majesty's government as the truly Christian pattern must entertain fervent hope that the advice proffered in this discourse will be attended to; more especially on reflecting that not only the good, but even the most barbarous kings have acted up to it in their respective dominions.

'Pharaoh was bad enough, nevertheless he judged that the children of Israel were dangerous to the state, because they appeared to him to be living without any certain occupation; and for this very reason the Chaldeans cast them out of Babylon. Amasis, king of Egypt, drove all the vagrants from his kingdom, forbidding them to return under pain of death. The Soldan of Egypt expelled the Torlaquis. The Moors did the same; and Bajazet cast them out of all the Ottoman empire, according to Leo Clavius.

'In the second place, the Christian princes have deemed it an important measure of state.

'The emperor our Lord, in the German Diets of the year 1548, expelled the Gitanos from all his empire, and these were the words of the decree: "Zigeuner quos compertum est proditores esse, et exploratores hostium nusquam in imperio locum inveniunto. In deprehensos vis et injuria sine fraude esto. Fides publica Zigeuners ne dator, nec data servator."

'The King of France, Francis, expelled them from thence; and the Duke of Terranova, when Governor of Milan for our lord the king, obliged them to depart from that territory under pain of death.

'Thirdly, there is one grand reason which ought to be conclusive in moving him who so much values himself in being a faithful son of the church, - I mean the example which Pope Pius the Fifth gave to all the princes; for he drove the Gitanos from all his domains, and in the year 1568, he expelled the Jews, assigning as reasons for their expulsion those which are more closely applicable to the Gitanos; - namely, that they sucked the vitals of the state, without being of any utility whatever; that they were thieves themselves, and harbourers of others; that they were wizards, diviners, and wretches who induced people to believe that they knew the future, which is what the Gitanos at present do by telling fortunes.

'Your Majesty has already freed us from greater and more dangerous enemies; finish, therefore, the enterprise begun, whence will result universal joy and security, and by which your Majesty will earn immortal honour. Amen.

'O Regum summe, horum plura ne temnas (absit) ne forte tempsisse Hispaniae periculosum existat.'

CHAPTER XI

PERHAPS there is no country in which more laws have been framed, having in view the extinction and suppression of the Gypsy name, race, and manner of life, than Spain. Every monarch, during a period of three hundred years, appears at his accession to the throne to have considered that one of his first and most imperative duties consisted in suppressing or checking the robberies, frauds, and other enormities of the Gitanos, with which the whole country seems to have resounded since the time of their first appearance.

They have, by royal edicts, been repeatedly banished from Spain, under terrible penalties, unless they renounced their inveterate habits; and for the purpose of eventually confounding them with the residue of the population, they have been forbidden, even when stationary, to reside together, every family being enjoined to live apart, and neither to seek nor to hold communication with others of the race.

We shall say nothing at present as to the wisdom which dictated these provisions, nor whether others might not have been devised, better calculated to produce the end desired. Certain it is, that the laws were never, or very imperfectly, put in force, and for reasons with which their expediency or equity (which no one at the time impugned) had no connection whatever.

It is true that, in a country like Spain, abounding in wildernesses and almost inaccessible mountains, the task of hunting down and exterminating or banishing the roving bands would have been found one of no slight difficulty, even if such had ever been attempted; but it must be remembered, that from an early period colonies of Gitanos have existed in the principal towns of Spain, where the men have plied the trades of jockeys and blacksmiths, and the women subsisted by divination, and all kinds of fraud. These colonies were, of course, always within the reach of the hand of justice, yet it does not appear that they were more interfered with than the roving and independent bands, and that any serious attempts were made to break them up, though notorious as nurseries and refuges of crime.

It is a lamentable fact, that pure and uncorrupt justice has never existed in Spain, as far at least as record will allow us to judge; not that the principles of justice have been less understood there than in other countries, but because the entire system of justiciary administration has ever been shamelessly profligate and vile.

Spanish justice has invariably been a mockery, a thing to be bought and sold, terrible only to the feeble and innocent, and an instrument of cruelty and avarice.

The tremendous satires of Le Sage upon Spanish corregidors and alguazils are true, even at the present day, and the most notorious offenders can generally escape, if able to administer sufficient bribes to the ministers [40] of what is misnamed justice.

The reader, whilst perusing the following extracts from the laws framed against the Gitanos, will be filled with wonder that the Gypsy sect still exists in Spain, contrary to the declared will of the sovereign and the nation, so often repeated during a period of three hundred years; yet such is the fact, and it can only be accounted for on the ground of corruption.

It was notorious that the Gitanos had powerful friends and favourers in every district, who sanctioned and encouraged them in their Gypsy practices. These their fautors were of all ranks and grades, from the corregidor of noble blood to the low and obscure escribano; and from the viceroy of the province to the archer of the Hermandad.

To the high and noble, they were known as Chalanes, and to the plebeian functionaries, as people who, notwithstanding their general poverty, could pay for protection.

A law was even enacted against these protectors of the Gitanos, which of course failed, as the execution of the law was confided to the very delinquents against whom it was directed. Thus, the Gitano bought, sold, and exchanged animals openly, though he subjected himself to the penalty of death by so doing, or left his habitation when he thought fit, though such an act, by the law of the land, was punishable with the galleys.

In one of their songs they have commemorated the impunity with which they wandered about. The escribano, to whom the Gitanos of the neighbourhood pay contribution, on a strange Gypsy being brought before him, instantly orders him to be liberated, assigning as a reason that he is no Gitano, but a legitimate Spaniard:-

'I left my house, and walked about
They seized me fast, and bound:
It is a Gypsy thief, they shout,
The Spaniards here have found.

'From out the prison me they led,
Before the scribe they brought;
It is no Gypsy thief, he said,
The Spaniards here have caught.'

In a word, nothing was to be gained by interfering with the Gitanos, by those in whose hands the power was vested; but, on the contrary, something was to be lost. The chief sufferers were the labourers, and they had no power to right themselves, though their wrongs were universally admitted, and laws for their protection continually being made, which their enemies contrived to set at nought; as will presently be seen.

The first law issued against the Gypsies appears to have been that of Ferdinand and Isabella, at Medina del Campo, in 1499. In this edict they were commanded, under certain penalties, to become stationary in towns and villages, and to provide themselves with masters whom they might serve for their maintenance, or in default thereof, to quit the kingdom at the end of sixty days. No mention is made of the country to which they were expected to betake themselves in the event of their quitting Spain. Perhaps, as they are called Egyptians, it was concluded that they would forthwith return to Egypt; but the framers of the law never seem to have considered what means these Egyptians possessed of transporting their families and themselves across the sea to such a distance, or if they betook themselves to other countries, what reception a host of people, confessedly thieves and vagabonds, were likely to meet with, or whether it was fair in the TWO CHRISTIAN PRINCES to get rid of such a nuisance at the expense of their neighbours. Such matters were of course left for the Gypsies themselves to settle.

In this edict, a class of individuals is mentioned in conjunction with the Gitanos, or Gypsies, but distinguished from them by the name of foreign tinkers, or Calderos estrangeros. By these, we presume, were meant the Calabrians, who are still to be seen upon the roads of Spain, wandering about from town to town, in much the same way as the itinerant tinkers of England at the present day. A man, half a savage, a haggard woman, who is generally a Spaniard, a wretched child, and still more miserable donkey, compose the group; the gains are of course exceedingly scanty, nevertheless this life, seemingly so wretched, has its charms for these outcasts, who live without care and anxiety, without a thought beyond the present hour, and who sleep as sound in ruined posadas and ventas, or in ravines amongst rocks and pines, as the proudest grandee in his palace at Seville or Madrid.

Don Carlos and Donna Juanna, at Toledo, 1539, confirmed the edict of Medina del Campo against the Egyptians, with the addition, that if any Egyptian, after the expiration of the sixty days, should be found wandering about, he should be sent to the galleys for six years, if above the age of twenty and under that of fifty, and if under or above those years, punished as the preceding law provides.

Philip the Second, at Madrid, 1586, after commanding that all the laws and edicts be observed, by which the Gypsies are forbidden to wander about, and commanded to establish themselves, ordains, with the view of restraining their thievish and cheating practices, that none of them be permitted to sell anything, either within or without fairs or markets, if not provided with a testimony signed by the notary public, to prove that they have a settled residence, and where it may be; which testimony must also specify and describe the horses, cattle, linen, and other things, which they carry forth for sale; otherwise they are to be punished as thieves, and what they attempt to sell considered as stolen property.

Philip the Third, at Belem, in Portugal, 1619, commands all the Gypsies of the kingdom to quit the same within the term of six months, and never to return, under pain of death; those who should wish to remain are to establish themselves in cities, towns, and villages, of one thousand families and upwards, and are not to be allowed the use of the dress, name, and language of Gypsies, IN ORDER THAT, FORASMUCH AS THEY ARE NOT SUCH BY NATION, THIS NAME AND MANNER OF LIFE MAY BE FOR EVERMORE CONFOUNDED AND FORGOTTEN. They are moreover forbidden, under the same penalty, to have anything to do with the buying or selling of cattle, whether great or small.

The most curious portion of the above law is the passage in which these people are declared not to be Gypsies by nation. If they are not Gypsies, who are they then? Spaniards? If so, what right had the King of Spain to send the refuse of his subjects abroad, to corrupt other lands, over which he had no jurisdiction?

The Moors were sent back to Africa, under some colour of justice, as they came originally from that part of the world; but what would have been said to such a measure, if the edict which banished them had declared that they were not Moors, but Spaniards?

The law, moreover, in stating that they are not Gypsies by nation, seems to have forgotten that in that case it would be impossible to distinguish them from other Spaniards, so soon as they should have dropped the name, language, and dress of Gypsies. How, provided they were like other Spaniards, and did not carry the mark of another nation on their countenances, could it be known whether or not they obeyed the law, which commanded them to live only in populous towns or villages, or how could they be detected in the buying or selling of cattle, which the law forbids them under pain of death?

The attempt to abolish the Gypsy name and manner of life might have been made without the assertion of a palpable absurdity.

Philip the Fourth, May 8, 1633, after reference to the evil lives and want of religion of the Gypsies, and the complaints made against them by prelates and others, declares 'that the laws hitherto adopted since the year 1499, have been inefficient to restrain their excesses; that they are not Gypsies by origin or nature, but have adopted this form of life'; and then, after forbidding them, according to custom, the dress and language of Gypsies, under the usual severe penalties, he ordains:-

'1st. That under the same penalties, the aforesaid people shall, within two months, leave the quarters (barrios) where they now live with the denomination of Gitanos, and that they shall separate from each other, and mingle with the other inhabitants, and that they shall hold no more meetings, neither in public nor in secret; that the ministers of justice are to observe, with particular diligence, how they fulfil these commands, and whether they hold communication with each other, or marry amongst themselves; and how they fulfil the obligations of Christians by assisting at sacred worship in the churches; upon which latter point they are to procure information with all possible secrecy from the curates and clergy of the parishes where the Gitanos reside.

'2ndly. And in order to extirpate, in every way, the name of Gitanos, we ordain that they be not called so, and that no one venture to call them so, and that such shall be esteemed a very heavy injury, and shall be punished as such, if proved, and that nought pertaining to the Gypsies, their name, dress, or actions, be represented, either in dances or in any other performance, under the penalty of two years' banishment, and a mulct of fifty thousand maravedis to whomsoever shall offend for the first time, and double punishment for the second.'

The above two articles seem to have in view the suppression and breaking up of the Gypsy colonies established in the large towns, more especially the suburbs; farther on, mention is made of the wandering bands.

'4thly. And forasmuch as we have understood that numerous Gitanos rove in bands through various parts of the kingdom, committing robberies in uninhabited places, and even invading some small villages, to the great terror and danger of the inhabitants, we give by this our law a general commission to all ministers of justice, whether appertaining to royal domains, lordships, or abbatial territories, that every one may, in his district, proceed to the imprisonment and chastisement of the delinquents, and may pass beyond his own jurisdiction in pursuit of them; and we also command all the ministers of justice aforesaid, that on receiving information that Gitanos or highwaymen are prowling in their districts, they do assemble at an appointed day, and with the necessary preparation of men and arms they do hunt down, take, and deliver them under a good guard to the nearest officer holding the royal commission.'

Carlos the Second followed in the footsteps of his predecessors, with respect to the Gitanos. By a law of the 20th of

November 1692, he inhibits the Gitanos from living in towns of less than one thousand heads of families (vecinos), and pursuing any trade or employment, save the cultivation of the ground; from going in the dress of Gypsies, or speaking the language or gibberish which they use; from living apart in any particular quarter of the town; from visiting fairs with cattle, great or small, or even selling or exchanging such at any time, unless with the testimonial of the public notary, that they were bred within their own houses. By this law they are also forbidden to have firearms in their possession.

So far from being abashed by this law, or the preceding one, the Gitanos seem to have increased in excesses of every kind. Only three years after (12th June 1695), the same monarch deemed it necessary to publish a new law for their persecution and chastisement. This law, which is exceedingly severe, consists of twenty-nine articles. By the fourth they are forbidden any other exercise or manner of life than that of the cultivation of the fields, in which their wives and children, if of competent age, are to assist them.

Of every other office, employment, or commerce, they are declared incapable, and especially of being BLACKSMITHS.

By the fifth, they are forbidden to keep horses or mares, either within or without their houses, or to make use of them in any way whatever, under the penalty of two months' imprisonment and the forfeiture of such animals; and any one lending them a horse or a mare is to forfeit the same, if it be found in their possession. They are declared only capable of keeping a mule, or some lesser beast, to assist them in their labour, or for the use of their families.

By the twelfth, they are to be punished with six years in the galleys, if they leave the towns or villages in which they are located, and pass to others, or wander in the fields or roads; and they are only to be permitted to go out, in order to exercise the pursuit of husbandry. In this edict, particular mention is made of the favour and protection shown to the Gitanos, by people of various descriptions, by means of which they had been enabled to follow their manner of life undisturbed, and to baffle the severity of the laws:-

'Article 16. - And because we understand that the continuance in these kingdoms of those who are called Gitanos has depended on the favour, protection, and assistance which they have experienced from persons of different stations, we do ordain, that whosoever, against whom shall be proved the fact of having, since the day of the publication hereof, favoured, received, or assisted the said Gitanos, in any manner whatever, whether within their houses or without, the said person, provided he is noble, shall be subjected to the fine of six thousand ducats, the half of which shall be applied to our treasury, and the other half to the expenses of the prosecution; and, if a plebeian, to a punishment of ten years in the galleys. And we declare, that in order to proceed to the infliction of such fine and punishment, the evidence of two respectable witnesses, without stain or suspicion, shall be esteemed legitimate and conclusive, although they depose to separate acts, or three depositions of the Gitanos themselves, MADE UPON THE RACK, although they relate to separate and different acts of abetting and harbouring.'

The following article is curious, as it bears evidence to Gypsy craft and cunning:-

'Article 18. - And whereas it is very difficult to prove against the Gitanos the robberies and delinquencies which they commit, partly because they happen in uninhabited places, but more especially on account of the MALICE and CUNNING with which they execute them; we do ordain, in order that they may receive the merited chastisement, that to convict, in these cases, those who are called Gitanos, the depositions of the persons whom they have robbed in uninhabited places shall be sufficient, provided there are at least two witnesses to one and the same fact, and these of good fame and reputation; and we also declare, that the CORPUS DELICTI may be proved in the same manner in these cases, in order that the culprits may be proceeded against, and condemned to the corresponding pains and punishments.'

The council of Madrid published a schedule, 18th of August 1705, from which it appears that the villages and roads were so much infested by the Gitano race, that there was neither peace nor safety for labourers and travellers; the corregidors and justices are therefore exhorted to use their utmost endeavour to apprehend these outlaws, and to execute upon them the punishments enjoined by the preceding law. The ministers of justice are empowered to fire upon them as public enemies, wherever they meet them, in case of resistance or refusal to deliver up the arms they carry about them.

Philip the Fifth, by schedule, October 1st, 1726, forbade any complaints which the Gitanos might have to make against the inferior justices being heard in the higher tribunals, and, on that account, banished all the Gypsy women from Madrid, and, indeed, from all towns where royal audiences were held, it being the custom of the women to flock up to the capital from the small towns and villages, under pretence of claiming satisfaction for wrongs inflicted upon their husbands and relations, and when there to practise the art of divination, and to sing obscene songs through the streets; by this law, also, the justices are particularly commanded not to permit the Gitanos to leave their places of domicile, except in cases of very urgent necessity.

This law was attended with the same success as the others; the Gitanos left their places of domicile whenever they thought proper, frequented the various fairs, and played off their jockey tricks as usual, or traversed the country in armed gangs, plundering the small villages, and assaulting travellers.

The same monarch, in October, published another law against them, from St. Lorenzo, of the Escurial. From the words of this edict, and the measures resolved upon, the reader may form some idea of the excesses of the Gitanos at this period. They are to be hunted down with fire and sword, and even the sanctity of the temples is to be invaded in their pursuit, and the Gitanos dragged from the horns of the altar, should they flee thither for refuge. It was impossible, in Spain, to carry the severity of persecution farther, as the very parricide was in perfect safety, could he escape to the church. Here follows part of this law:-

'I have resolved that all the lord-lieutenants, intendants, and corregidors shall publish proclamations, and fix edicts, to the effect that all the Gitanos who are domiciled in the cities and towns of their jurisdiction shall return within the space of fifteen days to their places of domicile, under penalty of being declared, at the expiration of that term, as public banditti, subject to be fired at in the event of being found with arms, or without them, beyond the limits of their places of domicile; and at the expiration of the term aforesaid, the lord-lieutenants, intendants, and corregidors are strictly commanded, that either they themselves, or suitable persons deputed by them, march out with armed soldiery, or if there be none at hand, with the militias, and their officers, accompanied by the horse rangers, destined for the protection of the revenue, for the purpose of scouring the whole district within their jurisdiction, making use of all possible diligence to apprehend such Gitanos as are to be found on the public roads and other places beyond their domiciliary bounds, and to inflict upon them the penalty of death, for the mere act of being found.

'And in the event of their taking refuge in sacred places, they are empowered to drag them forth, and conduct them to the neighbouring prisons and fortresses, and provided the ecclesiastical judges proceed against the secular, in order that they be restored to the church, they are at liberty to avail themselves of the recourse to force, countenanced by laws declaring, even as I now declare, that all the Gitanos who shall leave their allotted places of abode, are to be held as incorrigible rebels, and enemies of the public peace.'

From this period, until the year 1780, various other laws and schedules were directed against the Gitanos, which, as they contain nothing very new or remarkable, we may be well excused from particularising. In 1783, a law was passed by the government, widely differing in character from any which had hitherto been enacted in connection with the Gitano caste or religion in Spain.

CHAPTER XII

CARLOS TERCERO, or Charles the Third, ascended the throne of Spain in the year 1759, and died in 1788. No Spanish monarch has left behind a more favourable impression on the minds of the generality of his countrymen; indeed, he is the only one who is remembered at all by all ranks and conditions; - perhaps he took the surest means for preventing his name being forgotten, by erecting a durable monument in every large town, - we do not mean a pillar surmounted by a statue, or a colossal figure on horseback, but some useful and stately public edifice. All the magnificent modern buildings which attract the eye of the traveller in Spain, sprang up during the reign of Carlos Tercero, - for example, the museum at Madrid, the gigantic tobacco fabric at Seville, - half fortress, half manufactory, - and the Farol, at Coruna. We suspect that these erections, which speak to the eye, have gained him far greater credit amongst Spaniards than the support which he afforded to liberal opinions, which served to fan the flame of insurrection in the new world, and eventually lost for Spain her transatlantic empire.

We have said that he left behind him a favourable impression amongst the generality of his countrymen; by which we mean the great body found in every nation, who neither think nor reason, - for there are amongst the Spaniards not a few who deny that any of his actions entitle him to the gratitude of the nation. 'All his thoughts,' say they, 'were directed to hunting - and hunting alone; and all the days of the year he employed himself either in hunting or in preparation for the sport. In one expedition, in the parks of the Pardo, he spent several millions of reals. The noble edifices which adorn Spain, though built by his orders, are less due to his reign than to the anterior one, - to the reign of Ferdinand the Sixth, who left immense treasures, a small portion of which Carlos Tercero devoted to these purposes, squandering away the remainder. It is said that Carlos Tercero was no friend to superstition; yet how little did Spain during his time gain in religious liberty! The great part of the nation remained intolerant and theocratic as before, the other and smaller section turned philosophic, but after the insane manner of the French revolutionists, intolerant in its incredulity, and believing more in the ENCYCLOPEDIE than in the Gospel of the Nazarene.' [41]

We should not have said thus much of Carlos Tercero, whose character has been extravagantly praised by the multitude, and severely criticised by the discerning few who look deeper than the surface of things, if a law passed during his reign did not connect him intimately with the history of the Gitanos, whose condition to a certain extent it has already altered, and over whose future destinies there can be no doubt that it will exert considerable influence. Whether Carlos Tercero had anything farther to do with its enactment than subscribing it with his own hand, is a point difficult to determine; the chances are that he had not; there is damning evidence to prove that in many respects he was a mere Nimrod, and it is not probable that such a character would occupy his thoughts much with plans for the welfare of his people, especially such a class as the Gitanos, however willing to build public edifices, gratifying to his vanity, with the money which a provident predecessor had amassed.

The law in question is dated 19th September 1783. It is entitled, 'Rules for repressing and chastising the vagrant mode of life, and other excesses, of those who are called Gitanos.' It is in many respects widely different from all the preceding laws, and on that account we have separated it from them, deeming it worthy of particular notice. It is evidently the production of a comparatively enlightened spirit, for Spain had already begun to emerge from the dreary night of monachism and bigotry, though the light which beamed upon her was not that of the Gospel, but of modern philosophy. The spirit, however, of the writers of the ENCYCLOPEDIE is to be preferred to that of TORQUEMADA AND MONCADA, and however deeply we may lament the many grievous omissions in the law of Carlos Tercero (for no provision was made for the spiritual instruction of the Gitanos), we prefer it in all points to that of Philip the Third, and to the law passed during the reign of that unhappy victim of monkish fraud, perfidy, and poison, Charles the Second.

Whoever framed the law of Carlos Tercero with respect to the Gitanos, had sense enough to see that it would be impossible to reclaim and bring them within the pale of civilised society by pursuing the course invariably adopted on former occasions - to see that all the menacing edicts for the last three hundred years, breathing a spirit of blood and persecution, had been unable to eradicate Gitanismo from Spain; but on the contrary, had rather served to extend it. Whoever framed this law was, moreover, well acquainted with the manner of administering justice in Spain, and saw the folly of making statutes which were never put into effect. Instead, therefore, of relying on corregidors and alguazils for the extinction of the Gypsy sect, the statute addresses itself more particularly to the Gitanos themselves, and endeavours to convince them that it would be for their interest to renounce their much cherished Gitanismo. Those who framed the former laws had invariably done their best to brand this race with infamy, and had marked out for its members, in the event of abandoning their Gypsy habits, a life to which death itself must have been preferable in every respect. They were not to speak to each other, nor to intermarry, though, as they were considered of an impure caste, it was scarcely to be expected that the other Spaniards would form with them relations of love or amity, and they were debarred the exercise of any trade or occupation but hard labour, for which neither by nature nor habit they were at all adapted. The law of Carlos Tercero, on the contrary, flung open to them the whole career of arts and sciences, and declared them capable of following any trade or profession to which they might please to addict themselves. Here follow extracts from the above-mentioned law:-

'Art. 1 I declare that those who go by the name of Gitanos are not so by origin or nature, nor do they proceed from any infected root.

'2. I therefore command that neither they, nor any one of them shall use the language, dress, or vagrant kind of life which they have followed unto the present time, under the penalties here below contained.

‘3. I forbid all my vassals, of whatever state, class, and condition they may be, to call or name the above-mentioned people by the names of Gitanos, or new Castilians, under the same penalties to which those are subject who injure others by word or writing.

‘5. It is my will that those who abandon the said mode of life, dress, language, or jargon, be admitted to whatever offices or employments to which they may apply themselves, and likewise to any guilds or communities, without any obstacle or contradiction being offered to them, or admitted under this pretext within or without courts of law.

‘6. Those who shall oppose and refuse the admission of this class of reclaimed people to their trades and guilds shall be mulcted ten ducats for the first time, twenty for the second, and a double quantity for the third; and during the time they continue in their opposition they shall be prohibited from exercising the same trade, for a certain period, to be determined by the judge, and proportioned to the opposition which they display.

‘7. I grant the term of ninety days, to be reckoned from the publication of this law in the principal town of every district, in order that all the vagabonds of this and any other class may retire to the towns and villages where they may choose to locate themselves, with the exception, for the present, of the capital and the royal residences, in order that, abandoning the dress, language, and behaviour of those who are called Gitanos, they may devote themselves to some honest office, trade, or occupation, it being a matter of indifference whether the same be connected with labour or the arts.

‘8. It will not be sufficient for those who have been formerly known to follow this manner of life to devote themselves solely to the occupation of shearing and clipping animals, nor to the traffic of markets and fairs, nor still less to the occupation of keepers of inns and ventas in uninhabited places, although they may be innkeepers within towns, which employment shall be considered as sufficient, provided always there be no well-founded indications of their being delinquents themselves, or harbourers of such people.

'9. At the expiration of ninety days, the justices shall proceed against the disobedient in the following manner:- Those who, having abandoned the dress, name, language or jargon, association, and manners of Gitanos, and shall have moreover chosen and established a domicile, but shall not have devoted themselves to any office or employment, though it be only that of day-labourers, shall be considered as vagrants, and be apprehended and punished according to the laws in force against such people without any distinction being made between them and the other vassals.

'10. Those who henceforth shall commit any crimes, having abandoned the language, dress, and manners of Gitanos, chosen a domicile, and applied themselves to any office, shall be prosecuted and chastised like others guilty of the same crimes, without any difference being made between them.

'11. But those who shall have abandoned the aforesaid dress, language and behaviour, and those who, pretending to speak and dress like the other vassals, and even to choose a domiciliary residence, shall continue to go forth, wandering about the roads and uninhabited places, although it be with the pretext of visiting markets and fairs, such people shall be pursued and taken by the justices, and a list of them formed, with their names and appellations, age, description, with the places where they say they reside and were born.

'16. I, however, except from punishment the children and young people of both sexes who are not above sixteen years of age.

'17. Such, although they may belong to a family, shall be separated from their parents who wander about and have no employment, and shall be destined to learn something, or shall be placed out in hospices or houses of instruction.

‘20. When the register of the Gitanos who have proved disobedient shall have taken place, it shall be notified and made known to them, that in case of another relapse, the punishment of death shall be executed upon them without remission, on the examination of the register, and proof being adduced that they have returned to their former life.’

What effect was produced by this law, and whether its results at all corresponded to the views of those who enacted it, will be gathered from the following chapters of this work, in which an attempt will be made to delineate briefly the present condition of the Gypsies in Spain.

PART II

CHAPTER I

ABOUT twelve in the afternoon of the 6th of January 1836, I crossed the bridge of the Guadiana, a boundary river between Portugal and Spain, and entered Badajoz, a strong town in the latter kingdom, containing about eight thousand inhabitants, supposed to have been founded by the Romans. I instantly returned thanks to God for having preserved me in a journey of five days through the wilds of the Alemtejo, the province of Portugal the most infested by robbers and desperate characters, which I had traversed with no other human companion than a lad, almost an idiot, who was to convey back the mules which had brought me from Aldea Gallega. I intended to make but a short stay, and as a diligence would set out for Madrid the day next but one to my arrival, I purposed departing therein for the capital of Spain.

I was standing at the door of the inn where I had taken up my temporary abode; the weather was gloomy, and rain seemed to be at hand; I was thinking on the state of the country I had just entered, which was involved in bloody anarchy and confusion, and where the ministers of a religion falsely styled Catholic and Christian were blowing the trump of war, instead of preaching the love-engendering words of the blessed Gospel.

Suddenly two men, wrapped in long cloaks, came down the narrow and almost deserted street; they were about to pass, and the face of the nearest was turned full towards me; I knew to whom the countenance which he displayed must belong, and I touched him on the arm. The man stopped, and likewise his companion; I said a certain word, to which, after an exclamation of surprise, he responded in the manner I expected. The men were Gitanos or Gypsies, members of that singular family or race which has diffused itself over the face of the civilised globe, and which, in all lands, has preserved more or less its original customs and its own peculiar language.

We instantly commenced discoursing in the Spanish dialect of this language, with which I was tolerably well acquainted. I asked my two newly-made acquaintances whether there were many of their race in Badajoz and the vicinity: they informed me that there were eight or ten families in the town, and that there were others at Merida, a town about six leagues distant. I inquired by what means they lived, and they replied that they and their brethren principally gained a livelihood by trafficking in mules and asses, but that all those in Badajoz were very poor, with the exception of one man, who was exceedingly BALBALO, or rich, as he was in possession of many mules and other cattle. They removed their cloaks for a moment, and I found that their under-garments were rags.

They left me in haste, and went about the town informing the rest that a stranger had arrived who spoke Rommany as well as themselves, who had the face of a Gitano, and seemed to be of the 'errate,' or blood. In less than half an hour the street before the inn was filled with the men, women, and children of Egypt. I went out amongst them, and my heart sank within me as I surveyed them: so much vileness, dirt, and misery I had never seen amongst a similar number of human beings; but worst of all was the evil expression of their countenances, which spoke plainly that they were conversant with every species of crime, and it was not long before I found that their countenances did not belie them. After they had asked me an infinity of questions, and felt my hands, face, and clothes, they retired to their own homes.

That same night the two men of whom I have already particularly spoken came to see me. They sat down by the brasero in the middle of the apartment, and began to smoke small paper cigars. We continued for a considerable time in silence surveying each other. Of the two Gitanos one was an elderly man, tall and bony, with lean, skinny, and whimsical features, though perfectly those of a Gypsy; he spoke little, and his expressions were generally singular and grotesque. His companion, who was the man whom I had first noticed in the street, differed from him in many respects; he could be scarcely thirty, and his figure, which was about the middle height, was of Herculean proportions; shaggy black hair, like that of a wild beast, covered the greatest part of his immense head; his face was frightfully seamed with the small-pox, and his eyes, which glared like those of ferrets, peered from beneath bushy eyebrows; he wore immense moustaches, and his wide mouth was garnished with teeth exceedingly large and white. There was one peculiarity about him which must not be forgotten: his right arm was withered, and hung down from his shoulder a thin sapless stick, which contrasted strangely with the huge brawn of the left. A figure so perfectly wild and uncouth I had scarcely ever before seen. He had now flung aside his cloak, and sat before me gaunt in his rags and nakedness. In spite of his appearance, however, he seemed to be much the most sensible of the two; and the conversation which ensued was carried on chiefly between him and myself. This man, whom I shall call the first Gypsy, was the first to break silence; and he thus addressed me, speaking in Spanish, broken with words of the Gypsy tongue:-

FIRST GYPSY. - 'Arromali (in truth), I little thought when I saw the errano standing by the door of the posada that I was about to meet a brother - one too who, though well dressed, was not ashamed to speak to a poor Gitano; but tell me, I beg you, brother, from whence you come; I have heard that you have just arrived from Laloro, but I am sure you are no Portuguese; the Portuguese are very different from you; I know it, for I have been in Laloro; I rather take you to be one of the Corahai, for I have heard say that there is much of our blood there. You are a Corahano, are you not?'

MYSELF. - 'I am no Moor, though I have been in the country. I was born in an island in the West Sea, called England, which I suppose you have heard spoken of.'

FIRST GYPSY. - 'Yes, yes, I have a right to know something of the English. I was born in this foros, and remember the day when the English hundunares clambered over the walls, and took the town from the Gabine: well do I remember that day, though I was but a child; the streets ran red with blood and wine! Are there Gitanos then amongst the English?'

MYSELF. - 'There are numbers, and so there are amongst most nations of the world.'

SECOND GYPSY. - 'Vaya! And do the English Calore gain their bread in the same way as those of Spain? Do they shear and trim? Do they buy and change beasts, and (lowering his voice) do they now and then chore a gras?' [42]

MYSELF. - 'They do most of these things: the men frequent fairs and markets with horses, many of which they steal; and the women tell fortunes and perform all kinds of tricks, by which they gain more money than their husbands.'

FIRST GYPSY. - 'They would not be callees if they did not: I have known a Gitana gain twenty ounces of gold, by means of the hokkano baro, in a few hours, whilst the silly Gypsy, her husband, would be toiling with his shears for a fortnight, trimming the horses of the Busne, and yet not be a dollar richer at the end of the time.'

MYSELF. - 'You seem wretchedly poor. Are you married?'

FIRST GYPSY. - 'I am, and to the best-looking and cleverest callee in Badajoz; nevertheless we have never thriven since the day of our marriage, and a curse seems to rest upon us both. Perhaps I have only to thank myself; I was once rich, and had never less than six borricos to sell or exchange, but the day before my marriage I sold all I possessed, in order to have a grand fiesta. For three days we were merry enough; I entertained every one who chose to come in, and flung away my money by handfuls, so that when the affair was over I had not a cuarto in the world; and the very people who had feasted at my expense refused me a dollar to begin again, so we were soon reduced to the greatest misery. True it is, that I now and then shear a mule, and my wife tells the bahi (fortune) to the servant-girls, but these things stand us in little stead: the people are now very much on the alert, and my wife, with all her knowledge, has been unable to perform any grand trick which would set us up at once. She wished to come to see you, brother, this night, but was ashamed, as she has no more clothes than myself. Last summer our distress was so great that we crossed the frontier into Portugal: my wife sung, and I played the guitar, for though I have but one arm, and that a left one, I have never felt the want of the other. At Estremoz I was cast into prison as a thief and vagabond, and there I might have remained till I starved with hunger. My wife, however, soon got me out: she went to the lady of the corregidor, to whom she told a most wonderful bahi, promising treasures and titles, and I wot not what; so I was set at liberty, and returned to Spain as quick as I could.'

MYSELF. - 'Is it not the custom of the Gypsies of Spain to relieve each other in distress? - it is the rule in other countries.'

FIRST GYPSY. - 'El krallis ha nicobado la liri de los Cales - (The king has destroyed the law of the Gypsies); we are no longer the people we were once, when we lived amongst the sierras and deserts, and kept aloof from the Busne; we have lived amongst the Busne till we are become almost like them, and we are no longer united, ready to assist each other at all times and seasons, and very frequently the Gitano is the worst enemy of his brother.'

MYSELF. - 'The Gitanos, then, no longer wander about, but have fixed residences in the towns and villages?'

FIRST GYPSY. - 'In the summer time a few of us assemble together, and live about amongst the plains and hills, and by doing so we frequently contrive to pick up a horse or a mule for nothing, and sometimes we knock down a Busne, and strip him, but it is seldom we venture so far. We are much looked after by the Busne, who hold us in great dread, and abhor us. Sometimes, when wandering about, we are attacked by the labourers, and then we defend ourselves as well as we can. There is no better weapon in the hands of a Gitano than his "cachas," or shears, with which he trims the mules. I once snipped off the nose of a Busne, and opened the greater part of his cheek in an affray up the country near Trujillo.'

MYSELF. - 'Have you travelled much about Spain?'

FIRST GYPSY. - 'Very little; I have never been out of this province of Estremadura, except last year, as I told you, into Portugal. When we wander we do not go far, and it is very rare that we are visited by our brethren of other parts. I have never been in Andalusia, but I have heard say that the Gitanos are many in Andalusia, and are more wealthy than those here, and that they follow better the Gypsy law.'

MYSELF. - 'What do you mean by the Gypsy law?'

FIRST GYPSY. - 'Wherefore do you ask, brother? You know what is meant by the law of the Cales better even than ourselves.'

MYSELF. - 'I know what it is in England and in Hungary, but I can only give a guess as to what it is in Spain.'

BOTH GYPSIES. - 'What do you consider it to be in Spain?'

MYSELF. - 'Cheating and choring the Busne on all occasions, and being true to the errate in life and in death.'

At these words both the Gitanos sprang simultaneously from their seats, and exclaimed with a boisterous shout - 'Chachipe.'

This meeting with the Gitanos was the occasion of my remaining at Badajoz a much longer time than I originally intended. I wished to become better acquainted with their condition and manners, and above all to speak to them of Christ and His Word; for I was convinced, that should I travel to the end of the universe, I should meet with no people more in need of a little Christian exhortation, and I accordingly continued at Badajoz for nearly three weeks.

During this time I was almost constantly amongst them, and as I spoke their language, and was considered by them as one of themselves, I had better opportunity of arriving at a fair conclusion respecting their character than any other person could have had, whether Spanish or foreigner, without such an advantage. I found that their ways and pursuits were in almost every respect similar to those of their brethren in other countries. By cheating and swindling they gained their daily bread; the men principally by the arts of the jockey, - by buying, selling, and exchanging animals, at which they are wonderfully expert; and the women by telling fortunes, selling goods smuggled from Portugal, and dealing in love-draughts and diablerie. The most innocent occupation which I observed amongst them was trimming and shearing horses and mules, which in their language is called 'monrabar,' and in Spanish 'esquilar'; and even whilst exercising this art, they not unfrequently have recourse to foul play, doing the animal some covert injury, in hope that the proprietor will dispose of it to themselves at an inconsiderable price, in which event they soon restore it to health; for knowing how to inflict the harm, they know likewise how to remove it.

Religion they have none; they never attend mass, nor did I ever hear them employ the names of God, Christ, and the Virgin, but in execration and blasphemy. From what I could learn, it appeared that their fathers had entertained some belief in metempsychosis; but they themselves laughed at the idea, and were of opinion that the soul perished when the body ceased to breathe; and the argument which they used was rational enough, so far as it impugned metempsychosis: 'We have been wicked and miserable enough in this life,' they said; 'why should we live again?'

I translated certain portions of Scripture into their dialect, which I frequently read to them; especially the parable of Lazarus and the Prodigal Son, and told them that the latter had been as wicked as themselves, and both had suffered as much or more; but that the sufferings of the former, who always looked forward to a blessed resurrection, were recompensed by admission, in the life to come, to the society of Abraham and the Prophets, and that the latter, when he repented of his sins, was forgiven, and received into as much favour as the just son.

They listened with admiration; but, alas! not of the truths, the eternal truths, I was telling them, but to find that their broken jargon could be written and read. The only words denoting anything like assent to my doctrine which I ever obtained, were the following from the mouth of a woman: 'Brother, you tell us strange things, though perhaps you do not lie; a month since I would sooner have believed these tales, than that this day I should see one who could write Rommany.'

Two or three days after my arrival, I was again visited by the Gypsy of the withered arm, who I found was generally termed Paco, which is the diminutive of Francisco; he was accompanied by his wife, a rather good-looking young woman with sharp intelligent features, and who appeared in every respect to be what her husband had represented her on the former visit. She was very poorly clad, and notwithstanding the extreme sharpness of the weather, carried no mantle to protect herself from its inclemency, - her raven black hair depended behind as far down as her hips. Another Gypsy came with them, but not the old fellow whom I had before seen. This was a man about forty-five, dressed in a zamarra of sheep-skin, with a high-crowned Andalusian hat; his complexion was dark as pepper, and his eyes were full of sullen fire. In his appearance he exhibited a goodly compound of Gypsy and bandit.

PACO. - 'Laches chibeses te dinele Undebel (May God grant you good days, brother). This is my wife, and this is my wife's father.'

MYSELF. - 'I am glad to see them. What are their names?'

PACO. - 'Maria and Antonio; their other name is Lopez.'

MYSELF. - 'Have they no Gypsy names?'

PACO. - 'They have no other names than these.'

MYSELF. - 'Then in this respect the Gitanos of Spain are unlike those of my country. Every family there has two names; one by which they are known to the Busne, and another which they use amongst themselves.'

ANTONIO. - 'Give me your hand, brother! I should have come to see you before, but I have been to Olivenzas in search of a horse. What I have heard of you has filled me with much desire to know you, and I now see that you can tell me many things which I am ignorant of. I am Zincalo by the four sides - I love our blood, and I hate that of the Busne. Had I my will I would wash my face every day in the blood of the Busne, for the Busne are made only to be robbed and to be slaughtered; but I love the Calore, and I love to hear of things of the Calore, especially from those of foreign lands; for the Calore of foreign lands know more than we of Spain, and more resemble our fathers of old.'

MYSELF. - 'Have you ever met before with Calore who were not Spaniards?'

ANTONIO. - 'I will tell you, brother. I served as a soldier in the war of the independence against the French. War, it is true, is not the proper occupation of a Gitano, but those were strange times, and all those who could bear arms were compelled to go forth to fight: so I went with the English armies, and we chased the Gabine unto the frontier of France; and it happened once that we joined in desperate battle, and there was a confusion, and the two parties became intermingled and fought sword to sword and bayonet to bayonet, and a French soldier singled me out, and we fought for a long time, cutting, goring, and cursing each other, till at last we flung down our arms and grappled; long we wrestled, body to body, but I found that I was the weaker, and I fell. The French soldier's knee was on my breast, and his grasp was on my throat, and he seized his bayonet, and he raised it to thrust me through the jaws; and his cap had fallen off, and I lifted up my eyes wildly to his face, and our eyes met, and I gave a loud shriek, and cried Zincalo, Zincalo! and I felt him shudder, and he relaxed his grasp and started up, and he smote his forehead and wept, and then he came to me and knelt down by my side, for I was almost dead, and he took my hand and called me Brother and Zincalo, and he produced his flask and poured wine into my mouth, and I revived, and he raised me up, and led me from the concourse, and we sat down on a knoll, and the two parties were fighting all around, and he said, "Let the dogs fight, and tear each others' throats till they are all destroyed, what matters it to the Zincali? they are not of our blood, and shall that be shed for them?" So we sat for hours on the knoll and discoursed on matters pertaining to our people; and I could have listened for years, for he told me secrets which made my ears tingle, and I soon found that I knew nothing, though I had before considered myself quite Zincalo; but as for him, he knew the whole cuenta; the Bengui Lango [43] himself could have told him nothing but what he knew. So we sat till the sun went down and the battle was over, and he proposed that we should both flee to his own country and live there with the Zincali; but my heart failed me; so we embraced, and he departed to the Gabine, whilst I returned to our own battalions.'

MYSELF. - 'Do you know from what country he came?'

ANTONIO. - 'He told me that he was a Mayoro.'

MYSELF. - 'You mean a Magyar or Hungarian.'

ANTONIO. - 'Just so; and I have repented ever since that I did not follow him.'

MYSELF. - 'Why so?'

ANTONIO. - 'I will tell you: the king has destroyed the law of the Cales, and has put disunion amongst us. There was a time when the house of every Zincalo, however rich, was open to his brother, though he came to him naked; and it was then the custom to boast of the "errate." It is no longer so now: those who are rich keep aloof from the rest, will not speak in Calo, and will have no dealings but with the Busne. Is there not a false brother in this foros, the only rich man among us, the swine, the balichow? he is married to a Busnee and he would fain appear as a Busno! Tell me one thing, has he been to see you? The white blood, I know he has not; he was afraid to see you, for he knew that by Gypsy law he was bound to take you to his house and feast you, whilst you remained, like a prince, like a crallis of the Cales, as I believe you are, even though he sold the last gras from the stall. Who have come to see you, brother? Have they not been such as Paco and his wife, wretches without a house, or, at best, one filled with cold and poverty; so that you have had to stay at a mesuna, at a posada of the Busne; and, moreover, what have the Cales given you since you have been residing here? Nothing, I trow, better than this rubbish, which is all I can offer you, this Meligrana de los Bengues.'

Here he produced a pomegranate from the pocket of his zamarra, and flung it on the table with such force that the fruit burst, and the red grains were scattered on the floor.

The Gitanos of Estremadura call themselves in general Chai or Chabos, and say that their original country was Chal or Egypt. I frequently asked them what reason they could assign for calling themselves Egyptians, and whether they could remember the names of any places in their supposed fatherland; but I soon found that, like their brethren in other parts of the world, they were unable to give any rational account of themselves, and preserved no recollection of the places where their forefathers had wandered; their language, however, to a considerable extent, solved the riddle, the bulk of which being Hindui, pointed out India as the birthplace of their race, whilst the number of Persian, Sclavonian, and modern Greek words with which it is checkered, spoke plainly as to the countries through which these singular people had wandered before they arrived in Spain.

They said that they believed themselves to be Egyptians, because their fathers before them believed so, who must know much better than themselves. They were fond of talking of Egypt and its former greatness, though it was evident that they knew nothing farther of the country and its history than what they derived from spurious biblical legends current amongst the Spaniards; only from such materials could they have composed the following account of the manner of their expulsion from their native land.

'There was a great king in Egypt, and his name was Pharaoh. He had numerous armies, with which he made war on all countries, and conquered them all. And when he had conquered the entire world, he became sad and sorrowful; for as he delighted in war, he no longer knew on what to employ himself. At last he bethought him on making war on God; so he sent a defiance to God, daring him to descend from the sky with his angels, and contend with Pharaoh and his armies; but God said, I will not measure my strength with that of a man. But God was incensed against Pharaoh, and resolved to punish him; and he opened a hole in the side of an enormous mountain, and he raised a raging wind, and drove before it Pharaoh and his armies to that hole, and the abyss received them, and the mountain closed upon them; but whosoever goes to that mountain on the night of St. John can hear Pharaoh and his armies singing and yelling therein. And it came to pass, that when Pharaoh and his armies had disappeared, all the kings and the nations which had become subject to Egypt revolted against Egypt, which, having lost her king and her armies, was left utterly without defence; and they made war against her, and prevailed against her, and took her people and drove them forth, dispersing them over all the world.'

So that now, say the Chai, 'Our horses drink the water of the Guadiana' - (Apilyela gras Chai la panee Lucalee).

'THE STEEDS OF THE EGYPTIANS DRINK THE WATERS OF THE GUADIANA

'The region of Chal was our dear native soil,
Where in fulness of pleasure we lived without toil;
Till dispersed through all lands, 'twas our fortune to be -
Our steeds, Guadiana, must now drink of thee.

'Once kings came from far to kneel down at our gate,
And princes rejoic'd on our meanest to wait;
But now who so mean but would scorn our degree -
Our steeds, Guadiana, must now drink of thee.

'For the Undebel saw, from his throne in the cloud,
That our deeds they were foolish, our hearts they were proud;
And in anger he bade us his presence to flee -
Our steeds, Guadiana, must now drink of thee.

'Our horses should drink of no river but one;
It sparkles through Chal, 'neath the smile of the sun,
But they taste of all streams save that only, and see -
Apilyela gras Chai la panee Lucalee.'

CHAPTER II

IN Madrid the Gitanos chiefly reside in the neighbourhood of the 'mercado,' or the place where horses and other animals are sold, - in two narrow and dirty lanes, called the Calle de la Comadre and the Callejon de Lavapies. It is said that at the beginning of last century Madrid abounded with these people, who, by their lawless behaviour and dissolute lives, gave occasion to great scandal; if such were the case, their numbers must have considerably diminished since that period, as it would be difficult at any time to collect fifty throughout Madrid. These Gitanos seem, for the most part, to be either Valencians or of Valencian origin, as they in general either speak or understand the dialect of Valencia; and whilst speaking their own peculiar jargon, the Rommany, are in the habit of making use of many Valencian words and terms.

The manner of life of the Gitanos of Madrid differs in no material respect from that of their brethren in other places. The men, every market-day, are to be seen on the skirts of the mercado, generally with some miserable animal - for example, a foundered mule or galled borrico, by means of which they seldom fail to gain a dollar or two, either by sale or exchange. It must not, however, be supposed that they content themselves with such paltry earnings. Provided they have any valuable animal, which is not unfrequently the case, they invariably keep such at home snug in the stall, conducting thither the chapman, should they find any, and concluding the bargain with the greatest secrecy. Their general reason for this conduct is an unwillingness to exhibit anything calculated to excite the jealousy of the chalans, or jockeys of Spanish blood, who on the slightest umbrage are in the habit of ejecting them from the fair by force of palos or cudgels, in which violence the chalans are to a certain extent countenanced by law; for though by the edict of Carlos the Third the Gitanos were in other respects placed upon an equality with the rest of the Spaniards, they were still forbidden to obtain their livelihood by the traffic of markets and fairs.

They have occasionally however another excellent reason for not exposing the animal in the public mercado - having obtained him by dishonest means. The stealing, concealing, and receiving animals when stolen, are inveterate Gypsy habits, and are perhaps the last from which the Gitano will be reclaimed, or will only cease when the race has become extinct. In the prisons of Madrid, either in that of the Saladero or De la Corte, there are never less than a dozen Gitanos immured for stolen horses or mules being found in their possession, which themselves or their connections have spirited away from the neighbouring villages, or sometimes from a considerable distance. I say spirited away, for so well do the thieves take their measures, and watch their opportunity, that they are seldom or never taken in the fact.

The Madrilenian Gypsy women are indefatigable in the pursuit of prey, prowling about the town and the suburbs from morning till night, entering houses of all descriptions, from the highest to the lowest; telling fortunes, or attempting to play off various kinds of Gypsy tricks, from which they derive much greater profit, and of which we shall presently have occasion to make particular mention.

From Madrid let us proceed to Andalusia, casting a cursory glance on the Gitanos of that country. I found them very numerous at Granada, which in the Gitano language is termed Meligrana. Their general condition in this place is truly miserable, far exceeding in wretchedness the state of the tribes of Estremadura. It is right to state that Granada itself is the poorest city in Spain; the greatest part of the population, which exceeds sixty thousand, living in beggary and nakedness, and the Gitanos share in the general distress.

Many of them reside in caves scooped in the sides of the ravines which lead to the higher regions of the Alpujarras, on a skirt of which stands Granada. A common occupation of the Gitanos of Granada is working in iron, and it is not unfrequent to find these caves tenanted by Gypsy smiths and their families, who ply the hammer and forge in the bowels of the earth. To one standing at the mouth of the cave, especially at night, they afford a picturesque spectacle. Gathered round the forge, their bronzed and naked bodies, illuminated by the flame, appear like figures of demons;

while the cave, with its flinty sides and uneven roof, blackened by the charcoal vapours which hover about it in festoons, seems to offer no inadequate representation of fabled purgatory. Working in iron was an occupation strictly forbidden to the Gitanos by the ancient laws, on what account does not exactly appear; though, perhaps, the trade of the smith was considered as too much akin to that of the chalan to be permitted to them. The Gypsy smith of Granada is still a chalan, even as his brother in England is a jockey and tinker alternately.

Whilst speaking of the Gitanos of Granada, we cannot pass by in silence a tragedy which occurred in this town amongst them, some fifteen years ago, and the details of which are known to every Gitano in Spain, from Catalonia to Estremadura. We allude to the murder of Pindamonas by Pepe Conde. Both these individuals were Gitanos; the latter was a celebrated contrabandista, of whom many remarkable tales are told. On one occasion, having committed some enormous crime, he fled over to Barbary and turned Moor, and was employed by the Moorish emperor in his wars, in company with the other renegade Spaniards, whose grand depot or presidio is the town of Agurey in the kingdom of Fez. After the lapse of some years, when his crime was nearly forgotten, he returned to Granada, where he followed his old occupations of contrabandista and chalan. Pindamonas was a Gitano of considerable wealth, and was considered as the most respectable of the race at Granada, amongst whom he possessed considerable influence. Between this man and Pepe Conde there existed a jealousy, especially on the part of the latter, who, being a man of proud untamable spirit, could not well brook a superior amongst his own people. It chanced one day that Pindamonas and other Gitanos, amongst whom was Pepe Conde, were in a coffee-house. After they had all partaken of some refreshment, they called for the reckoning, the amount of which Pindamonas insisted on discharging. It will be necessary here to observe, that on such occasions in Spain it is considered as a species of privilege to be allowed to pay, which is an honour generally claimed by the principal man of the party. Pepe Conde did not fail to take umbrage at the attempt of Pindamonas, which he considered as an undue assumption of superiority, and put in his own claim; but Pindamonas insisted, and at last flung down the money on the table, whereupon Pepe Conde instantly unclasped one of those terrible Manchegan knives which are generally carried by the contrabandistas, and with a frightful gash opened the abdomen of Pindamonas, who presently expired.

After this exploit, Pepe Conde fled, and was not seen for some time. The cave, however, in which he had been in the habit of residing was watched, as a belief was entertained that sooner or later he would return to it, in the hope of being able to remove some of the property contained in it. This belief was well founded. Early one morning he was observed to enter it, and a band of soldiers was instantly despatched to seize him. This circumstance is alluded to in a Gypsy stanza:-

'Fly, Pepe Conde, seek the hill;
To flee's thy only chance;
With bayonets fixed, thy blood to spill,
See soldiers four advance.'

And before the soldiers could arrive at the cave, Pepe Conde had discovered their approach and fled, endeavouring to make his escape amongst the rocks and barrancos of the Alpujarras. The soldiers instantly pursued, and the chase continued a considerable time. The fugitive was repeatedly summoned to surrender himself, but refusing, the soldiers at last fired, and four balls entered the heart of the Gypsy contrabandista and murderer.

Once at Madrid I received a letter from the sister's son of Pindamonas, dated from the prison of the Saladero. In this letter the writer, who it appears was in durance for stealing a pair of mules, craved my charitable assistance and advice; and possibly in the hope of securing my favour, forwarded some uncouth lines commemorative of the death of his relation, and commencing thus:-

'The death of Pindamonas fill'd all the world with pain; At the coffee-house's portal, by Pepe he was slain.'

The faubourg of Triana, in Seville, has from time immemorial been noted as a favourite residence of the Gitanos; and here, at the present day, they are to be found in greater number than in any other town in Spain. This faubourg is indeed chiefly inhabited by desperate characters, as, besides the Gitanos, the principal part of the robber population of Seville is here congregated. Perhaps there is no part even of Naples where crime so much abounds, and the law is so little respected, as at Triana, the character of whose inmates was so graphically delineated two centuries and a half back by Cervantes, in one of the most amusing of his tales. [44]

In the vilest lanes of this suburb, amidst dilapidated walls and ruined convents, exists the grand colony of Spanish Gitanos. Here they may be seen wielding the hammer; here they may be seen trimming the fetlocks of horses, or shearing the backs of mules and borricos with their cachas; and from hence they emerge to ply the same trade in the town, or to officiate as terceros, or to buy, sell, or exchange animals in the mercado, and the women to tell the bahi through the streets, even as in other parts of Spain, generally attended by one or two tawny bantlings in their arms or by their sides; whilst others, with baskets and chafing-pans, proceed to the delightful banks of the Len Baro, [45] by the Golden Tower, where, squatting on the ground and kindling their charcoal, they roast the chestnuts which, when well prepared, are the favourite bonne bouche of the Sevillians; whilst not a few, in league with the contrabandistas, go from door to door offering for sale prohibited goods brought from the English at Gibraltar. Such is Gitano life at Seville; such it is in the capital of Andalusia.

It is the common belief of the Gitanos of other provinces that in Andalusia the language, customs, habits, and practices peculiar to their race are best preserved. This opinion, which probably originated from the fact of their being found in greater numbers in this province than in any other, may hold good in some instances, but certainly not in all. In various parts of Spain I have found the Gitanos retaining their primitive language and customs better than in Seville, where they most abound: indeed, it is not plain that their number has operated at all favourably in this respect. At Cordova, a town at the distance of twenty leagues from Seville, which scarcely contains a dozen Gitano families, I found them living in much more brotherly amity, and cherishing in a greater degree the observances of their forefathers.

I shall long remember these Cordovese Gitanos, by whom I was very well received, but always on the supposition that I was one of their own race. They said that they never admitted strangers to their houses save at their marriage festivals, when they flung their doors open to all, and save occasionally people of influence and distinction, who wished to hear their songs and converse with their women; but they assured me, at the same time, that these they invariably deceived, and merely made use of as instruments to serve their own purposes. As for myself, I was admitted without scruple to their private meetings, and was made a participator of their most secret thoughts. During our intercourse some remarkable scenes occurred. One night more than twenty of us, men and women, were assembled in a long low room on the ground floor, in a dark alley or court in the old gloomy town of Cordova. After the Gitanos had discussed several jockey plans, and settled some private bargains amongst themselves, we all gathered round a huge brasero of flaming charcoal, and began conversing SOBRE LAS COSAS DE EGYPTO, when I proposed that, as we had no better means of amusing ourselves, we should endeavour to turn into the Calo language some pieces of devotion, that we might see whether this language, the gradual decay of which I had frequently heard them lament, was capable of expressing any other matters than those which related to horses, mules, and Gypsy traffic. It was in this cautious manner that I first endeavoured to divert the attention of these singular people to matters of eternal importance. My suggestion was received with acclamations, and we forthwith proceeded to the translation of the Apostles' creed. I first recited in Spanish, in the usual manner and without pausing, this noble confession, and then repeated it again, sentence by sentence, the Gitanos translating as I proceeded. They exhibited the greatest eagerness and interest in their unwonted occupation, and frequently broke into loud disputes as to the best rendering - many being offered at the same time. In the meanwhile, I wrote down from their dictation; and at the conclusion I read aloud the translation, the result of the united wisdom of the assembly, whereupon they all raised a shout of exultation, and appeared not a little proud of the composition.

The Cordovese Gitanos are celebrated esquiladors. Connected with them and the exercise of the ARTE DE ESQUILAR, in Gypsy monrabar, I have a curious anecdote to relate. In the first place, however, it may not be amiss to say something about the art itself, of all relating to which it is possible that the reader may be quite ignorant.

Nothing is more deserving of remark in Spanish grooming than the care exhibited in clipping and trimming various parts of the horse, where the growth of hair is considered as prejudicial to the perfect health and cleanliness of the animal, particular attention being always paid to the pastern, that part of the foot which lies between the fetlock and the hoof, to guard against the arestin - that cutaneous disorder which is the dread of the Spanish groom, on which account the services of a skilful esquilador are continually in requisition.

The esquilador, when proceeding to the exercise of his vocation, generally carries under his arm a small box containing the instruments necessary, and which consist principally of various pairs of scissors, and the ACIAL, two short sticks tied together with whipcord at the end, by means of which the lower lip of the horse, should he prove restive, is twisted, and the animal reduced to speedy subjection. In the girdle of the esquilador are stuck the large scissors called in Spanish TIJERAS, and in the Gypsy tongue CACHAS, with which he principally works. He operates upon the backs, ears, and tails of mules and borricos, which are invariably sheared quite bare, that if the animals are galled, either by their harness or the loads which they carry, the wounds may be less liable to fester, and be more easy to cure. Whilst engaged with horses, he confines himself to the feet and ears. The esquiladores in the two Castiles, and in those provinces where the Gitanos do not abound, are for the most part Aragonese; but in the others, and especially in Andalusia, they are of the Gypsy race. The Gitanos are in general very expert in the use of the cachas, which they handle in a manner practised nowhere but in Spain; and with this instrument the poorer class principally obtain their bread.

In one of their couplets allusion is made to this occupation in the following manner:-

'I'll rise to-morrow bread to earn,
For hunger's worn me grim;
Of all I meet I'll ask in turn,
If they've no beasts to trim.'

Sometimes, whilst shearing the foot of a horse, exceedingly small scissors are necessary for the purpose of removing fine solitary hairs; for a Spanish groom will tell you that a horse's foot behind ought to be kept as clean and smooth as the hand of a senora: such scissors can only be procured at Madrid. My sending two pair of this kind to a Cordovese Gypsy, from whom I had experienced much attention whilst in that city, was the occasion of my receiving a singular epistle from another whom I scarcely knew, and which I shall insert as being an original Gypsy composition, and in some points not a little characteristic of the people of whom I am now writing.

'Cordova, 20th day of January, 1837.
'SENOR DON JORGE,

'After saluting you and hoping that you are well, I proceed to tell you that the two pair of scissors arrived at this town of Cordova with him whom you sent them by; but, unfortunately, they were given to another Gypsy, whom you neither knew nor spoke to nor saw in your life; for it chanced that he who brought them was a friend of mine, and he told me that he had brought two pair of scissors which an Englishman had given him for the Gypsies; whereupon I, understanding it was yourself, instantly said to him, "Those scissors are for me"; he told me, however, that he had already given them to another, and he is a Gypsy who was not even in Cordova during the time you were. Nevertheless, Don Jorge, I am very grateful for your thus remembering me, although I did not receive your present, and in order that you may know who I am, my name is Antonio Salazar, a man pitted with the small-pox, and the very first who spoke to you in Cordova in the posada where you were; and you told me to come and see you next day at eleven, and I went, and we conversed together alone. Therefore I should wish you to do me the favour to send me scissors for trimming beasts, - good scissors, mind you, - such would be a very great favour, and I should be ever grateful, for here in Cordova there are none, or if there be, they are good for nothing. Senor Don Jorge, you remember I told you that I was an esquilador by trade, and only by that I got bread for my babes. Senor Don Jorge, if you do send me the scissors for trimming, pray write and direct to the alley De la Londiga, No. 28, to Antonio Salazar, in Cordova.

This is what I have to tell you, and do you ever command your trusty servant, who kisses your hand and is eager to serve you.

'ANTONIO SALAZAR.'

FIRST COUPLET

'That I may clip and trim the beasts, a pair of cachas grant,
If not, I fear my luckless babes will perish all of want.'

SECOND COUPLET

'If thou a pair of cachas grant, that I my babes may feed,
I'll pray to the Almighty God, that thee he ever speed.'

It is by no means my intention to describe the exact state and condition of the Gitanos in every town and province where they are to be found; perhaps, indeed, it will be considered that I have already been more circumstantial and particular than the case required. The other districts which they inhabit are principally those of Catalonia, Murcia, and Valencia; and they are likewise to be met with in the Basque provinces, where they are called Egipcioac, or Egyptians. What I next purpose to occupy myself with are some general observations on the habits, and the physical and moral state of the Gitanos throughout Spain, and of the position which they hold in society.

CHAPTER III

ALREADY, from the two preceding chapters, it will have been perceived that the condition of the Gitanos in Spain has been subjected of late to considerable modification. The words of the Gypsy of Badajoz are indeed, in some respects, true; they are no longer the people that they were; the roads and 'despoblados' have ceased to be infested by them, and the traveller is no longer exposed to much danger on their account; they at present confine themselves, for the most part, to towns and villages, and if they occasionally wander abroad, it is no longer in armed bands, formidable for their numbers, and carrying terror and devastation in all directions, bivouacking near solitary villages, and devouring the substance of the unfortunate inhabitants, or occasionally threatening even large towns, as in the singular case of Logrono, mentioned by Francisco de Cordova. As the reader will probably wish to know the cause of this change in the lives and habits of these people, we shall, as briefly as possible, afford as much information on the subject as the amount of our knowledge will permit.

One fact has always struck us with particular force in the history of these people, namely, that Gitanismo - which means Gypsy villainy of every description - flourished and knew nothing of decay so long as the laws recommended and enjoined measures the most harsh and severe for the suppression of the Gypsy sect; the palmy days of Gitanismo were those in which the caste was proscribed, and its members, in the event of renouncing their Gypsy habits, had nothing farther to expect than the occupation of tilling the earth, a dull hopeless toil; then it was that the Gitanos paid tribute to the inferior ministers of justice, and were engaged in illicit connection with those of higher station, and by such means baffled the law, whose vengeance rarely fell upon their heads; and then it was that they bid it open defiance, retiring to the deserts and mountains, and living in wild independence by rapine and shedding of blood; for as the law then stood they would lose all by resigning their Gitanismo, whereas by clinging to it they lived either in the independence so dear to them, or beneath the protection of their confederates. It would appear that in proportion as the law was harsh and severe, so was the Gitano bold and secure. The fiercest of these laws was the one of Philip the Fifth, passed in the year 1745, which commands that the refractory Gitanos be hunted down with fire and sword; that it was quite inefficient is satisfactorily proved by its being twice reiterated, once in the year '46, and again in '49, which would scarcely have been deemed necessary had it quelled the Gitanos. This law, with some unimportant modifications, continued in force till the year '83, when the famous edict of Carlos Tercero superseded it. Will any feel disposed to doubt that the preceding laws had served to foster what they were intended to suppress, when we state the remarkable fact, that since the enactment of that law, as humane as the others were unjust, WE HAVE HEARD NOTHING MORE OF THE GITANOS FROM OFFICIAL QUARTERS; THEY HAVE CEASED TO PLAY A DISTINCT PART IN THE HISTORY OF SPAIN; AND THE LAW NO LONGER SPEAKS OF THEM AS A DISTINCT PEOPLE? The caste of the Gitano still exists, but it is neither so extensive nor so formidable as a century ago, when the law in denouncing Gitanismo proposed to the Gitanos the alternatives of death for persisting in their profession, or slavery for abandoning it.

There are fierce and discontented spirits amongst them, who regret such times, and say that Gypsy law is now no more, that the Gypsy no longer assists his brother, and that union has ceased among them. If this be true, can better proof be adduced of the beneficial working of the later law? A blessing has been conferred on society, and in a manner highly creditable to the spirit of modern times; reform has been accomplished, not by persecution, not by the gibbet and the rack, but by justice and tolerance. The traveller has flung aside his cloak, not compelled by the angry buffeting of the north wind, but because the mild, benignant weather makes such a defence no longer necessary. The law no longer compels the Gitanos to stand back to back, on the principal of mutual defence, and to cling to Gitanismo to escape from servitude and thraldom.

Taking everything into consideration, and viewing the subject in all its bearings with an impartial glance, we are compelled to come to the conclusion that the law of Carlos Tercero, the provisions of which were distinguished by justice and clemency, has been the principal if not the only cause of the decline of Gitanismo in Spain. Some importance ought to be attached to the opinion of the Gitanos themselves on this point. 'El Crallis ha nicobado la liri de los Cales,' is a proverbial saying among them. By Crallis, or King, they mean Carlos Tercero, so that the saying, the proverbial saying, may be thus translated: THE LAW OF CARLOS TERCERO HAS SUPERSEDED GYPSY LAW.

By the law the schools are open to them, and there is no art or science which they may not pursue, if they are willing. Have they availed themselves of the rights which the law has conferred upon them?

Up to the present period but little - they still continue jockeys and blacksmiths; but some of these Gypsy chalans, these bronzed smiths, these wild-looking esquiladors, can read or write in the proportion of one man in three or four; what more can be expected? Would you have the Gypsy bantling, born in filth and misery, 'midst mules and borricos, amidst the mud of a choza or the sand of a barranco, grasp with its swarthy hands the crayon and easel, the compass, or the microscope, or the tube which renders more distinct the heavenly orbs, and essay to become a Murillo, or a Feijoo, or a Lorenzo de Hervas, as soon as the legal disabilities are removed which doomed him to be a thievish jockey or a sullen husbandman? Much will have been accomplished, if, after the lapse of a hundred years, one hundred human beings shall have been evolved from the Gypsy stock, who shall prove sober, honest, and useful members of society, - that stock so degraded, so inveterate in wickedness and evil customs, and so hardened by brutalising laws. Should so many beings, should so many souls be rescued from temporal misery and eternal woe; should only the half of that number, should only the tenth, nay, should only one poor wretched sheep be saved, there will be joy in heaven, for much will have been accomplished on earth, and those lines will have been in part falsified which filled the stout heart of Mahmoud with dismay:-

'For the root that's unclean, hope if you can;
No washing e'er whitens the black Zigan:
The tree that's bitter by birth and race,
If in paradise garden to grow you place,
And water it free with nectar and wine,
From streams in paradise meads that shine,
At the end its nature it still declares,
For bitter is all the fruit it bears.
If the egg of the raven of noxious breed
You place 'neath the paradise bird, and feed
The splendid fowl upon its nest,
With immortal figs, the food of the blest,
And give it to drink from Silisbel, [46]
Whilst life in the egg breathes Gabriel,
A raven, a raven, the egg shall bear,
And the fostering bird shall waste its care.' -

FERDOUSI.

The principal evidence which the Gitanos have hitherto given that a partial reformation has been effected in their habits, is the relinquishment, in a great degree, of that wandering life of which the ancient laws were continually complaining, and which was the cause of infinite evils, and tended not a little to make the roads insecure.

Doubtless there are those who will find some difficulty in believing that the mild and conciliatory clauses of the law in question could have much effect in weaning the Gitanos from this inveterate habit, and will be more disposed to think that this relinquishment was effected by energetic measures resorted to by the government, to compel them to remain in their places of location. It does not appear, however, that such measures were ever resorted to. Energy, indeed, in the removal of a nuisance, is scarcely to be expected from Spaniards under any circumstances. All we can say on the subject, with certainty, is, that since the repeal of the tyrannical laws, wandering has considerably decreased among the Gitanos.

Since the law has ceased to brand them, they have come nearer to the common standard of humanity, and their general condition has been ameliorated. At present, only the very poorest, the parias of the race, are to be found wandering about the heaths and mountains, and this only in the summer time, and their principal motive, according to their own confession, is to avoid the expense of house rent; the rest remain at home, following their avocations, unless some immediate prospect of gain, lawful or unlawful, calls them forth; and such is frequently the case. They attend most fairs, women and men, and on the way frequently bivouac in the fields, but this practice must not be confounded with systematic wandering.

Gitanismo, therefore, has not been extinguished, only modified; but that modification has been effected within the memory of man, whilst previously near four centuries elapsed, during which no reform had been produced amongst them by the various measures devised, all of which were distinguished by an absence not only of true policy, but of common-sense; it is therefore to be hoped, that if the Gitanos are abandoned to themselves, by which we mean no arbitrary laws are again enacted for their extinction, the sect will eventually cease to be, and its members become confounded with the residue of the population; for certainly no Christian nor merely philanthropic heart can desire the continuance of any sect or association of people whose fundamental principle seems to be to hate all the rest of mankind, and to live by deceiving them; and such is the practice of the Gitanos.

During the last five years, owing to the civil wars, the ties which unite society have been considerably relaxed; the law has been trampled under foot, and the greatest part of Spain overrun with robbers and miscreants, who, under pretence of carrying on partisan warfare, and not unfrequently under no pretence at all, have committed the most frightful excesses, plundering and murdering the defenceless. Such a state of things would have afforded the Gitanos a favourable opportunity to resume their former kind of life, and to levy contributions as formerly, wandering about in bands. Certain it is, however, that they have not sought to repeat their ancient excesses, taking advantage of the troubles of the country; they have gone on, with a few exceptions, quietly pursuing that part of their system to which they still cling, their jockeyism, which, though based on fraud and robbery, is far preferable to wandering brigandage, which necessarily involves the frequent shedding of blood. Can better proof be adduced, that Gitanismo owes its decline, in Spain, not to force, not to persecution, not to any want of opportunity of exercising it, but to some other cause? - and we repeat that we consider the principal if not the only cause of the decline of Gitanismo to be the conferring on the Gitanos the rights and privileges of other subjects.

We have said that the Gitanos have not much availed themselves of the permission, which the law grants them, of embarking in various spheres of life. They remain jockeys, but they have ceased to be wanderers; and the grand object of the law is accomplished. The law forbids them to be jockeys, or to follow the trade of trimming and shearing animals, without some other visible mode of subsistence. This provision, except in a few isolated instances, they evade; and the law seeks not, and perhaps wisely, to disturb them, content with having achieved so much. The chief evils of Gitanismo which still remain consist in the systematic frauds of the Gypsy jockeys and the tricks of the women. It is incurring considerable risk to purchase a horse or a mule, even from the most respectable Gitano, without a previous knowledge of the animal and his former possessor, the chances being that it is either diseased or stolen from a distance. Of the practices of the females, something will be said in particular in a future chapter.

The Gitanos in general are very poor, a pair of large cachas and various scissors of a smaller description constituting their whole capital; occasionally a good hit is made, as they call it, but the money does not last long, being quickly squandered in feasting and revelry. He who has habitually in his house a couple of donkeys is considered a thriving Gitano; there are some, however, who are wealthy in the strict sense of the word, and carry on a very extensive trade in horses and mules. These, occasionally, visit the most distant fairs, traversing the greatest part of Spain. There is a celebrated cattle-fair held at Leon on St. John's or Midsummer Day, and on one of these occasions, being present, I observed a small family of Gitanos, consisting of a man of about fifty, a female of the same age, and a handsome young Gypsy, who was their son; they were richly dressed after the Gypsy fashion, the men wearing zamarras with massy clasps and knobs of silver, and the woman a species of riding-dress with much gold embroidery, and having immense gold rings attached to her ears. They came from Murcia, a distance of one hundred leagues and upwards. Some merchants, to whom

I was recommended, informed me that they had credit on their house to the amount of twenty thousand dollars.

They experienced rough treatment in the fair, and on a very singular account: immediately on their appearing on the ground, the horses in the fair, which, perhaps, amounted to three thousand, were seized with a sudden and universal panic; it was one of those strange incidents for which it is difficult to assign a rational cause; but a panic there was amongst the brutes, and a mighty one; the horses neighed, screamed, and plunged, endeavouring to escape in all directions; some appeared absolutely possessed, stamping and tearing, their manes and tails stiffly erect, like the bristles of the wild boar - many a rider lost his seat. When the panic had ceased, and it did cease almost as suddenly as it had arisen, the Gitanos were forthwith accused as the authors of it; it was said that they intended to steal the best horses during the confusion, and the keepers of the ground, assisted by a rabble of chalans, who had their private reasons for hating the Gitanos, drove them off the field with sticks and cudgels. So much for having a bad name.

These wealthy Gitanos, when they are not ashamed of their blood or descent, and are not addicted to proud fancies, or 'barbales,' as they are called, possess great influence with the rest of their brethren, almost as much as the rabbins amongst the Jews; their bidding is considered law, and the other Gitanos are at their devotion. On the contrary, when they prefer the society of the Busne to that of their own race, and refuse to assist their less fortunate brethren in poverty or in prison, they are regarded with unbounded contempt and abhorrence, as in the case of the rich Gypsy of Badajoz, and are not unfrequently doomed to destruction: such characters are mentioned in their couplets:-

'The Gypsy fiend of Manga mead,
Who never gave a straw,
He would destroy, for very greed,
The good Egyptian law.

'The false Juanito day and night
Had best with caution go;
The Gypsy carles of Yeira height
Have sworn to lay him low.'

However some of the Gitanos may complain that there is no longer union to be found amongst them, there is still much of that fellow- feeling which springs from a consciousness of proceeding from one common origin, or, as they love to term it, 'blood.' At present their system exhibits less of a commonwealth than when they roamed in bands amongst the wilds, and principally subsisted by foraging, each individual contributing to the common stock, according to his success. The interests of individuals are now more distinct, and that close connection is of course dissolved which existed when they wandered about, and their dangers, gains, and losses were felt in common; and it can never be too often repeated that they are no longer a proscribed race, with no rights nor safety save what they gained by a close and intimate union. Nevertheless, the Gitano, though he naturally prefers his own interest to that of his brother, and envies him his gain when he does not expect to share in it, is at all times ready to side with him against the Busno, because the latter is not a Gitano, but of a different blood, and for no other reason. When one Gitano confides his plans to another, he is in no fear that they will be betrayed to the Busno, for whom there is no sympathy, and when a plan is to be executed which requires co-operation, they seek not the fellowship of the Busne, but of each other, and if successful, share the gain like brothers.

As a proof of the fraternal feeling which is not unfrequently displayed amongst the Gitanos, I shall relate a circumstance which occurred at Cordova a year or two before I first visited it. One of the poorest of the Gitanos murdered a Spaniard with the fatal Manchegan knife; for this crime he was seized, tried, and found guilty. Blood-shedding in Spain is not looked upon with much abhorrence, and the life of the culprit is seldom taken, provided he can offer a bribe sufficient to induce the notary public to report favourably upon his case; but in this instance money was of no avail; the murdered individual left behind him powerful friends and connections, who were determined that justice should take its course. It was in vain that the Gitanos exerted all their influence with the authorities in behalf of their comrade, and such influence was not slight; it was in vain that they offered extravagant sums that the punishment of death might be commuted to perpetual slavery in the dreary presidio of Ceuta; I was credibly informed that one of the richest Gitanos, by name Fruto, offered for his own share of the ransom the sum of five thousand crowns, whilst there was not an individual but contributed according to his means - nought availed, and the Gypsy was executed in the Plaza. The day before the execution, the Gitanos, perceiving that the fate of their brother was sealed, one and all quitted Cordova, shutting up their houses and carrying with them their horses, their mules, their borricos, their wives and families, and the greatest part of their household furniture. No one knew whither they directed their course, nor were they seen in Cordova for some months, when they again suddenly made their appearance; a few, however, never returned. So great was the horror of the Gitanos at what had occurred, that they were in the habit of saying that the place was cursed for evermore; and when I knew them, there were many amongst them who, on no account, would enter the Plaza which had witnessed the disgraceful end of their unfortunate brother.

The position which the Gitanos hold in society in Spain is the lowest, as might be expected; they are considered at best as thievish chalans, and the women as half sorceresses, and in every respect thieves; there is not a wretch, however vile, the outcast of the prison and the presidio, who calls himself Spaniard, but would feel insulted by being termed Gitano, and would thank God that he is not; and yet, strange to say, there are numbers, and those of the higher classes, who seek their company, and endeavour to imitate their manners and way of speaking. The connections which they form with the Spaniards are not many; occasionally some wealthy Gitano marries a Spanish female, but to find a Gitana united to a Spaniard is a thing of the rarest occurrence, if it ever takes place. It is, of course, by intermarriage alone that the two races will ever commingle, and before that event is brought about, much modification must take place amongst the Gitanos, in their manners, in their habits, in their affections, and their dislikes, and, perhaps, even in their physical peculiarities; much must be forgotten on both sides, and everything is forgotten in the course of time.

The number of the Gitano population of Spain at the present day may be estimated at about forty thousand. At the commencement of the present century it was said to amount to sixty thousand. There can be no doubt that the sect is by no means so numerous as it was at former periods; witness those barrios in various towns still denominated Gitanerias, but from whence the

Gitanos have disappeared even like the Moors from the Morerias. Whether this diminution in number has been the result of a partial change of habits, of pestilence or sickness, of war or famine, or of all these causes combined, we have no means of determining, and shall abstain from offering conjectures on the subject.

CHAPTER IV

IN the autumn of the year 1839, I landed at Tarifa, from the coast of Barbary. I arrived in a small felouk laden with hides for Cadiz, to which place I was myself going. We stopped at Tarifa in order to perform quarantine, which, however, turned out a mere farce, as we were all permitted to come on shore; the master of the felouk having bribed the port captain with a few fowls. We formed a motley group. A rich Moor and his son, a child, with their Jewish servant Yusouf, and myself with my own man Hayim Ben Attar, a Jew. After passing through the gate, the Moors and their domestics were conducted by the master to the house of one of his acquaintance, where he intended they should lodge; whilst a sailor was despatched with myself and Hayim to the only inn which the place afforded. I stopped in the street to speak to a person whom I had known at Seville. Before we had concluded our discourse, Hayim, who had walked forward, returned, saying that the quarters were good, and that we were in high luck, for that he knew the people of the inn were Jews. 'Jews,' said I, 'here in Tarifa, and keeping an inn, I should be glad to see them.' So I left my acquaintance, and hastened to the house. We first entered a stable, of which the ground floor of the building consisted, and ascending a flight of stairs entered a very large room, and from thence passed into a kitchen, in which were several people. One of these was a stout, athletic, burly fellow of about fifty, dressed in a buff jerkin, and dark cloth pantaloons. His hair was black as a coal and exceedingly bushy, his face much marked from some disorder, and his skin as dark as that of a toad. A very tall woman stood by the dresser, much resembling him in feature, with the same hair and complexion, but with more intelligence in her eyes than the man, who looked heavy and dogged. A dark woman, whom I subsequently discovered to be lame, sat in a corner, and two or three swarthy girls, from fifteen to eighteen years of age, were flitting about the room. I also observed a wicked-looking boy, who might have been called handsome, had not one of his eyes been injured. 'Jews,' said I, in Moorish, to Hayim, as I glanced at these people and about the room; 'these are not Jews, but children of the Dar-bushi-fal.'

'List to the Corahai,' said the tall woman, in broken Gypsy slang, 'hear how they jabber (hunelad como chamulian), truly we will make them pay for the noise they raise in the house.' Then coming up to me, she demanded with a shout, fearing otherwise that I should not understand, whether I would not wish to see the room where I was to sleep. I nodded: whereupon she led me out upon a back terrace, and opening the door of a small room, of which there were three, asked me if it would suit. 'Perfectly,' said I, and returned with her to the kitchen.

'O, what a handsome face! what a royal person!' exclaimed the whole family as I returned, in Spanish, but in the whining, canting tones peculiar to the Gypsies, when they are bent on victimising. 'A more ugly Busno it has never been our chance to see,' said the same voices in the next breath, speaking in the jargon of the tribe. 'Won't your Moorish Royalty please to eat something?' said the tall hag. 'We have nothing in the house; but I will run out and buy a fowl, which I hope may prove a royal peacock to nourish and strengthen you.' 'I hope it may turn to drow in your entrails,' she muttered to the rest in Gypsy. She then ran down, and in a minute returned with an old hen, which, on my arrival, I had observed below in the stable. 'See this beautiful fowl,' said she, 'I have been running over all Tarifa to procure it for your kingship; trouble enough I have had to obtain it, and dear enough it has cost me. I will now cut its throat.' 'Before you kill it,' said I, 'I should wish to know what you paid for it, that there may be no dispute about it in the account.' 'Two dollars I paid for it, most valorous and handsome sir; two dollars it cost me, out of my own quisobi - out of my own little purse.' I saw it was high time to put an end to these zalamerias, and therefore exclaimed in Gitano, 'You mean two brujis (reals), O mother of all the witches, and that is twelve cuartos more than it is worth.' 'Ay Dios mio, whom have we here?' exclaimed the females. 'One,' I replied, 'who knows you well and all your ways. Speak! am I to have the hen for two reals? if not, I shall leave the house this moment.' 'O yes, to be sure, brother, and for nothing if you wish it,' said the tall woman, in natural and quite altered tones; 'but why did you enter the house speaking in Corahai like a Bengui? We thought you a Busno, but we now see that you are of our religion; pray sit down and tell us where you have been.' . .

MYSELF. - 'Now, my good people, since I have answered your questions, it is but right that you should answer some of mine; pray who are you? and how happens it that you are keeping this inn?'

GYPSY HAG. - 'Verily, brother, we can scarcely tell you who we are. All we know of ourselves is, that we keep this inn, to our trouble and sorrow, and that our parents kept it before us; we were all born in this house, where I suppose we shall die.'

MYSELF. - 'Who is the master of the house, and whose are these children?'

GYPSY HAG. - 'The master of the house is the fool, my brother, who stands before you without saying a word; to him belong these children, and the cripple in the chair is his wife, and my cousin. He has also two sons who are grown-up men; one is a chumajarri (shoemaker), and the other serves a tanner.'

MYSELF. - 'Is it not contrary to the law of the Cales to follow such trades?'

GYPSY HAG. - 'We know of no law, and little of the Cales themselves. Ours is the only Calo family in Tarifa, and we never left it in our lives, except occasionally to go on the smuggling lay to Gibraltar. True it is that the Cales, when they visit Tarifa, put up at our house, sometimes to our cost. There was one Rafael, son of the rich Fruto of Cordova, here last summer, to buy up horses, and he departed a baria and a half in our debt; however, I do not grudge it him, for he is a handsome and clever Chabo - a fellow of many capacities. There was more than one Busno had cause to rue his coming to Tarifa.'

MYSELF. - 'Do you live on good terms with the Busne of Tarifa?'

GYPSY HAG. - 'Brother, we live on the best terms with the Busne of Tarifa; especially with the errays. The first people in Tarifa come to this house, to have their baji told by the cripple in the chair and by myself. I know not how it is, but we are more considered by the grandees than the poor, who hate and loathe us. When my first and only infant died, for I have been married, the child of one of the principal people was put to me to nurse, but I hated it for its white blood, as you may well believe. It never throve, for I did it a private mischief, and though it grew up and is now a youth, it is - mad.'

MYSELF. - 'With whom will your brother's children marry? You say there are no Gypsies here.'

GYPSY HAG. - 'Ay de mi, hermano! It is that which grieves me. I would rather see them sold to the Moors than married to the Busne. When Rafael was here he wished to persuade the chumajarri to accompany him to Cordova, and promised to provide for him, and to find him a wife among the Callees of that town; but the faint heart would not, though I myself begged him to comply. As for the curtidor (tanner), he goes every night to the house of a Busnee; and once, when I reproached him with it, he threatened to marry her. I intend to take my knife, and to wait behind the door in the dark, and when she comes out to gash her over the eyes. I trow he will have little desire to wed with her then.'

MYSELF. - 'Do many Busne from the country put up at this house?'

GYPSY HAG. - 'Not so many as formerly, brother; the labourers from the Campo say that we are all thieves; and that it is impossible for any one but a Calo to enter this house without having the shirt stripped from his back. They go to the houses of their acquaintance in the town, for they fear to enter these doors. I scarcely know why, for my brother is the veriest fool in Tarifa. Were it not for his face, I should say that he is no Chabo, for he cannot speak, and permits every chance to slip through his fingers. Many a good mule and borrico have gone out of the stable below, which he might have secured, had he but tongue enough to have cozened the owners. But he is a fool, as I said before; he cannot speak, and is no Chabo.'

How far the person in question, who sat all the while smoking his pipe, with the most unperturbed tranquillity, deserved the character bestowed upon him by his sister, will presently appear. It is not my intention to describe here all the strange things I both saw and heard in this Gypsy inn. Several Gypsies arrived from the country during the six days that I spent within its walls; one of them, a man, from Moron, was received with particular cordiality, he having a son, whom he was thinking of betrothing to one of the Gypsy daughters. Some females of quality likewise visited the house to gossip, like true Andalusians. It was singular to observe the behaviour of the Gypsies to these people, especially that of the remarkable woman, some of whose conversation I have given above. She whined, she canted, she blessed, she talked of beauty of colour, of eyes, of eyebrows, and pestanas (eyelids), and of hearts which were aching for such and such a lady. Amongst others, came a very fine woman, the widow of a colonel lately slain in battle; she brought with her a beautiful innocent little girl, her daughter, between three and four years of age. The Gypsy appeared to adore her; she sobbed, she shed tears, she kissed the child, she blessed it, she fondled it. I had my eye upon her countenance, and it brought to my recollection that of a she-wolf, which I had once seen in Russia, playing with her whelp beneath a birch-tree. 'You seem to love that child very much, O my mother,' said I to her, as the lady was departing.

GYPSY HAG. - 'No lo camelo, hijo! I do not love it, O my son, I do not love it; I love it so much, that I wish it may break its leg as it goes downstairs, and its mother also.'

On the evening of the fourth day, I was seated on the stone bench at the stable door, taking the fresco; the Gypsy innkeeper sat beside me, smoking his pipe, and silent as usual; presently a man and woman with a borrico, or donkey, entered the portal. I took little or no notice of a circumstance so slight, but I was presently aroused by hearing the Gypsy's pipe drop upon the ground. I looked at him, and scarcely recognised his face. It was no longer dull, black, and heavy, but was lighted up with an expression so extremely villainous that I felt uneasy. His eyes were scanning the recent comers, especially the beast of burden, which was a beautiful female donkey. He was almost instantly at their side, assisting to remove its housings, and the alforjas, or bags. His tongue had become unloosed, as if by sorcery; and far from being unable to speak, he proved that, when it suited his purpose, he could discourse with wonderful volubility. The donkey was soon tied to the manger, and a large measure of barley emptied before it, the greatest part of which the Gypsy boy presently removed, his father having purposely omitted to mix the barley with the straw, with which the Spanish mangers are always kept filled. The guests were hurried upstairs as soon as possible. I remained below, and subsequently strolled about the town and on the beach. It was about nine o'clock when I returned to the inn to retire to rest; strange things had evidently been going on during my absence. As I passed through the large room on my way to my apartment, lo, the table was set out with much wine, fruits, and viands. There sat the man from the country, three parts intoxicated; the Gypsy, already provided with another pipe, sat on his knee, with his right arm most affectionately round his neck; on one side sat the chumajarri drinking and smoking, on the other the tanner. Behold, poor humanity, thought I to myself, in the hands of devils; in this manner are human souls ensnared to destruction by the fiends of the pit. The females had already taken possession of the woman at the other end of the table, embracing her, and displaying every mark of friendship and affection. I passed on, but ere I reached my apartment I heard the words mule and donkey. 'Adios,' said I, for I but too well knew what was on the carpet.

In the back stable the Gypsy kept a mule, a most extraordinary animal, which was employed in bringing water to the house, a task which it effected with no slight difficulty; it was reported to be eighteen years of age; one of its eyes had been removed by some accident, it was foundered, and also lame, the result of a broken leg. This animal was the laughing-stock of all Tarifa; the Gypsy grudged it the very straw on while alone he fed it, and had repeatedly offered it for sale at a dollar, which he could never obtain. During the night there was much merriment going on, and I could frequently distinguish the voice of the Gypsy raised to a boisterous pitch. In the morning the Gypsy hag entered my apartment, bearing the breakfast of myself and Hayim. 'What were you about last night?' said I.

'We were bargaining with the Busno, evil overtake him, and he has exchanged us the ass, for the mule and the reckoning,' said the hag, in whose countenance triumph was blended with anxiety.

'Was he drunk when he saw the mule?' I demanded.

'He did not see her at all, O my son, but we told him we had a beautiful mule, worth any money, which we were anxious to dispose of, as a donkey suited our purpose better. We are afraid that when he sees her he will repent his bargain, and if he calls off within four-and-twenty hours, the exchange is null, and the justicia will cause us to restore the ass; we have, however, already removed her to our huerta out of the town, where we have hid her below the ground. Dios sabe (God knows) how it will turn out.'

When the man and woman saw the lame, foundered, one-eyed creature, for which and the reckoning they had exchanged their own beautiful borrico, they stood confounded. It was about ten in the morning, and they had not altogether recovered from the fumes of the wine of the preceding night; at last the man, with a frightful oath, exclaimed to the innkeeper, 'Restore my donkey, you Gypsy villain!'

'It cannot be, brother,' replied the latter, 'your donkey is by this time three leagues from here: I sold her this morning to a man I do not know, and I am afraid I shall have a hard bargain with her, for he only gave two dollars, as she was unsound. O, you have taken me in, I am a poor fool as they call me here, and you understand much, very much, baribu.' [47]

'Her value was thirty-five dollars, thou demon,' said the countryman, 'and the justicia will make you pay that.'

'Come, come, brother,' said the Gypsy, 'all this is mere conversation; you have a capital bargain, to-day the mercado is held, and you shall sell the mule; I will go with you myself. O, you understand baribu; sister, bring the bottle of anise; the senor and the senora must drink a copita.' After much persuasion, and many oaths, the man and woman were weak enough to comply; when they had drunk several glasses, they departed for the market, the Gypsy leading the mule. In about two hours they returned with the wretched beast, but not exactly as they went; a numerous crowd followed, laughing and hooting. The man was now frantic, and the woman yet more so. They forced their way upstairs to collect their baggage, which they soon effected, and were about to leave the house, vowing revenge. Now ensued a truly terrific scene, there were no more blandishments; the Gypsy men and women were in arms, uttering the most frightful execrations; as the woman came downstairs, the females assailed her like lunatics; the cripple poked at her with a stick, the tall hag clawed at her hair, whilst the father Gypsy walked close beside the man, his hand on his clasp-knife, looking like nothing in this world: the man, however, on reaching the door, turned to him and said: 'Gypsy demon, my borrico by three o'clock - or you know the rest, the justicia.'

The Gypsies remained filled with rage and disappointment; the hag vented her spite on her brother. ''Tis your fault,' said she; 'fool! you have no tongue; you a Chabo, you can't speak'; whereas, within a few hours, he had perhaps talked more than an auctioneer during a three days' sale: but he reserved his words for fitting occasions, and now sat as usual, sullen and silent, smoking his pipe.

The man and woman made their appearance at three o'clock, but they came - intoxicated; the Gypsy's eyes glistened - blandishment was again had recourse to. 'Come and sit down with the cavalier here,' whined the family; 'he is a friend of ours, and will soon arrange matters to your satisfaction.' I arose, and went into the street; the hag followed me. 'Will you not assist us, brother, or are you no Chabo?' she muttered.

'I will have nothing to do with your matters,' said I.

'I know who will,' said the hag, and hurried down the street.

The man and woman, with much noise, demanded their donkey; the innkeeper made no answer, and proceeded to fill up several glasses with the ANISADO. In about a quarter of an hour, the Gypsy hag returned with a young man, well dressed, and with a genteel air, but with something wild and singular in his eyes. He seated himself by the table, smiled, took a glass of liquor, drank part of it, smiled again, and handed it to the countryman. The latter seeing himself treated in this friendly manner by a caballero, was evidently much flattered, took off his hat to the newcomer, and drank, as did the woman also. The glass was filled, and refilled, till they became yet more intoxicated. I did not hear the young man say a word: he appeared a passive automaton. The Gypsies, however, spoke for him, and were profuse of compliments. It was now proposed that the caballero should settle the dispute; a long and noisy conversation ensued, the young man looking vacantly on: the strange people had no money, and had already run up another bill at a wine-house to which they had retired. At last it was proposed, as if by the young man, that the Gypsy should purchase his own mule for two dollars, and forgive the strangers the reckoning of the preceding night. To this they agreed, being apparently stultified with the liquor, and the money being paid to them in the presence of witnesses, they thanked the friendly mediator, and reeled away.

Before they left the town that night, they had contrived to spend the entire two dollars, and the woman, who first recovered her senses, was bitterly lamenting that they had permitted themselves to be despoiled so cheaply of a PRENDA TAN PRECIOSA, as was the donkey. Upon the whole, however, I did not much pity them. The woman was certainly not the man's wife. The labourer had probably left his village with some strolling harlot, bringing with him the animal which had previously served to support himself and family.

I believe that the Gypsy read, at the first glance, their history, and arranged matters accordingly. The donkey was soon once more in the stable, and that night there was much rejoicing in the Gypsy inn.

Who was the singular mediator? He was neither more nor less than the foster child of the Gypsy hag, the unfortunate being whom she had privately injured in his infancy. After having thus served them as an instrument in their villainy, he was told to go home...

THE GYPSY SOLDIER OF VALDEPENAS

It was at Madrid one fine afternoon in the beginning of March 1838, that, as I was sitting behind my table in a cabinete, as it is called, of the third floor of No. 16, in the Calle de Santiago, having just taken my meal, my hostess entered and informed me that a military officer wished to speak to me, adding, in an undertone, that he looked a STRANGE GUEST. I was acquainted with no military officer in the Spanish service; but as at that time I expected daily to be arrested for having distributed the Bible, I thought that very possibly this officer might have been sent to perform that piece of duty. I instantly ordered him to be admitted, whereupon a thin active figure, somewhat above the middle height, dressed in a blue uniform, with a long sword hanging at his side, tripped into the room. Depositing his regimental hat on the ground, he drew a chair to the table, and seating himself, placed his elbows on the board, and supporting his face with his hands, confronted me, gazing steadfastly upon me, without uttering a word. I looked no less wistfully at him, and was of the same opinion as my hostess, as to the strangeness of my guest. He was about fifty, with thin flaxen hair covering the sides of his head, which at the top was entirely bald. His eyes were small, and, like ferrets', red and fiery.

His complexion like a brick, a dull red, checkered with spots of purple. 'May I inquire your name and business, sir?' I at length demanded.

STRANGER. - 'My name is Chaleco of Valdepenas; in the time of the French I served as bragante, fighting for Ferdinand VII. I am now a captain on half-pay in the service of Donna Isabel; as for my business here, it is to speak with you. Do you know this book?'

MYSELF. - 'This book is Saint Luke's Gospel in the Gypsy language; how can this book concern you?'

STRANGER. - 'No one more. It is in the language of my people.'

MYSELF. - 'You do not pretend to say that you are a Calo?'

STRANGER. - 'I do! I am Zincalo, by the mother's side. My father, it is true, was one of the Busne; but I glory in being a Calo, and care not to acknowledge other blood.'

MYSELF. - 'How became you possessed of that book?'

STRANGER. - 'I was this morning in the Prado, where I met two women of our people, and amongst other things they told me that they had a gabicote in our language. I did not believe them at first, but they pulled it out, and I found their words true. They then spoke to me of yourself, and told me where you live, so I took the book from them and am come to see you.'

MYSELF. - 'Are you able to understand this book?'

STRANGER. - 'Perfectly, though it is written in very crabbed language: [48] but I learnt to read Calo when very young. My mother was a good Calli, and early taught me both to speak and read it. She too had a gabicote, but not printed like this, and it treated of a different matter.'

MYSELF. - 'How came your mother, being a good Calli, to marry one of a different blood?'

STRANGER. - 'It was no fault of hers; there was no remedy. In her infancy she lost her parents, who were executed; and she was abandoned by all, till my father, taking compassion on her, brought her up and educated her: at last he made her his wife, though three times her age. She, however, remembered her blood and hated my father, and taught me to hate him likewise, and avoid him. When a boy, I used to stroll about the plains, that I might not see my father; and my father would follow me and beg me to look upon him, and would ask me what I wanted; and I would reply, Father, the only thing I want is to see you dead.'

MYSELF. - 'That was strange language from a child to its parent.'

STRANGER. - 'It was - but you know the couplet, [49] which says, "I do not wish to be a lord - I am by birth a Gypsy - I do not wish to be a gentleman - I am content with being a Calo!"'

MYSELF. - 'I am anxious to hear more of your history - pray proceed.'

STRANGER. - 'When I was about twelve years old my father became distracted, and died. I then continued with my mother for some years; she loved me much, and procured a teacher to instruct me in Latin. At last she died, and then there was a pleyto (law-suit). I took to the sierra and became a highwayman; but the wars broke out. My cousin Jara, of Valdepenas, raised a troop of brigantes. [50] I enlisted with him and distinguished myself very much; there is scarcely a man or woman in Spain but has heard of Jara and Chaleco. I am now captain in the service of Donna Isabel - I am covered with wounds - I am - ugh! ugh! ugh - !'

He had commenced coughing, and in a manner which perfectly astounded me. I had heard hooping coughs, consumptive coughs, coughs caused by colds, and other accidents, but a cough so horrible and unnatural as that of the Gypsy soldier, I had never witnessed in the course of my travels. In a moment he was bent double, his frame writhed and laboured, the veins of his forehead were frightfully swollen, and his complexion became black as the blackest blood; he screamed, he snorted, he barked, and appeared to be on the point of suffocation - yet more explosive became the cough; and the people of the house, frightened, came running into the apartment. I cries, 'The man is perishing, run instantly for a surgeon!' He heard me, and with a quick movement raised his left hand as if to countermand the order; another struggle, then one mighty throe, which seemed to search his deepest intestines; and he remained motionless, his head on his knee. The cough had left him, and within a minute or two he again looked up.

'That is a dreadful cough, friend,' said I, when he was somewhat recovered. 'How did you get it?'

GYPSY SOLDIER. - 'I am - shot through the lungs - brother! Let me but take breath, and I will show you the hole - the agujero.'

He continued with me a considerable time, and showed not the slightest disposition to depart; the cough returned twice, but not so violently; - at length, having an engagement, I arose, and apologising, told him I must leave him. The next day he came again at the same hour, but he found me not, as I was abroad dining with a friend. On the third day, however, as I was sitting down to dinner, in he walked, unannounced. I am rather hospitable than otherwise, so I cordially welcomed him, and requested him to partake of my meal. 'Con mucho gusto,' he replied, and instantly took his place at the table. I was again astonished, for if his cough was frightful, his appetite was yet more so. He ate like a wolf of the sierra; - soup, puchero, fowl and bacon disappeared before him in a twinkling. I ordered in cold meat, which he presently despatched; a large piece of cheese was then produced. We had been drinking water.

'Where is the wine?' said he.

'I never use it,' I replied.

He looked blank. The hostess, however, who was present waiting, said, 'If the gentleman wish for wine, I have a bota nearly full, which I will instantly fetch.'

The skin bottle, when full, might contain about four quarts. She filled him a very large glass, and was removing the skin, but he prevented her, saying, 'Leave it, my good woman; my brother here will settle with you for the little I shall use.'

He now lighted his cigar, and it was evident that he had made good his quarters. On the former occasion I thought his behaviour sufficiently strange, but I liked it still less on the present. Every fifteen minutes he emptied his glass, which contained at least a pint; his conversation became horrible. He related the atrocities which he had committed when a robber and bragante in La Mancha. 'It was our custom,' said he, 'to tie our prisoners to the olive-trees, and then, putting our horses to full speed, to tilt at them with our spears.' As he continued to drink he became waspish and quarrelsome: he had hitherto talked Castilian, but he would now only converse in Gypsy and in Latin, the last of which languages he spoke with great fluency, though ungrammatically. He told me that he had killed six men in duels; and, drawing his sword, fenced about the room. I saw by the manner in which he handled it, that he was master of his weapon. His cough did not return, and he said it seldom afflicted him when he dined well. He gave me to understand that he had received no pay for two years. 'Therefore you visit me,' thought I. At the end of three hours, perceiving that he exhibited no signs of taking his departure, I arose, and said I must again leave him. 'As you please, brother,' said he; 'use no ceremony with me, I am fatigued, and will wait a little while.' I did not return till eleven at night, when my hostess informed me that he had just departed, promising to return next day. He had emptied the bota to the last drop, and the cheese produced being insufficient for him, he sent for an entire Dutch cheese on my account; part of which he had eaten and the rest carried away. I now saw that I had formed a most troublesome acquaintance, of whom it was highly necessary to rid myself, if possible; I therefore dined out for the next nine days.

For a week he came regularly at the usual hour, at the end of which time he desisted; the hostess was afraid of him, as she said that he was a brujo or wizard, and only spoke to him through the wicket.

On the tenth day I was cast into prison, where I continued several weeks. Once, during my confinement, he called at the house, and being informed of my mishap, drew his sword, and vowed with horrible imprecations to murder the prime minister of Ofalia, for having dared to imprison his brother. On my release, I did not revisit my lodgings for some days, but lived at an hotel. I returned late one afternoon, with my servant Francisco, a Basque of Hernani, who had served me with the utmost fidelity during my imprisonment, which he had voluntarily shared with me. The first person I saw on entering was the Gypsy soldier, seated by the table, whereon were several bottles of wine which he had ordered from the tavern, of course on my account. He was smoking, and looked savage and sullen; perhaps he was not much pleased with the reception he had experienced. He had forced himself in, and the woman of the house sat in a corner looking upon him with dread. I addressed him, but he would scarcely return an answer. At last he commenced discoursing with great volubility in Gypsy and Latin. I did not understand much of what he said. His words were wild and incoherent, but he repeatedly threatened some person. The last bottle was now exhausted: he demanded more. I told him in a gentle manner that he had drunk enough. He looked on the ground for some time, then slowly, and somewhat hesitatingly, drew his sword and laid it on the table. It was become dark. I was not afraid of the fellow, but I wished to avoid anything unpleasant. I called to Francisco to bring lights, and obeying a sign which I made him, he sat down at the table. The Gypsy glared fiercely upon him - Francisco laughed, and began with great glee to talk in Basque, of which the Gypsy understood not a word. The Basques, like all Tartars, [51] and such they are, are paragons of fidelity and good nature; they are only dangerous when outraged, when they are terrible indeed. Francisco, to the strength of a giant joined the disposition of a lamb. He was beloved even in the patio of the prison, where he used to pitch the bar and wrestle with the murderers and felons, always coming off victor. He continued speaking Basque. The Gypsy was incensed; and, forgetting the languages in which, for the last hour, he had been speaking, complained to Francisco of his rudeness in speaking any tongue but Castilian. The Basque replied by a loud carcajada, and slightly touched the Gypsy on the knee. The latter sprang up like a mine discharged, seized his sword, and, retreating a few steps, made a desperate lunge at Francisco.

The Basques, next to the Pasiegos, [52] are the best cudgel-players in Spain, and in the world. Francisco held in his hand part of a broomstick, which he had broken in the stable, whence he had just ascended. With the swiftness of lightning he foiled the stroke of Chaleco, and, in another moment, with a dexterous blow, struck the sword out of his hand, sending it ringing against the wall.

The Gypsy resumed his seat and his cigar. He occasionally looked at the Basque. His glances were at first atrocious, but presently changed their expression, and appeared to me to become prying and eagerly curious. He at last arose, picked up his sword, sheathed it, and walked slowly to the door; when there he stopped, turned round, advanced close to Francisco, and looked him steadfastly in the face. 'My good fellow,' said he, 'I am a Gypsy, and can read baji. Do you know where you will be at this time to-morrow?'[53] Then, laughing like a hyena, he departed, and I never saw him again.

At that time on the morrow, Francisco was on his death-bed. He had caught the jail fever, which had long raged in the Carcel de la Corte, where I was imprisoned. In a few days he was buried, a mass of corruption, in the Campo Santo of Madrid.

CHAPTER V

THE Gitanos, in their habits and manner of life, are much less cleanly than the Spaniards. The hovels in which they reside exhibit none of the neatness which is observable in the habitations of even the poorest of the other race. The floors are unswept, and abound with filth and mud, and in their persons they are scarcely less vile. Inattention to cleanliness is a characteristic of the Gypsies, in all parts of the world.

The Bishop of Forli, as far back as 1422, gives evidence upon this point, and insinuates that they carried the plague with them; as he observes that it raged with peculiar violence the year of their appearance at Forli.[54]

At the present day they are almost equally disgusting, in this respect, in Hungary, England, and Spain. Amongst the richer Gitanos, habits of greater cleanliness of course exist than amongst the poorer. An air of sluttishness, however, pervades their dwellings, which, to an experienced eye, would sufficiently attest that the inmates were Gitanos, in the event of their absence.

What can be said of the Gypsy dress, of which such frequent mention is made in the Spanish laws, and which is prohibited together with the Gypsy language and manner of life? Of whatever it might consist in former days, it is so little to be distinguished from the dress of some classes amongst the Spaniards, that it is almost impossible to describe the difference. They generally wear a high- peaked, narrow-brimmed hat, a zamarra of sheep-skin in winter, and, during summer, a jacket of brown cloth; and beneath this they are fond of exhibiting a red plush waistcoat, something after the fashion of the English jockeys, with numerous buttons and clasps. A faja, or girdle of crimson silk, surrounds the waist, where, not unfrequently, are stuck the cachas which we have already described. Pantaloons of coarse cloth or leather descend to the knee; the legs are protected by woollen stockings, and sometimes by a species of spatterdash, either of cloth or leather; stout high-lows complete the equipment.

Such is the dress of the Gitanos of most parts of Spain. But it is necessary to remark that such also is the dress of the chalans, and of the muleteers, except that the latter are in the habit of wearing broad sombreros as preservatives from the sun. This dress appears to be rather Andalusian than Gitano; and yet it certainly beseems the Gitano better than the chalan or muleteer. He wears it with more easy negligence or jauntiness, by which he may be recognised at some distance, even from behind.

It is still more difficult to say what is the peculiar dress of the Gitanas; they wear not the large red cloaks and immense bonnets of coarse beaver which distinguish their sisters of England; they have no other headgear than a handkerchief, which is occasionally resorted to as a defence against the severity of the weather; their hair is sometimes confined by a comb, but more frequently is permitted to stray dishevelled down their shoulders; they are fond of large ear-rings, whether of gold, silver, or metal, resembling in this respect the poissardes of France. There is little to distinguish them from the Spanish women save the absence of the mantilla, which they never carry. Females of fashion not unfrequently take pleasure in dressing a la Gitana, as it is called; but this female Gypsy fashion, like that of the men, is more properly the fashion of Andalusia, the principal characteristic of which is the saya, which is exceedingly short, with many rows of flounces.

True it is that the original dress of the Gitanos, male and female, whatever it was, may have had some share in forming the Andalusian fashion, owing to the great number of these wanderers who found their way to that province at an early period. The Andalusians are a mixed breed of various nations, Romans, Vandals, Moors; perhaps there is a slight sprinkling of Gypsy blood in their veins, and of Gypsy fashion in their garb.

The Gitanos are, for the most part, of the middle size, and the proportions of their frames convey a powerful idea of strength and activity united; a deformed or weakly object is rarely found amongst them in persons of either sex; such probably perish in their infancy, unable to support the hardships and privations to which the race is still subjected from its great poverty, and these same privations have given and still give a coarseness and harshness to their features, which are all strongly marked and expressive. Their complexion is by no means uniform, save that it is invariably darker than the general olive hue of the Spaniards; not unfrequently countenances as dark as those of mulattos present themselves, and in some few instances of almost negro blackness. Like most people of savage ancestry, their teeth are white and strong; their mouths are not badly formed, but it is in the eye more than in any other feature that they differ from other human beings.

There is something remarkable in the eye of the Gitano: should his hair and complexion become fair as those of the Swede or the Finn, and his jockey gait as grave and ceremonious as that of the native of Old Castile, were he dressed like a king, a priest, or a warrior, still would the Gitano be detected by his eye, should it continue unchanged. The Jew is known by his eye, but then in the Jew that feature is peculiarly small; the Chinese has a remarkable eye, but then the eye of the Chinese is oblong, and even with the face, which is flat; but the eye of the Gitano is neither large nor small, and exhibits no marked difference in its shape from the eyes of the common cast. Its peculiarity consists chiefly in a strange staring expression, which to be understood must be seen, and in a thin glaze, which steals over it when in repose, and seems to emit phosphoric light. That the Gypsy eye has sometimes a peculiar effect, we learn from the following stanza:-

> 'A Gypsy stripling's glossy eye
> Has pierced my bosom's core,
> A feat no eye beneath the sky
> Could e'er effect before.'

The following passages are extracted from a Spanish work,[55] and cannot be out of place here, as they relate to those matters to which we have devoted this chapter.

'The Gitanos have an olive complexion and very marked physiognomy; their cheeks are prominent, their lips thick, their eyes vivid and black; their hair is long, black, and coarse, and their teeth very white. The general expression of their physiognomy is a compound of pride, slavishness, and cunning. They are, for the most part, of good stature, well formed, and support with facility fatigue and every kind of hardship. When they discuss any matter, or speak among themselves, whether in Catalan, in Castilian, or in Germania, which is their own peculiar jargon, they always make use of much gesticulation, which contributes to give to their conversation and to the vivacity of their physiognomy a certain expression, still more penetrating and characteristic.

To this work we shall revert on a future occasion.

'When a Gitano has occasion to speak of some business in which his interest is involved, he redoubles his gestures in proportion as he knows the necessity of convincing those who hear him, and fears their impassibility. If any rancorous idea agitate him in the course of his narrative; if he endeavour to infuse into his auditors sentiments of jealousy, vengeance, or any violent passion, his features become exaggerated, and the vivacity of his glances, and the contraction of his lips, show clearly, and in an imposing manner, the foreign origin of the Gitanos, and all the customs of barbarous people. Even his very smile has an expression hard and disagreeable. One might almost say that joy in him is a forced sentiment, and that, like unto the savage man, sadness is the dominant feature of his physiognomy.

'The Gitana is distinguished by the same complexion, and almost the same features. In her frame she is as well formed, and as flexible as the Gitano. Condemned to suffer the same privations and wants, her countenance, when her interest does not oblige her to dissemble her feelings, presents the same aspect of melancholy, and shows besides, with more energy, the rancorous passions of which the female heart is susceptible. Free in her actions, her carriage, and her pursuits, she speaks, vociferates, and makes more gestures than the Gitano, and, in imitation of him, her arms are in continual motion, to give more expression to the imagery with which she accompanies her discourse; her whole body contributes to her gesture, and to increase its force; endeavouring by these means to sharpen the effect of language in itself insufficient; and her vivid and disordered imagination is displayed in her appearance and attitude.

'When she turns her hand to any species of labour, her hurried action, the disorder of her hair, which is scarcely subjected by a little comb, and her propensity to irritation, show how little she loves toil, and her disgust for any continued occupation.

'In her disputes, the air of menace and high passion, the flow of words, and the facility with which she provokes and despises danger, indicate manners half barbarous, and ignorance of other means of defence. Finally, both in males and females, their physical constitution, colour, agility, and flexibility, reveal to us a caste sprung from a burning clime, and devoted to all those exercises which contribute to evolve bodily vigour, and certain mental faculties.

'The dress of the Gitano varies with the country which he inhabits. Both in Rousillon and Catalonia his habiliments generally consist of jacket, waistcoat, pantaloons, and a red faja, which covers part of his waistcoat; on his feet he wears hempen sandals, with much ribbon tied round the leg as high as the calf; he has, moreover, either woollen or cotton stockings; round his neck he wears a handkerchief, carelessly tied; and in the winter he uses a blanket or mantle, with sleeves, cast over the shoulder; his head is covered with the indispensable red cap, which appears to be the favourite ornament of many nations in the vicinity of the Mediterranean and Caspian Sea.

'The neck and the elbows of the jacket are adorned with pieces of blue and yellow cloth embroidered with silk, as well as the seams of the pantaloons; he wears, moreover, on the jacket or the waistcoat, various rows of silver buttons, small and round, sustained by rings or chains of the same metal. The old people, and those who by fortune, or some other cause, exercise, in appearance, a kind of authority over the rest, are almost always dressed in black or dark-blue velvet. Some of those who affect elegance amongst them keep for holidays a complete dress of sky- blue velvet, with embroidery at the neck, pocket-holes, arm-pits, and in all the seams; in a word, with the exception of the turban, this was the fashion of dress of the ancient Moors of Granada, the only difference being occasioned by time and misery.

'The dress of the Gitanas is very varied: the young girls, or those who are in tolerably easy circumstances, generally wear a black bodice laced up with a string, and adjusted to their figures, and contrasting with the scarlet-coloured saya, which only covers a part of the leg; their shoes are cut very low, and are adorned with little buckles of silver; the breast, and the upper part of the bodice, are covered either with a white handkerchief, or one of some vivid colour; and on the head is worn another handkerchief, tied beneath the chin, one of the ends of which falls on the shoulder, in the manner of a hood. When the cold or the heat permit, the Gitana removes the hood, without untying the knots, and exhibits her long and shining tresses restrained by a comb. The old women, and the very poor, dress in the same manner, save that their habiliments are more coarse and the colours less in harmony. Amongst them misery appears beneath the most revolting aspect; whilst the poorest Gitano preserves a certain deportment which would make his aspect supportable, if his unquiet and ferocious glance did not inspire us with aversion.'

CHAPTER VI

WHILST their husbands are engaged in their jockey vocation, or in wielding the cachas, the Callees, or Gypsy females, are seldom idle, but are endeavouring, by various means, to make all the gain they can. The richest amongst them are generally contrabandistas, and in the large towns go from house to house with prohibited goods, especially silk and cotton, and occasionally with tobacco. They likewise purchase cast-off female wearing-apparel, which, when vamped up and embellished, they sometimes contrive to sell as new, with no inconsiderable profit.

Gitanas of this description are of the most respectable class; the rest, provided they do not sell roasted chestnuts, or esteras, which are a species of mat, seek a livelihood by different tricks and practices, more or less fraudulent; for example -

LA BAHI, or fortune-telling, which is called in Spanish, BUENA VENTURA. - This way of extracting money from the credulity of dupes is, of all those practised by the Gypsies, the readiest and most easy; promises are the only capital requisite, and the whole art of fortune-telling consists in properly adapting these promises to the age and condition of the parties who seek for information. The Gitanas are clever enough in the accomplishment of this, and in most cases afford perfect satisfaction. Their practice chiefly lies amongst females, the portion of the human race most given to curiosity and credulity. To the young maidens they promise lovers, handsome invariably, and sometimes rich; to wives children, and perhaps another husband; for their eyes are so penetrating, that occasionally they will develop your most secret thoughts and wishes; to the old, riches - and nothing but riches; for they have sufficient knowledge of the human heart to be aware that avarice is the last passion that becomes extinct within it. These riches are to proceed either from the discovery of hidden treasures or from across the water; from the Americas, to which the Spaniards still look with hope, as there is no individual in Spain, however poor, but has some connection in those realms of silver and gold, at whose death he considers it probable that he may succeed to a brilliant 'herencia.' The Gitanas, in the exercise of this practice, find dupes almost as readily amongst the superior classes, as the veriest dregs of the population. It is their boast, that the best houses are open to them; and perhaps in the space of one hour, they will spae the bahi to a duchess, or countess, in one of the hundred palaces of Madrid, and to half a dozen of the lavanderas engaged in purifying the linen of the capital, beneath the willows which droop on the banks of the murmuring Manzanares. One great advantage which the Gypsies possess over all other people is an utter absence of MAUVAISE HONTE; their speech is as fluent, and their eyes as unabashed, in the presence of royalty, as before those from whom they have nothing to hope or fear; the result being, that most minds quail before them. There were two Gitanas at Madrid, one Pepita by name, and the other La Chicharona; the first was a spare, shrewd, witch- like female, about fifty, and was the mother-in-law of La Chicharona, who was remarkable for her stoutness. These women subsisted entirely by fortune-telling and swindling. It chanced that the son of Pepita, and husband of Chicharona, having spirited away a horse, was sent to the presidio of Malaga for ten years of hard labour. This misfortune caused inexpressible affliction to his wife and mother, who determined to make every effort to procure his liberation. The readiest way which occurred to them was to procure an interview with the Queen Regent Christina, who they doubted not would forthwith pardon the culprit, provided they had an opportunity of assailing her with their Gypsy discourse; for, to use their own words, 'they well knew what to say.' I at that time lived close by the palace, in the street of Santiago, and daily, for the space of a month, saw them bending their steps in that direction.

One day they came to me in a great hurry, with a strange expression on both their countenances. 'We have seen Christina, hijo' (my son), said Pepita to me.

'Within the palace?' I inquired.

'Within the palace, O child of my garlochin,' answered the sibyl: 'Christina at last saw and sent for us, as I knew she would; I told her "bahi," and Chicharona danced the Romalis (Gypsy dance) before her.'

'What did you tell her?'

'I told her many things,' said the hag, 'many things which I need not tell you: know, however, that amongst other things, I told her that the chabori (little queen) would die, and then she would be Queen of Spain. I told her, moreover, that within three years she would marry the son of the King of France, and it was her bahi to die Queen of France and Spain, and to be loved much, and hated much.'

'And did you not dread her anger, when you told her these things?'

'Dread her, the Busnee?' screamed Pepita: 'No, my child, she dreaded me far more; I looked at her so - and raised my finger so - and Chicharona clapped her hands, and the Busnee believed all I said, and was afraid of me; and then I asked for the pardon of my son, and she pledged her word to see into the matter, and when we came away, she gave me this baria of gold, and to Chicharona this other, so at all events we have hokkanoed the queen. May an evil end overtake her body, the Busnee!'

Though some of the Gitanas contrive to subsist by fortune-telling alone, the generality of them merely make use of it as an instrument towards the accomplishment of greater things. The immediate gains are scanty; a few cuartos being the utmost which they receive from the majority of their customers. But the bahi is an excellent passport into houses, and when they spy a convenient opportunity, they seldom fail to avail themselves of it. It is necessary to watch them strictly, as articles frequently disappear in a mysterious manner whilst Gitanas are telling fortunes. The bahi, moreover, is occasionally the prelude to a device which we shall now attempt to describe, and which is called HOKKANO BARO, or the great trick, of which we have already said something in the former part of this work. It consists in persuading some credulous person to deposit whatever money and valuables the party can muster in a particular spot, under the promise that the deposit will increase many manifold. Some of our readers will have difficulty in believing that any people can be found sufficiently credulous to allow themselves to be duped by a trick of this description, the grossness of the intended fraud seeming too palpable. Experience, however, proves the contrary. The deception is frequently practised at the present day, and not only in Spain but in England - enlightened England - and in France likewise; an instance being given in the memoirs of Vidocq, the late celebrated head of the secret police of Paris, though, in that instance, the perpetrator of the fraud was not a Gypsy. The most subtle method of accomplishing the hokkano baro is the following:-

When the dupe - a widow we will suppose, for in these cases the dupes are generally widows - has been induced to consent to make the experiment, the Gitana demands of her whether she has in the house some strong chest with a safe lock. On receiving an affirmative answer, she will request to see all the gold and silver of any description which she may chance to have in her possession. The treasure is shown her; and when the Gitana has carefully inspected and counted it, she produces a white handkerchief, saying, Lady, I give you this handkerchief, which is blessed. Place in it your gold and silver, and tie it with three knots. I am going for three days, during which period you must keep the bundle beneath your pillow, permitting no one to go near it, and observing the greatest secrecy, otherwise the money will take wings and fly away. Every morning during the three days it will be well to open the bundle, for your own satisfaction, to see that no misfortune has befallen your treasure; be always careful, however, to fasten it again with the three knots. On my return, we will place the bundle, after having inspected it, in the chest, which you shall yourself lock, retaining the key in your possession. But, thenceforward, for three weeks, you must by no means unlock the chest, nor look at the treasure - if you do it will fly away. Only follow my directions, and you will gain much, very much, baribu.

The Gitana departs, and, during the three days, prepares a bundle as similar as possible to the one which contains the money of her dupe, save that instead of gold ounces, dollars, and plate, its contents consist of copper money and pewter articles of little or no value. With this bundle concealed beneath her cloak, she returns at the end of three days to her intended victim. The bundle of real treasure is produced and inspected, and again tied up by the Gitana, who then requests the other to open the chest, which done, she formally places A BUNDLE in it; but, in the meanwhile, she has contrived to substitute the fictitious for the real one. The chest is then locked, the lady retaining the key. The Gitana promises to return at the end of three weeks, to open the chest, assuring the lady that if it be not unlocked until that period, it will be found filled with gold and silver; but threatening that in the event of her injunctions being disregarded, the money deposited will vanish. She then walks off with great deliberation, bearing away the spoil. It is needless to say that she never returns.

There are other ways of accomplishing the hokkano baro. The most simple, and indeed the one most generally used by the Gitanas, is to persuade some simple individual to hide a sum of money in the earth, which they afterwards carry away. A case of this description occurred within my own knowledge, at Madrid, towards the latter part of the year 1837. There was a notorious Gitana, of the name of Aurora; she was about forty years of age, a Valencian by birth, and immensely fat. This amiable personage, by some means, formed the acquaintance of a wealthy widow lady; and was not slow in attempting to practise the hokkano baro upon her. She succeeded but too well. The widow, at the instigation of Aurora, buried one hundred ounces of gold beneath a ruined arch in a field, at a short distance from the wall of Madrid. The inhumation was effected at night by the widow alone. Aurora was, however, on the watch, and, in less than ten minutes after the widow had departed, possessed herself of the treasure; perhaps the largest one ever acquired by this kind of deceit. The next day the widow had certain misgivings, and, returning to the spot, found her money gone. About six months after this event, I was imprisoned in the Carcel de la Corte, at Madrid, and there I found Aurora, who was in durance for defrauding the widow. She said that it had been her intention to depart for Valencia with the 'barias,' as she styled her plunder, but the widow had discovered the trick too soon, and she had been arrested. She added, however, that she had contrived to conceal the greatest part of the property, and that she expected her liberation in a few days, having been prodigal of bribes to the 'justicia.' In effect, her liberation took place sooner than my own. Nevertheless, she had little cause to triumph, as before she left the prison she had been fleeced of the last cuarto of her ill- gotten gain, by alguazils and escribanos, who, she admitted, understood hokkano baro much better than herself.

When I next saw Aurora, she informed me that she was once more on excellent terms with the widow, whom she had persuaded that the loss of the money was caused by her own imprudence, in looking for it before the appointed time; the spirit of the earth having removed it in anger. She added that her dupe was quite disposed to make another venture, by which she hoped to retrieve her former loss.

USTILAR PASTESAS. - Under this head may be placed various kinds of theft committed by the Gitanos. The meaning of the words is stealing with the hands; but they are more generally applied to the filching of money by dexterity of hand, when giving or receiving change. For example: a Gitana will enter a shop, and purchase some insignificant article, tendering in payment a baria or golden ounce. The change being put down before her on the counter, she counts the money, and complains that she has received a dollar and several pesetas less than her due. It seems impossible that there can be any fraud on her part, as she has not even taken the pieces in her hand, but merely placed her fingers upon them; pushing them on one side. She now asks the merchant what he means by attempting to deceive the poor woman. The merchant, supposing that he has made a mistake, takes up the money, counts it, and finds in effect that the just sum is not there. He again hands out the change, but there is now a greater deficiency than before, and the merchant is convinced that he is dealing with a witch. The Gitana now pushes the money to him, uplifts her voice, and talks of the justicia. Should the merchant become frightened, and, emptying a bag of dollars, tell her to pay herself, as has sometimes been the case, she will have a fine opportunity to exercise her powers, and whilst taking the change will contrive to convey secretly into her sleeves five or six dollars at least; after which she will depart with much vociferation, declaring that she will never again enter the shop of so cheating a picaro.

Of all the Gitanas at Madrid, Aurora the fat was, by their own confession, the most dexterous at this species of robbery; she having been known in many instances, whilst receiving change for an ounce, to steal the whole value, which amounts to sixteen dollars. It was not without reason that merchants in ancient times were, according to Martin Del Rio, advised to sell nothing out of their shops to Gitanas, as they possessed an infallible secret for attracting to their own purses from the coffers of the former the money with which they paid for the articles they purchased. This secret consisted in stealing a pastesas, which they still practise. Many accounts of witchcraft and sorcery, which are styled old women's tales, are perhaps equally well founded. Real actions have been attributed to wrong causes.

Shoplifting, and other kinds of private larceny, are connected with stealing a pastesas, for in all dexterity of hand is required. Many of the Gitanas of Madrid are provided with large pockets, or rather sacks, beneath their gowns, in which they stow away their plunder. Some of these pockets are capacious enough to hold, at one time, a dozen yards of cloth, a Dutch cheese and a bottle of wine. Nothing that she can eat, drink, or sell, comes amiss to a veritable Gitana; and sometimes the contents of her pocket would afford materials for an inventory far more lengthy and curious than the one enumerating the effects found on the person of the man-mountain at Lilliput.

CHIVING DRAO. - In former times the Spanish Gypsies of both sexes were in the habit of casting a venomous preparation into the mangers of the cattle for the purpose of causing sickness. At present this practice has ceased, or nearly so; the Gitanos, however, talk of it as universal amongst their ancestors. They were in the habit of visiting the stalls and stables secretly, and poisoning the provender of the animals, who almost immediately became sick. After a few days the Gitanos would go to the labourers and offer to cure the sick cattle for a certain sum, and if their proposal was accepted would in effect perform the cure.

Connected with the cure was a curious piece of double dealing. They privately administered an efficacious remedy, but pretended to cure the animals not by medicines but by charms, which consisted of small variegated beans, called in their language bobis,[56] dropped into the mangers. By this means they fostered the idea, already prevalent, that they were people possessed of supernatural gifts and powers, who could remove diseases without having recourse to medicine. By means of drao, they likewise procured themselves food; poisoning swine, as their brethren in England still do,[57] and then feasting on the flesh, which was abandoned as worthless: witness one of their own songs:-

'By Gypsy drow the Porker died,
I saw him stiff at evening tide,
But I saw him not when morning shone,
For the Gypsies ate him flesh and bone.'

By drao also they could avenge themselves on their enemies by destroying their cattle, without incurring a shadow of suspicion. Revenge for injuries, real or imaginary, is sweet to all unconverted minds; to no one more than the Gypsy, who, in all parts of the world, is, perhaps, the most revengeful of human beings.

Vidocq in his memoirs states, that having formed a connection with an individual whom he subsequently discovered to be the captain of a band of Walachian Gypsies, the latter, whose name was Caroun, wished Vidocq to assist in scattering certain powders in the mangers of the peasants' cattle; Vidocq, from prudential motives, refused the employment. There can be no doubt that these powders were, in substance, the drao of the Spanish Gitanos.

LA BAR LACHI, OR THE LOADSTONE. - If the Gitanos in general be addicted to any one superstition, it is certainly with respect to this stone, to which they attribute all kinds of miraculous powers. There can be no doubt, that the singular property which it possesses of attracting steel, by filling their untutored minds with amazement, first gave rise to this veneration, which is carried beyond all reasonable bounds.

They believe that he who is in possession of it has nothing to fear from steel or lead, from fire or water, and that death itself has no power over him. The Gypsy contrabandistas are particularly anxious to procure this stone, which they carry upon their persons in their expeditions; they say, that in the event of being pursued by the jaracanallis, or revenue officers, whirlwinds of dust will arise, and conceal them from the view of their enemies; the horse-stealers say much the same thing, and assert that they are uniformly successful, when they bear about them the precious stone. But it is said to be able to effect much more. Extraordinary things are related of its power in exciting the amorous passions, and, on this account, it is in great request amongst the Gypsy hags; all these women are procuresses, and find persons of both sexes weak and wicked enough to make use of their pretended knowledge in the composition of love-draughts and decoctions.

In the case of the loadstone, however, there is no pretence, the Gitanas believing all they say respecting it, and still more; this is proved by the eagerness with which they seek to obtain the stone in its natural state, which is somewhat difficult to accomplish.

In the museum of natural curiosities at Madrid there is a large piece of loadstone originally extracted from the American mines. There is scarcely a Gitana in Madrid who is not acquainted with this circumstance, and who does not long to obtain the stone, or a part of it; its being placed in a royal museum serving to augment, in their opinion, its real value. Several attempts have been made to steal it, all of which, however, have been unsuccessful. The Gypsies seem not to be the only people who envy royalty the possession of this stone. Pepita, the old Gitana of whose talent at telling fortunes such honourable mention has already been made, informed me that a priest, who was muy enamorado (in love), proposed to her to steal the loadstone, offering her all his sacerdotal garments in the event of success: whether the singular reward that was promised had but slight temptations for her, or whether she feared that her dexterity was not equal to the accomplishment of the task, we know not, but she appears to have declined attempting it. According to the Gypsy account, the person in love, if he wish to excite a corresponding passion in another quarter by means of the loadstone, must swallow, IN AGUARDIENTE, a small portion of the stone pulverised, at the time of going to rest, repeating to himself the following magic rhyme:-

'To the Mountain of Olives one morning I hied,
Three little black goats before me I spied,
Those three little goats on three cars I laid,
Black cheeses three from their milk I made;
The one I bestow on the loadstone of power,
That save me it may from all ills that lower;
The second to Mary Padilla I give,
And to all the witch hags about her that live;
The third I reserve for Asmodeus lame,
That fetch me he may whatever I name.'

LA RAIZ DEL BUEN BARON, OR THE ROOT OF THE GOOD BARON. - On this subject we cannot be very explicit. It is customary with the Gitanas to sell, under this title, various roots and herbs, to unfortunate females who are desirous of producing a certain result; these roots are boiled in white wine, and the abominable decoction is taken fasting. I was once shown the root of the good baron, which, in this instance, appeared to be parsley root. By the good baron is meant his Satanic majesty, on whom the root is very appropriately fathered.

CHAPTER VII

IT is impossible to dismiss the subject of the Spanish Gypsies without offering some remarks on their marriage festivals. There is nothing which they retain connected with their primitive rites and principles, more characteristic perhaps of the sect of the Rommany, of the sect of the HUSBANDS AND WIVES, than what relates to the marriage ceremony, which gives the female a protector, and the man a helpmate, a sharer of his joys and sorrows. The Gypsies are almost entirely ignorant of the grand points of morality; they have never had sufficient sense to perceive that to lie, to steal, and to shed human blood violently, are crimes which are sure, eventually, to yield bitter fruits to those who perpetrate them; but on one point, and that one of no little importance as far as temporal happiness is concerned, they are in general wiser than those who have had far better opportunities than such unfortunate outcasts, of regulating their steps, and distinguishing good from evil. They know that chastity is a jewel of high price, and that conjugal fidelity is capable of occasionally flinging a sunshine even over the dreary hours of a life passed in the contempt of almost all laws, whether human or divine.

There is a word in the Gypsy language to which those who speak it attach ideas of peculiar reverence, far superior to that connected with the name of the Supreme Being, the creator of themselves and the universe. This word is LACHA, which with them is the corporeal chastity of the females; we say corporeal chastity, for no other do they hold in the slightest esteem; it is lawful amongst them, nay praiseworthy, to be obscene in look, gesture, and discourse, to be accessories to vice, and to stand by and laugh at the worst abominations of the Busne, provided their LACHA YE TRUPOS, or corporeal chastity, remains unblemished. The Gypsy child, from her earliest years, is told by her strange mother, that a good Calli need only dread one thing in this world, and that is the loss of Lacha, in comparison with which that of life is of little consequence, as in such an event she will be provided for, but what provision is there for a Gypsy who has lost her Lacha? 'Bear this in mind, my child,' she will say, 'and now eat this bread, and go forth and see what you can steal.'

A Gypsy girl is generally betrothed at the age of fourteen to the youth whom her parents deem a suitable match, and who is generally a few years older than herself. Marriage is invariably preceded by betrothment; and the couple must then wait two years before their union can take place, according to the law of the Cales. During this period it is expected that they treat each other as common acquaintance; they are permitted to converse, and even occasionally to exchange slight presents. One thing, however, is strictly forbidden, and if in this instance they prove contumacious, the betrothment is instantly broken and the pair are never united, and thenceforward bear an evil reputation amongst their sect. This one thing is, going into the campo in each other's company, or having any rendezvous beyond the gate of the city, town, or village, in which they dwell. Upon this point we can perhaps do no better than quote one of their own stanzas:-

'Thy sire and mother wrath and hate
Have vowed against us, love!
The first, first night that from the gate
We two together rove.'

With all the other Gypsies, however, and with the Busne or Gentiles, the betrothed female is allowed the freest intercourse, going whither she will, and returning at all times and seasons. With respect to the Busne, indeed, the parents are invariably less cautious than with their own race, as they conceive it next to an impossibility that their child should lose her Lacha by any intercourse with THE WHITE BLOOD; and true it is that experience has proved that their confidence in this respect is not altogether idle. The Gitanas have in general a decided aversion to the white men; some few instances, however, to the contrary are said to have occurred.

A short time previous to the expiration of the term of the betrothment, preparations are made for the Gypsy bridal. The wedding-day is certainly an eventful period in the life of every individual, as he takes a partner for better or for worse, whom he is bound to cherish through riches and poverty; but to the Gypsy particularly the wedding festival is an important affair. If he is rich, he frequently becomes poor before it is terminated; and if he is poor, he loses the little which he possesses, and must borrow of his brethren; frequently involving himself throughout life, to procure the means of giving a festival; for without a festival, he could not become a Rom, that is, a husband, and would cease to belong to this sect of Rommany.

There is a great deal of what is wild and barbarous attached to these festivals. I shall never forget a particular one at which I was present. After much feasting, drinking, and yelling, in the Gypsy house, the bridal train sallied forth - a frantic spectacle. First of all marched a villainous jockey-looking fellow, holding in his hands, uplifted, a long pole, at the top of which fluttered in the morning air a snow-white cambric handkerchief, emblem of the bride's purity. Then came the betrothed pair, followed by their nearest friends; then a rabble rout of Gypsies, screaming and shouting, and discharging guns and pistols, till all around rang with the din, and the village dogs barked. On arriving at the church gate, the fellow who bore the pole stuck it into the ground with a loud huzza, and the train, forming two ranks, defiled into the church on either side of the pole and its strange ornaments. On the conclusion of the ceremony, they returned in the same manner in which they had come.

Throughout the day there was nothing going on but singing, drinking, feasting, and dancing; but the most singular part of the festival was reserved for the dark night. Nearly a ton weight of sweetmeats had been prepared, at an enormous expense, not for the gratification of the palate, but for a purpose purely Gypsy. These sweetmeats of all kinds, and of all forms, but principally yemas, or yolks of eggs prepared with a crust of sugar (a delicious bonne-bouche), were strewn on the floor of a large room, at least to the depth of three inches. Into this room, at a given signal, tripped the bride and bridegroom DANCING ROMALIS, followed amain by all the Gitanos and Gitanas, DANCING ROMALIS. To convey a slight idea of the scene is almost beyond the power of words. In a few minutes the sweetmeats were reduced to a powder, or rather to a mud, the dancers were soiled to the knees with sugar, fruits, and yolks of eggs. Still more terrific became the lunatic merriment. The men sprang high into the air, neighed, brayed, and crowed; whilst the Gitanas snapped their fingers in their own fashion, louder than castanets, distorting their forms into all kinds of obscene attitudes, and uttering words to repeat which were an abomination. In a corner of the apartment capered the while Sebastianillo, a convict Gypsy from Melilla, strumming the guitar most furiously, and producing demoniacal sounds which had some resemblance to Malbrun (Malbrouk), and, as he strummed, repeating at intervals the Gypsy modification of the song:-

'Chala Malbrun chinguerar,
Birandon, birandon, birandera -
Chala Malbrun chinguerar,
No se bus trutera -
No se bus trutera.
No se bus trutera.
La romi que le camela,
Birandon, birandon,' etc.

The festival endures three days, at the end of which the greatest part of the property of the bridegroom, even if he were previously in easy circumstances, has been wasted in this strange kind of riot and dissipation. Paco, the Gypsy of Badajoz, attributed his ruin to the extravagance of his marriage festival; and many other Gitanos have confessed the same thing of themselves. They said that throughout the three days they appeared to be under the influence of infatuation, having no other wish or thought but to make away with their substance; some have gone so far as to cast money by handfuls into the street. Throughout the three days all the doors are kept open, and all corners, whether Gypsies or Busne, welcomed with a hospitality which knows no bounds.

In nothing do the Jews and Gitanos more resemble each other than in their marriages, and what is connected therewith. In both sects there is a betrothment: amongst the Jews for seven, amongst the Gitanos for a period of two years. In both there is a wedding festival, which endures amongst the Jews for fifteen and amongst the Gitanos for three days, during which, on both sides, much that is singular and barbarous occurs, which, however, has perhaps its origin in antiquity the most remote. But the wedding ceremonies of the Jews are far more complex and allegorical than those of the Gypsies, a more simple people. The Nazarene gazes on these ceremonies with mute astonishment; the washing of the bride - the painting of the face of herself and her companions with chalk and carmine - her ensconcing herself within the curtains of the bed with her female bevy, whilst the bridegroom hides himself within his apartment with the youths his companions - her envelopment in the white sheet, in which she appears like a corse, the bridegroom's going to sup with her, when he places himself in the middle of the apartment with his eyes shut, and without tasting a morsel. His going to the synagogue, and then repairing to breakfast with the bride, where he practises the same self-denial - the washing of the bridegroom's plate and sending it after him, that he may break his fast - the binding his hands behind him - his ransom paid by the bride's mother - the visit of the sages to the bridegroom - the mulct imposed in case he repent - the killing of the bullock at the house of the bridegroom - the present of meat and fowls, meal and spices, to the bride - the gold and silver - that most imposing part of the ceremony, the walking of the bride by torchlight to the house of her betrothed, her eyes fixed in vacancy, whilst the youths of her kindred sing their wild songs around her - the cup of milk and the spoon presented to her by the bridegroom's mother - the arrival of the sages in the morn - the reading of the Ketuba - the night - the half-enjoyment - the old woman - the tantalising knock at the door - and then the festival of fishes which concludes all, and leaves the jaded and wearied couple to repose after a fortnight of persecution.

The Jews, like the Gypsies, not unfrequently ruin themselves by the riot and waste of their marriage festivals. Throughout the entire fortnight, the houses, both of bride and bridegroom, are flung open to all corners; - feasting and song occupy the day - feasting and song occupy the hours of the night, and this continued revel is only broken by the ceremonies of which we have endeavoured to convey a faint idea. In these festivals the sages or ULEMMA take a distinguished part, doing their utmost to ruin the contracted parties, by the wonderful despatch which they make of the fowls and viands, sweetmeats, AND STRONG WATERS provided for the occasion.

After marriage the Gypsy females generally continue faithful to their husbands through life; giving evidence that the exhortations of their mothers in early life have not been without effect. Of course licentious females are to be found both amongst the matrons and the unmarried; but such instances are rare, and must be considered in the light of exceptions to a principle. The Gypsy women (I am speaking of those of Spain), as far as corporeal chastity goes, are very paragons; but in other respects, alas! - little can be said in praise of their morality.

CHAPTER VIII

WHILST in Spain I devoted as much time as I could spare from my grand object, which was to circulate the Gospel through that benighted country, to attempt to enlighten the minds of the Gitanos on the subject of religion. I cannot say that I experienced much success in my endeavours; indeed, I never expected much, being fully acquainted with the stony nature of the ground on which I was employed; perhaps some of the seed that I scattered may eventually spring up and yield excellent fruit. Of one thing I am certain: if I did the Gitanos no good, I did them no harm.

It has been said that there is a secret monitor, or conscience, within every heart, which immediately upbraids the individual on the commission of a crime; this may be true, but certainly the monitor within the Gitano breast is a very feeble one, for little attention is ever paid to its reproofs. With regard to conscience, be it permitted to observe, that it varies much according to climate, country, and religion; perhaps nowhere is it so terrible and strong as in England; I need not say why. Amongst the English, I have seen many individuals stricken low, and broken-hearted, by the force of conscience; but never amongst the Spaniards or Italians; and I never yet could observe that the crimes which the Gitanos were daily and hourly committing occasioned them the slightest uneasiness.

One important discovery I made among them: it was, that no individual, however wicked and hardened, is utterly GODLESS. Call it superstition, if you will, still a certain fear and reverence of something sacred and supreme would hang about them. I have heard Gitanos stiffly deny the existence of a Deity, and express the utmost contempt for everything holy; yet they subsequently never failed to contradict themselves, by permitting some expression to escape which belied their assertions, and of this I shall presently give a remarkable instance.

I found the women much more disposed to listen to anything I had to say than the men, who were in general so taken up with their traffic that they could think and talk of nothing else; the women, too, had more curiosity and more intelligence; the conversational powers of some of them I found to be very great, and yet they were destitute of the slightest rudiments of education, and were thieves by profession. At Madrid I had regular conversaziones, or, as they are called in Spanish, tertulias, with these women, who generally visited me twice a week; they were perfectly unreserved towards me with respect to their actions and practices, though their behaviour, when present, was invariably strictly proper. I have already had cause to mention Pepa the sibyl, and her daughter-in-law, Chicharona; the manners of the first were sometimes almost elegant, though, next to Aurora, she was the most notorious she-thug in Madrid; Chicharona was good-humoured, like most fat personages. Pepa had likewise two daughters, one of whom, a very remarkable female, was called La Tuerta, from the circumstance of her having but one eye, and the other, who was a girl of about thirteen, La Casdami, or the scorpion, from the malice which she occasionally displayed.

Pepa and Chicharona were invariably my most constant visitors. One day in winter they arrived as usual; the One-eyed and the Scorpion following behind.

MYSELF. - 'I am glad to see you, Pepa: what have you been doing this morning?'

PEPA. - 'I have been telling baji, and Chicharona has been stealing a pastesas; we have had but little success, and have come to warm ourselves at the brasero. As for the One-eyed, she is a very sluggard (holgazana), she will neither tell fortunes nor steal.'

THE ONE-EYED. - 'Hold your peace, mother of the Bengues; I will steal, when I see occasion, but it shall not be a pastesas, and I will hokkawar (deceive), but it shall not be by telling fortunes. If I deceive, it shall be by horses, by jockeying.[58] If I steal, it shall be on the road - I'll rob. You know already what I am capable of, yet knowing that, you would have me tell fortunes like yourself, or steal like Chicharona. Me dinela conche (it fills me with fury) to be asked to tell fortunes, and the next Busnee that talks to me of bajis, I will knock all her teeth out.'

THE SCORPION. - 'My sister is right; I, too, would sooner be a salteadora (highwaywoman), or a chalana (she-jockey), than steal with the hands, or tell bajis.'

MYSELF. - 'You do not mean to say, O Tuerta, that you are a jockey, and that you rob on the highway.'

THE ONE-EYED. - 'I am a chalana, brother, and many a time I have robbed upon the road, as all our people know. I dress myself as a man, and go forth with some of them. I have robbed alone, in the pass of the Guadarama, with my horse and escopeta. I alone once robbed a cuadrilla of twenty Gallegos, who were returning to their own country, after cutting the harvests of Castile; I stripped them of their earnings, and could have stripped them of their very clothes had I wished, for they were down on their knees like cowards. I love a brave man, be he Busne or Gypsy. When I was not much older than the Scorpion, I went with several others to rob the cortijo of an old man; it was more than twenty leagues from here. We broke in at midnight, and bound the old man: we knew he had money; but he said no, and would not tell us where it was; so we tortured him, pricking him with our knives and burning his hands over the lamp; all, however, would not do. At last I said, "Let us try the PIMIENTOS"; so we took the green pepper husks, pulled open his eyelids, and rubbed the pupils with the green pepper fruit. That was the worst pinch of all. Would you believe it? the old man bore it. Then our people said, "Let us kill him," but I said, no, it were a pity: so we spared him, though we got nothing. I have loved that old man ever since for his firm heart, and should have wished him for a husband.'

THE SCORPION. - 'Ojala, that I had been in that cortijo, to see such sport!'

MYSELF. - 'Do you fear God, O Tuerta?'

THE ONE-EYED. - 'Brother, I fear nothing.'

MYSELF. - 'Do you believe in God, O Tuerta?'

THE ONE-EYED. - 'Brother, I do not; I hate all connected with that name; the whole is folly; me dinela conche. If I go to church, it is but to spit at the images. I spat at the bulto of Maria this morning; and I love the Corojai, and the Londone,[59] because they are not baptized.'

MYSELF. - 'You, of course, never say a prayer.'

THE ONE-EYED. - 'No, no; there are three or four old words, taught me by some old people, which I sometimes say to myself; I believe they have both force and virtue.'

MYSELF. - 'I would fain hear; pray tell me them.'

THE ONE-EYED. - 'Brother, they are words not to be repeated.'

MYSELF. - 'Why not?'

THE ONE-EYED. - 'They are holy words, brother.'

MYSELF. - 'Holy! You say there is no God; if there be none, there can be nothing holy; pray tell me the words, O Tuerta.'

THE ONE-EYED. - 'Brother, I dare not.'

MYSELF. - 'Then you do fear something.'

THE ONE-EYED.- 'Not I -

'SABOCA ENRECAR MARIA ERERIA,[60] and now I wish I had not said them.'

MYSELF. - 'You are distracted, O Tuerta: the words say simply, 'Dwell within us, blessed Maria.' You have spitten on her bulto this morning in the church, and now you are afraid to repeat four words, amongst which is her name.'

THE ONE-EYED. - 'I did not understand them; but I wish I had not said them.'

* * * * *

I repeat that there is no individual, however hardened, who is utterly GODLESS.

The reader will have already gathered from the conversations reported in this volume, and especially from the last, that there is a wide difference between addressing Spanish Gitanos and Gitanas and English peasantry: of a certainty what will do well for the latter is calculated to make no impression on these thievish half- wild people. Try them with the Gospel, I hear some one cry, which speaks to all: I did try them with the Gospel, and in their own language. I commenced with Pepa and Chicharona. Determined that they should understand it, I proposed that they themselves should translate it. They could neither read nor write, which, however, did not disqualify them from being translators. I had myself previously translated the whole Testament into the Spanish Rommany, but I was desirous to circulate amongst the Gitanos a version conceived in the exact language in which they express their ideas. The women made no objection, they were fond of our tertulias, and they likewise reckoned on one small glass of Malaga wine, with which I invariably presented them. Upon the whole, they conducted themselves much better than could have been expected. We commenced with Saint Luke: they rendering into Rommany the sentences which I delivered to them in Spanish. They proceeded as far as the eighth chapter, in the middle of which they broke down. Was that to be wondered at? The only thing which astonished me was, that I had induced two such strange beings to advance so far in a task so unwonted, and so entirely at variance with their habits, as translation.

These chapters I frequently read over to them, explaining the subject in the best manner I was able. They said it was lacho, and jucal, and misto, all of which words express approval of the quality of a thing. Were they improved, were their hearts softened by these Scripture lectures? I know not. Pepa committed a rather daring theft shortly afterwards, which compelled her to conceal herself for a fortnight; it is quite possible, however, that she may remember the contents of those chapters on her death-bed; if so, will the attempt have been a futile one?

I completed the translation, supplying deficiencies from my own version begun at Badajoz in 1836. This translation I printed at Madrid in 1838; it was the first book which ever appeared in Rommany, and was called 'Embeo e Majaro Lucas,' or Gospel of Luke the Saint. I likewise published, simultaneously, the same Gospel in Basque, which, however, I had no opportunity of circulating.

The Gitanos of Madrid purchased the Gypsy Luke freely: many of the men understood it, and prized it highly, induced of course more by the language than the doctrine; the women were particularly anxious to obtain copies, though unable to read; but each wished to have one in her pocket, especially when engaged in thieving expeditions, for they all looked upon it in the light of a charm, which would preserve them from all danger and mischance; some even went so far as to say, that in this respect it was equally efficacious as the Bar Lachi, or loadstone, which they are in general so desirous of possessing. Of this Gospel[61] five hundred copies were printed, of which the greater number I contrived to circulate amongst the Gypsies in various parts; I cast the book upon the waters and left it to its destiny.

I have counted seventeen Gitanas assembled at one time in my apartment in the Calle de Santiago in Madrid; for the first quarter of an hour we generally discoursed upon indifferent matters, I then by degrees drew their attention to religion and the state of souls. I finally became so bold that I ventured to speak against their inveterate practices, thieving and lying, telling fortunes, and stealing a pastesas; this was touching upon delicate ground, and I experienced much opposition and much feminine clamour. I persevered, however, and they finally assented to all I said, not that I believe that my words made much impression upon their hearts. In a few months matters were so far advanced that they would sing a hymn; I wrote one expressly for them in Rommany, in which their own wild couplets were, to a certain extent, imitated.

The people of the street in which I lived, seeing such numbers of these strange females continually passing in and out, were struck with astonishment, and demanded the reason. The answers which they obtained by no means satisfied them. 'Zeal for the conversion of souls, - the souls too of Gitanas, - disparate! the fellow is a scoundrel. Besides he is an Englishman, and is not baptized; what cares he for souls? They visit him for other purposes. He makes base ounces, which they carry away and circulate. Madrid is already stocked with false money.' Others were of opinion that we met for the purposes of sorcery and abomination. The Spaniard has no conception that other springs of action exist than interest or villainy.

My little congregation, if such I may call it, consisted entirely of women; the men seldom or never visited me, save they stood in need of something which they hoped to obtain from me. This circumstance I little regretted, their manners and conversation being the reverse of interesting. It must not, however, be supposed that, even with the women, matters went on invariably in a smooth and satisfactory manner. The following little anecdote will show what slight dependence can be placed upon them, and how disposed they are at all times to take part in what is grotesque and malicious. One day they arrived, attended by a Gypsy jockey whom I had never previously seen. We had scarcely been seated a minute, when this fellow, rising, took me to the window, and without any preamble or circumlocution, said - 'Don Jorge, you shall lend me two barias' (ounces of gold). 'Not to your whole race, my excellent friend,' said I; 'are you frantic? Sit down and be discreet.' He obeyed me literally, sat down, and when the rest departed, followed with them. We did not invariably meet at my own house, but occasionally at one in a street inhabited by Gypsies. On the appointed day I went to this house, where I found the women assembled; the jockey was also present. On seeing me he advanced, again took me aside, and again said - 'Don Jorge, you shall lend me two barias.' I made him no answer, but at once entered on the subject which brought me thither. I spoke for some time in Spanish; I chose for the theme of my discourse the situation of the Hebrews in Egypt, and pointed out its similarity to that of the Gitanos in Spain. I spoke of the power of God, manifested in preserving both as separate and distinct people amongst the nations until the present day. I warmed with my subject. I subsequently produced a manuscript book, from which I read a portion of Scripture, and the Lord's Prayer and Apostles' Creed, in Rommany. When I had concluded I looked around me.

The features of the assembly were twisted, and the eyes of all turned upon me with a frightful squint; not an individual present but squinted, - the genteel Pepa, the good-humoured Chicharona, the Casdami, etc. etc. The Gypsy fellow, the contriver of the jest, squinted worst of all. Such are Gypsies.

PART III

CHAPTER I

THERE is no nation in the world, however exalted or however degraded, but is in possession of some peculiar poetry. If the Chinese, the Hindoos, the Greeks, and the Persians, those splendid and renowned races, have their moral lays, their mythological epics, their tragedies, and their immortal love songs, so also have the wild and barbarous tribes of Soudan, and the wandering Esquimaux, their ditties, which, however insignificant in comparison with the compositions of the former nations, still are entitled in every essential point to the name of poetry; if poetry mean metrical compositions intended to soothe and recreate the mind fatigued by the cares, distresses, and anxieties to which mortality is subject.

The Gypsies too have their poetry. Of that of the Russian Zigani we have already said something. It has always been our opinion, and we believe that in this we are by no means singular, that in nothing can the character of a people be read with greater certainty and exactness than in its songs. How truly do the warlike ballads of the Northmen and the Danes, their DRAPAS and KOEMPE-VISER, depict the character of the Goth; and how equally do the songs of the Arabians, replete with homage to the one high, uncreated, and eternal God, 'the fountain of blessing,' 'the only conqueror,' lay bare to us the mind of the Moslem of the desert, whose grand characteristic is religious veneration, and uncompromising zeal for the glory of the Creator.

And well and truly do the coplas and gachaplas of the Gitanos depict the character of the race. This poetry, for poetry we will call it, is in most respects such as might be expected to originate among people of their class; a set of Thugs, subsisting by cheating and villainy of every description; hating the rest of the human species, and bound to each other by the bonds of common origin, language, and pursuits. The general themes of this poetry are the various incidents of Gitano life and the feelings of the Gitanos. A Gypsy sees a pig running down a hill, and imagines that it cries 'Ustilame Caloro!'[62] - a Gypsy reclining sick on the prison floor beseeches his wife to intercede with the alcayde for the removal of the chain, the weight of which is bursting his body - the moon arises, and two Gypsies, who are about to steal a steed, perceive a Spaniard, and instantly flee - Juanito Ralli, whilst going home on his steed, is stabbed by a Gypsy who hates him - Facundo, a Gypsy, runs away at the sight of the burly priest of Villa Franca, who hates all Gypsies. Sometimes a burst of wild temper gives occasion to a strain - the swarthy lover threatens to slay his betrothed, even AT THE FEET OF JESUS, should she prove unfaithful. It is a general opinion amongst the Gitanos that Spanish women are very fond of Rommany chals and Rommany. There is a stanza in which a Gitano hopes to bear away a beauty of Spanish race by means of a word of Rommany whispered in her ear at the window.

Amongst these effusions are even to be found tender and beautiful thoughts; for Thugs and Gitanos have their moments of gentleness. True it is that such are few and far between, as a flower or a shrub is here and there seen springing up from the interstices of the rugged and frightful rocks of which the Spanish sierras are composed: a wicked mother is afraid to pray to the Lord with her own lips, and calls on her innocent babe to beseech him to restore peace and comfort to her heart - an imprisoned youth appears to have no earthly friend on whom he can rely, save his sister, and wishes for a messenger to carry unto her the tale of his sufferings, confident that she would hasten at once to his assistance. And what can be more touching than the speech of the relenting lover to the fair one whom he has outraged?

'Extend to me the hand so small,
Wherein I see thee weep,
For O thy balmy tear-drops all
I would collect and keep.'

This Gypsy poetry consists of quartets, or rather couplets, but two rhymes being discernible, and those generally imperfect, the vowels alone agreeing in sound. Occasionally, however, sixains, or stanzas of six lines, are to be found, but this is of rare occurrence. The thought, anecdote or adventure described, is seldom carried beyond one stanza, in which everything is expressed which the poet wishes to impart. This feature will appear singular to those who are unacquainted with the character of the popular poetry of the south, and are accustomed to the redundancy and frequently tedious repetition of a more polished muse. It will be well to inform such that the greater part of the poetry sung in the south, and especially in Spain, is extemporary. The musician composes it at the stretch of his voice, whilst his fingers are tugging at the guitar; which style of composition is by no means favourable to a long and connected series of thought. Of course, the greater part of this species of poetry perishes as soon as born. A stanza, however, is sometimes caught up by the bystanders, and committed to memory; and being frequently repeated, makes, in time, the circuit of the country. For example, the stanza about Coruncho Lopez, which was originally made at the gate of a venta by a Miquelet,[63] who was conducting the said Lopez to the galleys for a robbery. It is at present sung through the whole of the peninsula, however insignificant it may sound to foreign ears:-

'Coruncho Lopez, gallant lad,
A smuggling he would ride;
He stole his father's ambling prad,
And therefore to the galleys sad
Coruncho now I guide.'

The couplets of the Gitanos are composed in the same off-hand manner, and exactly resemble in metre the popular ditties of the Spaniards. In spirit, however, as well as language, they are in general widely different, as they mostly relate to the Gypsies and their affairs, and not unfrequently abound with abuse of the Busne or Spaniards. Many of these creations have, like the stanza of Coruncho Lopez, been wafted over Spain amongst the Gypsy tribes, and are even frequently repeated by the

Spaniards themselves; at least, by those who affect to imitate the phraseology of the Gitanos. Those which appear in the present collection consist partly of such couplets, and partly of such as we have ourselves taken down, as soon as they originated, not unfrequently in the midst of a circle of these singular people, dancing and singing to their wild music. In no instance have they been subjected to modification; and the English translation is, in general, very faithful to the original, as will easily be perceived by referring to the lexicon. To those who may feel disposed to find fault with or criticise these songs, we have to observe, that the present work has been written with no other view than to depict the Gitanos such as they are, and to illustrate their character; and, on that account, we have endeavoured, as much as possible, to bring them before the reader, and to make them speak for themselves. They are a half-civilised, unlettered people, proverbial for a species of knavish acuteness, which serves them in lieu of wisdom. To place in the mouth of such beings the high-flown sentiments of modern poetry would not answer our purpose, though several authors have not shrunk from such an absurdity.

These couplets have been collected in Estremadura and New Castile, in Valencia and Andalusia; the four provinces where the Gitano race most abounds. We wish, however, to remark, that they constitute scarcely a tenth part of our original gleanings, from which we have selected one hundred of the most remarkable and interesting.

The language of the originals will convey an exact idea of the Rommany of Spain, as used at the present day amongst the Gitanos in the fairs, when they are buying and selling animals, and wish to converse with each other in a way unintelligible to the Spaniards. We are free to confess that it is a mere broken jargon, but it answers the purpose of those who use it; and it is but just to remark that many of its elements are of the most remote antiquity, and the most illustrious descent, as will be shown hereafter. We have uniformly placed the original by the side of the translation; for though unwilling to make the Gitanos speak in any other manner than they are accustomed, we are equally averse to have it supposed that many of the thoughts and expressions which occur in these songs, and which are highly objectionable, originated with ourselves.[64]

RHYMES OF THE GITANOS

Unto a refuge me they led,
To save from dungeon drear;
Then sighing to my wife I said,
I leave my baby dear.

Back from the refuge soon I sped,
My child's sweet face to see;
Then sternly to my wife I said,
You've seen the last of me.

O when I sit my courser bold,
My bantling in my rear,
And in my hand my musket hold,
O how they quake with fear.

Pray, little baby, pray the Lord,
Since guiltless still thou art,
That peace and comfort he afford
To this poor troubled heart.

The false Juanito, day and night,
Had best with caution go,
The Gypsy carles of Yeira height
Have sworn to lay him low.

There runs a swine down yonder hill,
As fast as e'er he can,
And as he runs he crieth still,
Come, steal me, Gypsy man.

I wash'd not in the limpid flood
The shirt which binds my frame;
But in Juanito Ralli's blood
I bravely wash'd the same.

I sallied forth upon my grey,
With him my hated foe,
And when we reach'd the narrow way

I dealt a dagger blow.
To blessed Jesus' holy feet
I'd rush to kill and slay
My plighted lass so fair and sweet,
Should she the wanton play.

I for a cup of water cried,
But they refus'd my prayer,
Then straight into the road I hied,
And fell to robbing there.

I ask'd for fire to warm my frame,
But they'd have scorn'd my prayer,
If I, to pay them for the same,
Had stripp'd my body bare.

Then came adown the village street,
With little babes that cry,
Because they have no crust to eat,
A Gypsy company;
And as no charity they meet,
They curse the Lord on high.

I left my house and walk'd about,
They seized me fast and bound;
It is a Gypsy thief, they shout,
The Spaniards here have found.

From out the prison me they led,
Before the scribe they brought;
It is no Gypsy thief, he said,
The Spaniards here have caught.

Throughout the night, the dusky night,
I prowl in silence round,
And with my eyes look left and right,
For him, the Spanish hound,
That with my knife I him may smite,
And to the vitals wound.

Will no one to the sister bear
News of her brother's plight,
How in this cell of dark despair,
To cruel death he's dight?

The Lord, as e'en the Gentiles state,
By Egypt's race was bred,
And when he came to man's estate,
His blood the Gentiles shed.

O never with the Gentiles wend,
Nor deem their speeches true;
Or else, be certain in the end
Thy blood will lose its hue.

From out the prison me they bore,
Upon an ass they placed,
And scourg'd me till I dripp'd with gore,
As down the road it paced.

They bore me from the prison nook,
They bade me rove at large;
When out I'd come a gun I took,
And scathed them with its charge.

My mule so bonny I bestrode,
To Portugal I'd flee,
And as I o'er the water rode
A man came suddenly;
And he his love and kindness show'd
By setting his dog on me.

Unless within a fortnight's space
Thy face, O maid, I see;
Flamenca, of Egyptian race,
My lady love shall be.
Flamenca, of Egyptian race,
If thou wert only mine,
Within a bonny crystal case
For life I'd thee enshrine.

Sire nor mother me caress,
For I have none on earth;
One little brother I possess,
And he's a fool by birth.

Thy sire and mother wrath and hate
Have vow'd against me, love!
The first, first night that from the gate
We two together rove.

Come to the window, sweet love, do,
And I will whisper there,
In Rommany, a word or two,
And thee far off will bear.

A Gypsy stripling's sparkling eye
Has pierced my bosom's core,
A feat no eye beneath the sky
Could e'er effect before.

Dost bid me from the land begone,
And thou with child by me?
Each time I come, the little one,
I'll greet in Rommany.

With such an ugly, loathly wife
The Lord has punish'd me;
I dare not take her for my life
Where'er the Spaniards be.

O, I am not of gentle clan,
I'm sprung from Gypsy tree;
And I will be no gentleman,
But an Egyptian free.
On high arose the moon so fair,
The Gypsy 'gan to sing:
I see a Spaniard coming there,
I must be on the wing.

This house of harlotry doth smell,
I flee as from the pest;
Your mother likes my sire too well;
To hie me home is best.

The girl I love more dear than life,
Should other gallant woo,
I'd straight unsheath my dudgeon knife
And cut his weasand through;
Or he, the conqueror in the strife,
The same to me should do.

Loud sang the Spanish cavalier,
And thus his ditty ran:
God send the Gypsy lassie here,
And not the Gypsy man.

At midnight, when the moon began
To show her silver flame,
There came to him no Gypsy man,
The Gypsy lassie came.

CHAPTER II

THE Gitanos, abject and vile as they have ever been, have nevertheless found admirers in Spain, individuals who have taken pleasure in their phraseology, pronunciation, and way of life; but above all, in the songs and dances of the females. This desire for cultivating their acquaintance is chiefly prevalent in Andalusia, where, indeed, they most abound; and more especially in the town of Seville, the capital of the province, where, in the barrio or Faubourg of Triana, a large Gitano colon has long flourished, with the denizens of which it is at all times easy to have intercourse, especially to those who are free of their money, and are willing to purchase such a gratification at the expense of dollars and pesetas.

When we consider the character of the Andalusians in general, we shall find little to surprise us in this predilection for the Gitanos. They are an indolent frivolous people, fond of dancing and song, and sensual amusements. They live under the most glorious sun and benign heaven in Europe, and their country is by nature rich and fertile, yet in no province of Spain is there more beggary and misery; the greater part of the land being uncultivated, and producing nothing but thorns and brushwood, affording in itself a striking emblem of the moral state of its inhabitants.

Though not destitute of talent, the Andalusians are not much addicted to intellectual pursuits, at least in the present day. The person in most esteem among them is invariably the greatest MAJO, and to acquire that character it is necessary to appear in the dress of a Merry Andrew, to bully, swagger, and smoke continually, to dance passably, and to strum the guitar. They are fond of obscenity and what they term PICARDIAS. Amongst them learning is at a terrible discount, Greek, Latin, or any of the languages generally termed learned, being considered in any light but accomplishments, but not so the possession of thieves' slang or the dialect of the

Gitanos, the knowledge of a few words of which invariably creates a certain degree of respect, as indicating that the individual is somewhat versed in that kind of life or TRATO for which alone the Andalusians have any kind of regard.

In Andalusia the Gitano has been studied by those who, for various reasons, have mingled with the Gitanos. It is tolerably well understood by the chalans, or jockeys, who have picked up many words in the fairs and market-places which the former frequent. It has, however, been cultivated to a greater degree by other individuals, who have sought the society of the Gitanos from a zest for their habits, their dances, and their songs; and such individuals have belonged to all classes, amongst them have been noblemen and members of the priestly order.

Perhaps no people in Andalusia have been more addicted in general to the acquaintance of the Gitanos than the friars, and pre-eminently amongst these the half-jockey half-religious personages of the Cartujan convent at Xeres. This community, now suppressed, was, as is well known, in possession of a celebrated breed of horses, which fed in the pastures of the convent, and from which they derived no inconsiderable part of their revenue. These reverend gentlemen seem to have been much better versed in the points of a horse than in points of theology, and to have understood thieves' slang and Gitano far better than the language of the Vulgate. A chalan, who had some knowledge of the Gitano, related to me the following singular anecdote in connection with this subject.

He had occasion to go to the convent, having been long in treaty with the friars for a steed which he had been commissioned by a nobleman to buy at any reasonable price. The friars, however, were exorbitant in their demands. On arriving at the gate, he sang to the friar who opened it a couplet which he had composed in the Gypsy tongue, in which he stated the highest price which he was authorised to give for the animal in question; whereupon the friar instantly answered in the same tongue in an extemporary couplet full of abuse of him and his employer, and forthwith slammed the door in the face of the disconcerted jockey.

An Augustine friar of Seville, called, we believe, Father Manso, who lived some twenty years ago, is still remembered for his passion for the Gitanos; he seemed to be under the influence of fascination, and passed every moment that he could steal from his clerical occupations in their company. His conduct at last became so notorious that he fell under the censure of the Inquisition, before which he was summoned; whereupon he alleged, in his defence, that his sole motive for following the Gitanos was zeal for their spiritual conversion. Whether this plea availed him we know not; but it is probable that the Holy Office dealt mildly with him; such offenders, indeed, have never had much to fear from it. Had he been accused of liberalism, or searching into the Scriptures, instead of connection with the Gitanos, we should, doubtless, have heard either of his execution or imprisonment for life in the cells of the cathedral of Seville.

Such as are thus addicted to the Gitanos and their language, are called, in Andalusia, Los del' Aficion, or those of the predilection. These people have, during the last fifty years, composed a spurious kind of Gypsy literature: we call it spurious because it did not originate with the Gitanos, who are, moreover, utterly unacquainted with it, and to whom it would be for the most part unintelligible. It is somewhat difficult to conceive the reason which induced these individuals to attempt such compositions; the only probable one seems to have been a desire to display to each other their skill in the language of their predilection. It is right, however, to observe, that most of these compositions, with respect to language, are highly absurd, the greatest liberties being taken with the words picked up amongst the Gitanos, of the true meaning of which the writers, in many instances, seem to have been entirely ignorant. From what we can learn, the composers of this literature flourished chiefly at the commencement of the present century: Father Manso is said to have been one of the last. Many of their compositions, which are both in poetry and prose, exist in manuscript in a compilation made by one Luis Lobo. It has never been our fortune to see this compilation, which, indeed, we scarcely regret, as a rather curious circumstance has afforded us a perfect knowledge of its contents.

Whilst at Seville, chance made us acquainted with a highly extraordinary individual, a tall, bony, meagre figure, in a tattered Andalusian hat, ragged capote, and still more ragged pantaloons, and seemingly between forty and fifty years of age. The only appellation to which he answered was Manuel. His occupation, at the time we knew him, was selling tickets for the lottery, by which he obtained a miserable livelihood in Seville and the neighbouring villages. His appearance was altogether wild and uncouth, and there was an insane expression in his eye. Observing us one day in conversation with a Gitana, he addressed us, and we soon found that the sound of the Gitano language had struck a chord which vibrated through the depths of his soul. His history was remarkable; in his early youth a manuscript copy of the compilation of Luis Lobo had fallen into his hands. This book had so taken hold of his imagination, that he studied it night and day until he had planted it in his memory from beginning to end; but in so doing, his brain, like that of the hero of Cervantes, had become dry and heated, so that he was unfitted for any serious or useful occupation. After the death of his parents he wandered about the streets in great distress, until at last he fell into the hands of certain toreros, or bull-fighters, who kept him about them, in order that he might repeat to them the songs of the AFICION. They subsequently carried him to Madrid, where, however, they soon deserted him after he had experienced much brutality from their hands. He returned to Seville, and soon became the inmate of a madhouse, where he continued several years. Having partially recovered from his malady, he was liberated, and wandered about as before. During the cholera at Seville, when nearly twenty thousand human beings perished, he was appointed conductor of one of the death-carts, which went through the streets for the purpose of picking up the dead bodies. His perfect inoffensiveness eventually procured him friends, and he obtained the situation of vendor of lottery tickets. He frequently visited us, and would then recite long passages from the work of Lobo. He was wont to say that he was the only one in Seville, at the present day, acquainted with the language of the Aficion; for though there were many pretenders, their knowledge was confined to a few words.

From the recitation of this individual, we wrote down the Brijindope, or Deluge, and the poem on the plague which broke out in Seville in the year 1800. These and some songs of less consequence, constitute the poetical part of the compilation in question; the rest, which is in prose, consisting chiefly of translations from the Spanish, of proverbs and religious pieces.

BRIJINDOPE. - THE DELUGE[65]
A POEM: IN TWO PARTS

PART THE FIRST

I with fear and terror quake,
Whilst the pen to write I take;
I will utter many a pray'r
To the heaven's Regent fair,
That she deign to succour me,
And I'll humbly bend my knee;
For but poorly do I know
With my subject on to go;
Therefore is my wisest plan
Not to trust in strength of man.
I my heavy sins bewail,
Whilst I view the wo and wail
Handed down so solemnly
In the book of times gone by.
Onward, onward, now I'll move
In the name of Christ above,
And his Mother true and dear,
She who loves the wretch to cheer.
All I know, and all I've heard
I will state - how God appear'd
And to Noah thus did cry:
Weary with the world am I;
Let an ark by thee be built,
For the world is lost in guilt;

And when thou hast built it well,
Loud proclaim what now I tell:
Straight repent ye, for your Lord
In his hand doth hold a sword.
And good Noah thus did call:
Straight repent ye one and all,
For the world with grief I see
Lost in vileness utterly.
God's own mandate I but do,
He hath sent me unto you.
Laugh'd the world to bitter scorn,
I his cruel sufferings mourn;
Brawny youths with furious air
Drag the Patriarch by the hair;
Lewdness governs every one:
Leaves her convent now the nun,
And the monk abroad I see
Practising iniquity. Now
I'll tell how God, intent
To avenge, a vapour sent,
With full many a dreadful sign -
Mighty, mighty fear is mine:
As I hear the thunders roll,
Seems to die my very soul;
As I see the world o'erspread
All with darkness thick and dread;
I the pen can scarcely ply
For the tears which dim my eye,
And o'ercome with grievous wo,
Fear the task I must forego
I have purposed to perform. -
Hark, I hear upon the storm
Thousand, thousand devils fly,
Who with awful howlings cry:
Now's the time and now's the hour,
We have licence, we have power
To obtain a glorious prey. -
I with horror turn away;
Tumbles house and tumbles wall;
Thousands lose their lives and all,

Voiding curses, screams and groans,
For the beams, the bricks and stones
Bruise and bury all below -
Nor is that the worst,
I trow, For the clouds begin to pour
Floods of water more and more,
Down upon the world with might,
Never pausing day or night.
Now in terrible distress
All to God their cries address,
And his Mother dear adore, -
But the time of grace is o'er,
For the Almighty in the sky
Holds his hand upraised on high.
Now's the time of madden'd rout,
Hideous cry, despairing shout;
Whither, whither shall they fly?
For the danger threat'ningly
Draweth near on every side,
And the earth, that's opening wide,
Swallows thousands in its womb,
Who would 'scape the dreadful doom.
Of dear hope exists no gleam,
Still the water down doth stream;
Ne'er so little a creeping thing
But from out its hold doth spring:
See the mouse, and see its mate
Scour along, nor stop, nor wait;
See the serpent and the snake
For the nearest highlands make;
The tarantula I view,
Emmet small and cricket too,
All unknowing where to fly,
In the stifling waters die.
See the goat and bleating sheep,
See the bull with bellowings deep.
And the rat with squealings shrill,
They have mounted on the hill:
See the stag, and see the doe,
How together fond they go;

Lion, tiger-beast, and pard,
To escape are striving hard:
Followed by her little ones,
See the hare how swift she runs:
Asses, he and she, a pair.
Mute and mule with bray and blare,
And the rabbit and the fox,
Hurry over stones and rocks,
With the grunting hog and horse,
Till at last they stop their course -
On the summit of the hill
All assembled stand they still;
In the second part I'll tell
Unto them what there befell.

PART THE SECOND

When I last did bid farewell,
I proposed the world to tell,
Higher as the Deluge flow'd,
How the frog and how the toad,
With the lizard and the eft,
All their holes and coverts left,
And assembled on the height;
Soon I ween appeared in sight
All that's wings beneath the sky,
Bat and swallow, wasp and fly,
Gnat and sparrow, and behind
Comes the crow of carrion kind;
Dove and pigeon are descried,
And the raven fiery-eyed,
With the beetle and the crane
Flying on the hurricane:
See they find no resting-place,
For the world's terrestrial space
Is with water cover'd o'er,
Soon they sink to rise no more:

'To our father let us flee!'
Straight the ark-ship openeth he,
And to everything that lives
Kindly he admission gives.
Of all kinds a single pair,
And the members safely there
Of his house he doth embark,
Then at once he shuts the ark;
Everything therein has pass'd,
There he keeps them safe and fast.
O'er the mountain's topmost peak
Now the raging waters break.
Till full twenty days are o'er,
'Midst the elemental roar,
Up and down the ark forlorn,
Like some evil thing is borne:
O what grief it is to see
Swimming on the enormous sea
Human corses pale and white,
More, alas! than I can write:
O what grief, what grief profound,
But to think the world is drown'd:
True a scanty few are left,
All are not of life bereft,
So that, when the Lord ordain,
They may procreate again,
In a world entirely new,
Better people and more true,
To their Maker who shall bow;
And I humbly beg you now,
Ye in modern times who wend,
That your lives ye do amend;
For no wat'ry punishment,
But a heavier shall be sent;
For the blessed saints pretend
That the latter world shall end
To tremendous fire a prey,
And to ashes sink away.
To the Ark I now go back,

Which pursues its dreary track,
Lost and 'wilder'd till the Lord
In his mercy rest accord.
Early of a morning tide
They unclosed a window wide,
Heaven's beacon to descry,
And a gentle dove let fly,
Of the world to seek some trace,
And in two short hours' space
It returns with eyes that glow,
In its beak an olive bough.
With a loud and mighty sound,
They exclaim: 'The world we've found.'
To a mountain nigh they drew,
And when there themselves they view,
Bound they swiftly on the shore,
And their fervent thanks outpour,
Lowly kneeling to their God;
Then their way a couple trod,
Man and woman, hand in hand,
Bent to populate the land,
To the Moorish region fair -
And another two repair
To the country of the Gaul;
In this manner wend they all,
And the seeds of nations lay.
I beseech ye'll credence pay,
For our father, high and sage,
Wrote the tale in sacred page,
As a record to the world,
Record sad of vengeance hurl'd.
I, a low and humble wight,
Beg permission now to write
Unto all that in our land
Tongue Egyptian understand.
May our Virgin Mother mild
Grant to me, her erring child,
Plenteous grace in every way,
And success. Amen I say.

THE PESTILENCE

I'm resolved now to tell
In the speech of Gypsy-land
All the horror that befell
In this city huge and grand.

In the eighteenth hundred year
In the midst of summertide,
God, with man dissatisfied,
His right hand on high did rear,
With a rigour most severe;
Whence we well might understand
He would strict account demand
Of our lives and actions here.
The dread event to render clear
Now the pen I take in hand.

At the dread event aghast,
Straight the world reform'd its course;
Yet is sin in greater force,
Now the punishment is past;
For the thought of God is cast
All and utterly aside,
As if death itself had died.
Therefore to the present race
These memorial lines I trace
In old Egypt's tongue of pride.

As the streets you wander'd through
How you quail'd with fear and dread,
Heaps of dying and of dead
At the leeches' door to view.
To the tavern O how few
To regale on wine repair;
All a sickly aspect wear.
Say what heart such sights could brook -
Wail and woe where'er you look -
Wail and woe and ghastly care.

Plying fast their rosaries,
See the people pace the street,
And for pardon God entreat
Long and loud with streaming eyes.
And the carts of various size,
Piled with corses, high in air,
To the plain their burden bear.
O what grief it is to me
Not a friar or priest to see
In this city huge and fair.

ON THE LANGUAGE OF THE GITANOS

'I am not very willing that any language should be totally extinguished; the similitude and derivation of languages afford the most indubitable proof of the traduction of nations, and the genealogy of mankind; they add often physical certainty to historical evidence of ancient migrations, and of the revolutions of ages which left no written monuments behind them.'

- JOHNSON.

THE Gypsy dialect of Spain is at present very much shattered and broken, being rather the fragments of the language which the Gypsies brought with them from the remote regions of the East than the language itself: it enables, however, in its actual state, the Gitanos to hold conversation amongst themselves, the import of which is quite dark and mysterious to those who are not of their race, or by some means have become acquainted with their vocabulary. The relics of this tongue, singularly curious in themselves, must be ever particularly interesting to the philological antiquarian, inasmuch as they enable him to arrive at a satisfactory conclusion respecting the origin of the Gypsy race. During the later part of the last century, the curiosity of some learned individuals, particularly Grellmann, Richardson, and Marsden, induced them to collect many words of the Romanian language, as spoken in Germany, Hungary, and England, which, upon analysing, they discovered to be in general either pure Sanscrit or Hindustani words, or modifications thereof; these investigations have been continued to the present time by men of equal curiosity and no less erudition, the result of which has been the establishment of the fact, that the Gypsies of those countries are the descendants of a tribe of Hindus who for some particular reason had abandoned their native country. In England, of late, the Gypsies have excited particular attention; but a desire far more noble and laudable than mere antiquarian curiosity has given rise to it, namely, the desire of propagating the glory of Christ amongst those who know Him not, and of saving souls from the jaws of the infernal wolf. It is, however, with the Gypsies of Spain, and not with those of England and other countries, that we are now occupied, and we shall merely mention the latter so far as they may serve to elucidate the case of the Gitanos, their brethren by blood and language. Spain for many centuries has been the country of error; she has mistaken stern and savage tyranny for rational government; base, low, and grovelling superstition for clear, bright, and soul-ennobling religion; sordid cheating she has considered as the path to riches; vexatious persecution as the path to power; and the consequence has been, that she is now poor and powerless, a pagan amongst the pagans, with a dozen kings, and with none. Can we be surprised, therefore, that, mistaken in policy, religion, and moral conduct, she should have fallen into error on points so naturally dark and mysterious as the history and origin of those remarkable people whom for the last four hundred years she has supported under the name of Gitanos? The idea entertained at the present day in Spain respecting this race is, that they are the descendants of the Moriscos who remained in Spain, wandering about amongst the mountains and wildernesses, after the expulsion of the great body of the nation from the country in the time of Philip the Third, and that they form a distinct body, entirely unconnected with the wandering tribes known in other countries by the names of Bohemians, Gypsies, etc. This, like all unfounded opinions, of course originated in ignorance, which is always ready to have recourse to conjecture and guesswork, in preference to travelling through the long, mountainous, and stony road of patient investigation; it is, however, an error far more absurd and more destitute of tenable grounds than the ancient belief that the Gitanos were Egyptians, which they themselves have always professed to be, and which the original written documents which they brought with them on their first arrival in Western Europe, and which bore the signature of the king of Bohemia, expressly stated them to be. The only clue to arrive at any certainty respecting their origin, is the language which they still speak amongst themselves; but before we can avail ourselves of the evidence of this language, it will be necessary to make a few remarks respecting the principal languages and dialects of that immense tract of country, peopled by at least eighty millions of human beings, generally known by the name of Hindustan, two Persian words tantamount to the land of Ind, or, the land watered by the river Indus.

The most celebrated of these languages is the Sanskrida, or, as it is known in Europe, the Sanscrit, which is the language of religion of all those nations amongst whom the faith of Brahma has been adopted; but though the language of religion, by which we mean the tongue in which the religious books of the Brahmanic sect were originally written and are still preserved, it has long since ceased to be a spoken language; indeed, history is silent as to any period when it was a language in common use amongst any of the various tribes of the Hindus; its knowledge, as far as reading and writing it went, having been entirely confined to the priests of Brahma, or Brahmans, until within the last half-century, when the British, having subjugated the whole of Hindustan, caused it to be openly taught in the colleges which they established for the instruction of their youth in the languages of the country. Though sufficiently difficult to acquire, principally on account of its prodigious richness in synonyms, it is no longer a sealed language, - its laws, structure, and vocabulary being sufficiently well known by means of numerous elementary works, adapted to facilitate its study. It has been considered by famous philologists as the mother not only of all the languages of Asia, but of all others in the world. So wild and preposterous an idea, however, only serves to prove that a devotion to philology, whose principal object should be the expansion of the mind by the various treasures of learning and wisdom which it can unlock, sometimes only tends to its bewilderment, by causing it to embrace shadows for reality. The most that can be allowed, in reason, to the Sanscrit is that it is the mother of a certain class or family of languages, for example, those spoken in Hindustan, with which most of the European, whether of the Sclavonian, Gothic, or Celtic stock, have some connection. True it is that in this case we know not how to dispose of the ancient Zend, the mother of the modern Persian, the language in which were written those writings generally attributed to Zerduscht, or Zoroaster, whose affinity to the said tongues is as easily established as that of the Sanscrit, and which, in respect to antiquity, may well dispute the palm with its Indian rival. Avoiding, however, the discussion of this point, we shall content ourselves with observing, that closely connected with the Sanscrit, if not derived from it, are the Bengali, the high Hindustani, or grand popular language of Hindustan, generally used by the learned in their intercourse and writings, the languages of Multan, Guzerat, and other provinces, without mentioning the mixed dialect called Mongolian Hindustani, a corrupt jargon of Persian, Turkish, Arabic, and Hindu words, first used by the Mongols, after the conquest, in their intercourse with the natives. Many of the principal languages of Asia are totally unconnected with the Sanscrit, both in words and grammatical structure; these are mostly of the great Tartar family, at the head of which there is good reason for placing the Chinese and Tibetian.

Bearing the same analogy to the Sanscrit tongue as the Indian dialects specified above, we find the Rommany, or speech of the Roma, or Zincali, as they style themselves, known in England and Spain as Gypsies and Gitanos. This speech, wherever it is spoken, is, in all principal points, one and the same, though more or less corrupted by foreign words, picked up in the various countries to which those who use it have penetrated. One remarkable feature must not be passed over without notice, namely, the very considerable number of Sclavonic words, which are to be found embedded within it, whether it be spoken in Spain or Germany, in England or Italy; from which circumstance we are led to the conclusion, that these people, in their way from the East, travelled in one large compact body, and that their route lay through some region where the Sclavonian language, or a dialect thereof, was spoken. This region I have no hesitation in asserting to have been Bulgaria, where they probably tarried for a considerable period, as nomad herdsmen, and where numbers of them are still to be found at the present day. Besides the many Sclavonian words in the Gypsy tongue, another curious feature attracts the attention of the philologist - an equal or still greater quantity of terms from the modern Greek; indeed, we have full warranty for assuming that at one period the Spanish section, if not the rest of the Gypsy nation, understood the Greek language well, and that, besides their own Indian dialect, they occasionally used it for considerably upwards of a century subsequent to their arrival, as amongst the Gitanos there were individuals to whom it was intelligible so late as the year 1540.

Where this knowledge was obtained it is difficult to say, - perhaps in Bulgaria, where two-thirds of the population profess the Greek religion, or rather in Romania, where the Romaic is generally understood; that they DID understand the Romaic in 1540, we gather from a very remarkable work, called EL ESTUDIOSO CORTESANO, written by Lorenzo Palmireno: this learned and highly extraordinary individual was by birth a Valencian, and died about 1580; he was professor at various universities - of rhetoric at Valencia, of Greek at Zaragossa, where he gave lectures, in which he explained the verses of Homer; he was a proficient in Greek, ancient and modern, and it should be observed that, in the passage which we are about to cite, he means himself by the learned individual who held conversation with the Gitanos.[66] EL ESTUDIOSO CORTESANO was reprinted at Alcala in 1587, from which edition we now copy.

'Who are the Gitanos? I answer; these vile people first began to show themselves in Germany, in the year 1417, where they call them Tartars or Gentiles; in Italy they are termed Ciani. They pretend that they come from Lower Egypt, and that they wander about as a penance, and to prove this, they show letters from the king of Poland. They lie, however, for they do not lead the life of penitents, but of dogs and thieves. A learned person, in the year 1540, prevailed with them, by dint of much persuasion, to show him the king's letter, and he gathered from it that the time of their penance was already expired; he spoke to them in the Egyptian tongue; they said, however, as it was a long time since their departure from Egypt, they did not understand it; he then spoke to them in the vulgar Greek, such as is used at present in the Morea and Archipelago; SOME UNDERSTOOD IT, others did not; so that as all did not understand it, we may conclude that the language which they use is a feigned one,[67] got up by thieves for the purpose of concealing their robberies, like the jargon of blind beggars.'

Still more abundant, however, than the mixture of Greek, still more abundant than the mixture of Sclavonian, is the alloy in the Gypsy language, wherever spoken, of modern Persian words, which circumstance will compel us to offer a few remarks on the share which the Persian has had in the formation of the dialects of India, as at present spoken.

The modern Persian, as has been already observed, is a daughter of the ancient Zend, and, as such, is entitled to claim affinity with the Sanscrit, and its dialects. With this language none in the world would be able to vie in simplicity and beauty, had not the Persians, in adopting the religion of Mahomet, unfortunately introduces into their speech an infinity of words of the rude coarse language used by the barbaric Arab tribes, the immediate followers of the warlike Prophet. With the rise of Islam the modern Persian was doomed to be carried into India. This country, from the time of Alexander, had enjoyed repose from external aggression, had been ruled by its native princes, and been permitted by Providence to exercise, without control or reproof, the degrading superstitions, and the unnatural and bloody rites of a religion at the formation of which the fiends of cruelty and lust seem to have presided; but reckoning was now about to be demanded of the accursed ministers of this system for the pain, torture, and misery which they had been instrumental in inflicting on their countrymen for the gratification of their avarice, filthy passions, and pride; the new Mahometans were at hand - Arab, Persian, and Afghan, with the glittering scimitar upraised, full of zeal for the glory and adoration of the one high God, and the relentless persecutors of the idol-worshippers. Already, in the four hundred and twenty-sixth year of the Hegeira, we read of the destruction of the great Butkhan, or image-house of Sumnaut, by the armies of the far-conquering Mahmoud, when the dissevered heads of the Brahmans rolled down the steps of the gigantic and Babel-like temple of the great image -

[Text which cannot be reproduced - Arabic?]

(This image grim, whose name was Laut, Bold Mahmoud found when he took Sumnaut.)

It is not our intention to follow the conquests of the Mahometans from the days of Walid and Mahmoud to those of Timour and Nadir; sufficient to observe, that the greatest part of

India was subdued, new monarchies established, and the old religion, though far too powerful and widely spread to be extirpated, was to a considerable extent abashed and humbled before the bright rising sun of Islam. The Persian language, which the conquerors[68] of whatever denomination introduced with them to Hindustan, and which their descendants at the present day still retain, though not lords of the ascendant, speedily became widely extended in these regions, where it had previously been unknown. As the language of the court, it was of course studied and acquired by all those natives whose wealth, rank, and influence necessarily brought them into connection with the ruling powers; and as the language of the camp, it was carried into every part of the country where the duties of the soldiery sooner or later conducted them; the result of which relations between the conquerors and conquered was the adoption into the popular dialects of India of an infinity of modern Persian words, not merely those of science, such as it exists in the East, and of luxury and refinement, but even those which serve to express many of the most common objects, necessities, and ideas, so that at the present day a knowledge of the Persian is essential for the thorough understanding of the principal dialects of Hindustan, on which account, as well as for the assistance which it affords in communication with the Mahometans, it is cultivated with peculiar care by the present possessors of the land.

No surprise, therefore, can be entertained that the speech of the Gitanos in general, who, in all probability, departed from Hindustan long subsequent to the first Mahometan invasions, abounds, like other Indian dialects, with words either purely Persian, or slightly modified to accommodate them to the genius of the language. Whether the Rommany originally constituted part of the natives of Multan or Guzerat, and abandoned their native land to escape from the torch and sword of Tamerlane and his Mongols, as Grellmann and others have supposed, or whether, as is much more probable, they were a thievish caste, like some others still to be found in Hindustan, who fled westward, either from the vengeance of justice, or in pursuit of plunder, their speaking Persian is alike satisfactorily accounted for. With the view of exhibiting how closely their language is connected with the Sanscrit and Persian, we subjoin the first ten numerals in the three tongues, those of the Gypsy according to the Hungarian dialect.[69]

	Gypsy.	Persian.	Sanscrit.[70]
1	Jek	Ek	Ega
2	Dui	Du	Dvaya
3	Trin	Se	Treya
4	Schtar	Chehar	Tschatvar
5	Pansch	Pansch	Pantscha
6	Tschov	Schesche	Schasda
7	Efta	Heft	Sapta
8	Ochto	Hescht	Aschta
9	Enija	Nu	Nava
10	Dosch	De	Dascha

It would be easy for us to adduce a thousand instances, as striking as the above, of the affinity of the Gypsy tongue to the Persian, Sanscrit, and the Indian dialects, but we have not space for further observation on a point which long since has been sufficiently discussed by others endowed with abler pens than our own; but having made these preliminary remarks, which we deemed necessary for the elucidation of the subject, we now hasten to speak of the Gitano language as used in Spain, and to determine, by its evidence (and we again repeat, that the language is the only criterion by which the question can be determined), how far the Gitanos of Spain are entitled to claim connection with the tribes who, under the names of Zingani, etc., are to be found in various parts of Europe, following, in general, a life of wandering adventure, and practising the same kind of thievish arts which enable those in Spain to obtain a livelihood at the expense of the more honest and industrious of the community.

The Gitanos of Spain, as already stated, are generally believed to be the descendants of the Moriscos, and have been asserted to be such in printed books.[71] Now they are known to speak a language or jargon amongst themselves which the other natives of Spain do not understand; of course, then, supposing them to be of Morisco origin, the words of this tongue or jargon, which are not Spanish, are the relics of the Arabic or Moorish tongue once spoken in Spain, which they have inherited from their Moorish ancestors. Now it is well known, that the Moorish of Spain was the same tongue as that spoken at present by the Moors of Barbary, from which country Spain was invaded by the Arabs, and to which they again retired when unable to maintain their ground against the armies of the Christians. We will, therefore, collate the numerals of the Spanish Gitano with those of the Moorish tongue, preceding both with those of the Hungarian Gypsy, of which we have already made use, for the purpose of making clear the affinity of that language to the Sanscrit and Persian. By this collation we shall at once perceive whether the Gitano of Spain bears most resemblance to the Arabic, or the Rommany of other lands.

Hungarian Spanish Moorish Gypsy. Gitano. Arabic.

1 Jek Yeque Wahud 2 Dui Dui Snain 3 Trin Trin Slatza 4 Schtar Estar Arba 5 Pansch Pansche Khamsa 6 Tschov Job. Zoi Seta 7 Efta Hefta Sebea 8 Ochto Otor Sminia 9 Enija Esnia (Nu. PERS.) Tussa 10 Dosch Deque Aschra

We believe the above specimens will go very far to change the opinion of those who have imbibed the idea that the Gitanos of Spain are the descendants of Moors, and are of an origin different from that of the wandering tribes of Rommany in other parts of the world, the specimens of the two dialects of the Gypsy, as far as they go, being so strikingly similar, as to leave no doubt of their original identity, whilst, on the contrary, with the Moorish neither the one nor the other exhibits the slightest point of similarity or connection. But with these specimens we shall not content ourselves, but proceed to give the names of the most common things and objects in the Hungarian and Spanish Gitano, collaterally, with their equivalents in the Moorish Arabic; from which it will appear that whilst the former are one and the same language, they are in every respect at variance with the latter. When we consider that the Persian has adopted so many words and phrases from the Arabic, we are at first disposed to wonder that a considerable portion of these words are not to be discovered in every dialect of the Gypsy tongue, since the Persian has lent it so much of its vocabulary. Yet such is by no means the case, as it is very uncommon, in any one of these dialects, to discover words derived from the Arabic. Perhaps, however, the following consideration will help to solve this point. The Gitanos, even before they left India, were probably much the same rude, thievish, and ignorant people as they are at the present day. Now the words adopted by the Persian from the Arabic, and which it subsequently introduced into the dialects of India, are sounds representing objects and ideas with which such a people as the Gitanos could necessarily be but scantily acquainted, a people whose circle of ideas only embraces physical objects, and who never commune with their own minds, nor exert them but in devising low and vulgar schemes of pillage and deceit. Whatever is visible and common is seldom or never represented by the Persians, even in their books, by the help of Arabic words: the sun and stars, the sea and river, the earth, its trees, its fruits, its flowers, and all that it produces and supports, are seldom named by them by other terms than those which their own language is capable of affording; but in expressing the abstract thoughts of their minds, and they are a people who think much and well, they borrow largely from the language of their religion - the Arabic. We therefore, perhaps, ought not to be surprised that in the scanty phraseology of the Gitanos, amongst so much Persian, we find so little that is Arabic; had their pursuits been less vile, their desires less animal, and their thoughts less circumscribed, it would probably have been otherwise; but from time immemorial they have shown themselves a nation of petty thieves, horse-traffickers, and the like, without a thought of the morrow, being content to provide against the evil of the passing day.

The following is a comparison of words in the three languages:-

	Hungarian Gypsy.(72)	Spanish Gitano.	Moorish Arabic.
Bone	Cokalos	Cocal	Adorn
City	Forjus	Foros	Beled
Day	Dives	Chibes	Youm
Drink (to)	Piava	Piyar	Yeschrab
Ear	Kan	Can	Oothin
Eye	Jakh	Aquia	Ein
Feather	Por	Porumia	Risch
Fire	Vag	Yaque	Afia
Fish	Maczo	Macho	Hutz
Foot	Pir	Piro, pindro	Rjil
Gold	Sonkai	Sonacai	Dahab
Great	Baro	Baro	Quibir
Hair	Bala	Bal	Schar
He, pron.	Wow	O	Hu

Head	Tschero	Jero	Ras
House	Ker	Quer	Dar
Husband	Rom	Ron	Zooje
Lightning	Molnija	Maluno	Brak
Love (to)	Camaba	Camelar	Yehib
Man	Manusch	Manu	Rajil
Milk	Tud	Chuti	Helib
Mountain	Bar	Bur	Djibil
Mouth	Mui	Mui	Fum
Name	Nao	Nao	Ism
Night	Rat	Rachi	Lila
Nose	Nakh	Naqui	Munghar
Old	Puro	Puro	Shaive
Red	Lal	Lalo	Hamr
Salt	Lon	Lon	Mela
Sing	Gjuwawa	Gilyabar	Iganni
Sun	Cam	Can	Schems
Thief	Tschor	Choro	Haram
Thou	Tu	Tucue	Antsin
Tongue	Tschib	Chipe	Lsan
Tooth	Dant	Dani	Sinn
Tree	Karscht	Caste	Schizara
Water	Pani	Pani	Ma
Wind	Barbar	Barban	Ruhk

We shall offer no further observations respecting the affinity of the Spanish Gitano to the other dialects, as we conceive we have already afforded sufficient proof of its original identity with them, and consequently shaken to the ground the absurd opinion that the Gitanos of Spain are the descendants of the Arabs and Moriscos. We shall now conclude with a few remarks on the present state of the Gitano language in Spain, where, perhaps, within the course of a few years, it will have perished, without leaving a vestige of its having once existed; and where, perhaps, the singular people who speak it are likewise doomed to disappear, becoming sooner or later engulfed and absorbed in the great body of the nation, amongst whom they have so long existed a separate and peculiar class.

Though the words or a part of the words of the original tongue still remain, preserved by memory amongst the Gitanos, its grammatical peculiarities have disappeared, the entire language having been modified and subjected to the rules of Spanish grammar, with which it now coincides in syntax, in the conjugation of verbs, and in the declension of its nouns. Were it possible or necessary to collect all the relics of this speech, they would probably amount to four or five thousand words; but to effect such an achievement, it would be necessary to hold close and long intercourse with almost every Gitano in Spain, and to extract, by various means, the peculiar information which he might be capable of affording; for it is necessary to state here, that though such an amount of words may still exist amongst the Gitanos in general, no single individual of their sect is in possession of one-third part thereof, nor indeed, we may add, those of any single city or province of Spain; nevertheless all are in possession, more or less, of the language, so that, though of different provinces, they are enabled to understand each other tolerably well, when discoursing in this their characteristic speech. Those who travel most are of course best versed in it, as, independent of the words of their own village or town, they acquire others by intermingling with their race in various places. Perhaps there is no part of Spain where it is spoken better than in Madrid, which is easily accounted for by the fact, that Madrid, as the capital, has always been the point of union of the Gitanos, from all those provinces of Spain where they are to be found. It is least of all preserved in Seville, notwithstanding that its Gitano population is very considerable, consisting, however, almost entirely of natives of the place. As may well be supposed, it is in all places best preserved amongst the old people, their children being comparatively ignorant of it, as perhaps they themselves are in comparison with their own parents. We are persuaded that the Gitano language of Spain is nearly at its last stage of existence, which persuasion has been our main instigator to the present attempt to collect its scanty remains, and by the assistance of the press, rescue it in some degree from destruction. It will not be amiss to state here, that it is only by listening attentively to the speech of the Gitanos, whilst discoursing amongst themselves, that an acquaintance with their dialect can be formed, and by seizing upon all unknown words as they fall in succession from their lips. Nothing can be more useless and hopeless than the attempt to obtain possession of their vocabulary by inquiring of them how particular objects and ideas are styled; for with the exception of the names of the most common things, they are totally incapable, as a Spanish writer has observed, of yielding the required information, owing to their great ignorance, the shortness of their memories, or rather the state of bewilderment to which their minds are brought by any question which tends to bring their reasoning faculties into action, though not unfrequently the very words which have been in vain required of them will, a minute subsequently, proceed inadvertently from their mouths.

We now take leave of their language. When wishing to praise the proficiency of any individual in their tongue, they are in the habit of saying, 'He understands the seven jargons.' In the Gospel which we have printed in this language, and in the dictionary which we have compiled, we have endeavoured, to the utmost of our ability, to deserve that compliment; and at all times it will afford us sincere and heartfelt pleasure to be informed that any Gitano, capable of appreciating the said little works, has observed, whilst reading them or hearing them read: It is clear that the writer of these books understood

THE SEVEN JARGONS.

ON ROBBER LANGUAGE; OR, AS IT IS CALLED IN SPAIN, GERMANIA

'So I went with them to a music booth, where they made me almost drunk with gin, and began to talk their FLASH LANGUAGE, which I did not understand.' - Narrative of the Exploits of Henry Simms, executed at Tyburn, 1746.

'Hablaronse los dos en Germania, de lo qual resulto darme un abraco, y ofrecerseme.' - QUEVEDO. Vida dal gran Tacano.

HAVING in the preceding article endeavoured to afford all necessary information concerning the Rommany, or language used by the Gypsies amongst themselves, we now propose to turn our attention to a subject of no less interest, but which has hitherto never been treated in a manner calculated to lead to any satisfactory result or conclusion; on the contrary, though philosophic minds have been engaged in its consideration, and learned pens have not disdained to occupy themselves with its details, it still remains a singular proof of the errors into which the most acute and laborious writers are apt to fall, when they take upon themselves the task of writing on matters which cannot be studied in the closet, and on which no information can be received by mixing in the society of the wise, the lettered, and the respectable, but which must be investigated in the fields, and on the borders of the highways, in prisons, and amongst the dregs of society. Had the latter system been pursued in the matter now before us, much clearer, more rational, and more just ideas would long since have been entertained respecting the Germania, or language of thieves.

In most countries of Europe there exists, amongst those who obtain their existence by the breach of the law, and by preying upon the fruits of the labours of the quiet and orderly portion of society, a particular jargon or dialect, in which the former discuss their schemes and plans of plunder, without being in general understood by those to whom they are obnoxious. The name of this jargon varies with the country in which it is spoken. In Spain it is called 'Germania'; in France, 'Argot'; in Germany, 'Rothwelsch,' or Red Italian; in Italy, 'Gergo'; whilst in England it is known by many names; for example, 'cant, slang, thieves' Latin,' etc. The most remarkable circumstance connected with the history of this jargon is, that in all the countries in which it is spoken, it has invariably, by the authors who have treated of it, and who are numerous, been confounded with the Gypsy language, and asserted to be the speech of those wanderers who have so long infested Europe under the name of Gitanos, etc. How far this belief is founded in justice we shall now endeavour to show, with the premise that whatever we advance is derived, not from the assertions or opinions of others, but from our own observation; the point in question being one which no person is capable of solving, save him who has mixed with Gitanos and thieves, - not with the former merely or the latter, but with both.

We have already stated what is the Rommany or language of the Gypsies. We have proved that when properly spoken it is to all intents and purposes entitled to the appellation of a language, and that wherever it exists it is virtually the same; that its origin is illustrious, it being a daughter of the Sanscrit, and in consequence in close connection with some of the most celebrated languages of the East, although it at present is only used by the most unfortunate and degraded of beings, wanderers without home and almost without country, as wherever they are found they are considered in the light of foreigners and interlopers. We shall now state what the language of thieves is, as it is generally spoken in Europe; after which we shall proceed to analyse it according to the various countries in which it is used.

The dialect used for their own peculiar purposes amongst thieves is by no means entitled to the appellation of a language, but in every sense to that of a jargon or gibberish, it being for the most part composed of words of the native language of those who use it, according to the particular country, though invariably in a meaning differing more or less from the usual and received one, and for the most part in a metaphorical sense. Metaphor and allegory, indeed, seem to form the nucleus of this speech, notwithstanding that other elements are to be distinguished; for it is certain that in every country where it is spoken, it contains many words differing from the language of that country, and which may either be traced to foreign tongues, or are of an origin at which, in many instances, it is impossible to arrive. That which is most calculated to strike the philosophic mind when considering this dialect, is doubtless the fact of its being formed everywhere upon the same principle - that of metaphor, in which point all the branches agree, though in others they differ as much from each other as the languages on which they are founded; for example, as the English and German from the Spanish and Italian. This circumstance naturally leads to the conclusion that the robber language has not arisen fortuitously in the various countries where it is at present spoken, but that its origin is one and the same, it being probably invented by the outlaws of one particular country; by individuals of which it was, in course of time, carried to others, where its principles, if not its words, were adopted; for upon no other supposition can we account for its general metaphorical character in regions various and distant. It is, of course, impossible to state with certainty the country in which this jargon first arose, yet there is cogent reason for supposing that it may have been Italy. The Germans call it Rothwelsch, which signifies 'Red Italian,' a name which appears to point out Italy as its birthplace; and which, though by no means of sufficient importance to determine the question, is strongly corroborative of the supposition, when coupled with the following fact. We have already intimated, that wherever it is spoken, this speech, though composed for the most part of words of the language of the particular country, applied in a metaphorical sense, exhibits a considerable sprinkling of foreign words; now of these words no slight number are Italian or bastard Latin, whether in Germany, whether in Spain, or in other countries more or less remote from Italy. When we consider the ignorance of thieves in general, their total want of education, the slight knowledge which they possess even of their mother tongue, it is hardly reasonable to suppose that in any country they were ever capable of having recourse to foreign languages, for the purpose of enriching any peculiar vocabulary or phraseology which they might deem convenient to use among themselves; nevertheless, by associating with foreign thieves, who had either left their native country for their crimes, or from a hope of reaping a rich harvest of plunder in other lands, it would be easy for them to adopt a considerable number of words belonging to the languages of their foreign associates, from whom perhaps they derived an increase of knowledge in thievish arts of every description. At the commencement of the fifteenth century no nation in Europe was at all calculated to vie with the Italian in arts of any kind, whether those whose tendency was the benefit or improvement of society, or those the practice of which serves to injure and undermine it. The artists and artisans of Italy were to be found in all the countries of Europe, from Madrid to Moscow, and so were its charlatans, its jugglers, and multitudes of its children, who lived by fraud and cunning. Therefore, when a comprehensive view of the subject is taken, there appears to be little improbability in supposing, that not only were the Italians the originators of the metaphorical robber jargon, which has been termed 'Red Italian,' but that they were mainly instrumental in causing it to be adopted by the thievish race in various countries of Europe.

It is here, however, necessary to state, that in the robber jargon of Europe, elements of another language are to be discovered, and perhaps in greater number than the Italian words. The language which we allude to is the Rommany; this language has been, in general, confounded with the vocabulary used among thieves, which, however, is a gross error, so gross, indeed, that it is almost impossible to conceive the manner in which it originated: the speech of the Gypsies being a genuine language of Oriental origin, and the former little more than a phraseology of convenience, founded upon particular European tongues. It will be sufficient here to remark, that the Gypsies do not understand the jargon of the thieves, whilst the latter, with perhaps a few exceptions, are ignorant of the language of the former. Certain words, however, of the Rommany have found admission into the said jargon, which may be accounted for by the supposition that the Gypsies, being themselves by birth, education, and profession, thieves of the first water, have, on various occasions, formed alliances with the outlaws of the various countries in which they are at present to be found, which association may have produced the result above alluded to; but it will be as well here to state, that in no country of Europe have the Gypsies forsaken or forgotten their native tongue, and in its stead adopted the 'Germania,' 'Red Italian,' or robber jargon, although in some they preserve their native language in a state of less purity than in others. We are induced to make this statement from an assertion of the celebrated Lorenzo Hervas, who, in the third volume of his CATALOGO DE LAS LENGUAS, trat. 3, cap. vi., p. 311, expresses himself to the following effect:- 'The proper language of the Gitanos neither is nor can be found amongst those who scattered themselves through the western kingdoms of Europe, but only amongst those who remained in the eastern, where they are still to be found. The former were notably divided and disunited, receiving into their body a great number of European outlaws, on which account the language in question was easily adulterated and soon perished. In Spain, and also in Italy, the Gitanos have totally forgotten and lost their native language; yet still wishing to converse with each other in a language unknown to the Spaniards and Italians, they have invented some words, and have transformed many others by changing the signification which properly belongs to them in Spanish and Italian.' In proof of which assertion he then exhibits a small number of words of the 'Red Italian,' or allegorical tongue of the thieves of Italy.

It is much to be lamented that a man like Hervas, so learned, of such knowledge, and upon the whole well-earned celebrity, should have helped to propagate three such flagrant errors as are contained in the passages above quoted: 1st. That the Gypsy language, within a very short period after the arrival of those who spoke it in the western kingdoms of Europe, became corrupted, and perished by the admission of outlaws into the Gypsy fraternity. 2ndly. That the Gypsies, in order to supply the loss of their native tongue, invented some words, and modified others, from the Spanish and Italian. 3rdly. That the Gypsies of the present day in Spain and Italy speak the allegorical robber dialect. Concerning the first assertion, namely, that the Gypsies of the west lost their language shortly after their arrival, by mixing with the outlaws of those parts, we believe that its erroneousness will be sufficiently established by the publication of the present volume, which contains a dictionary of the Spanish Gitano, which we have proved to be the same language in most points as that spoken by the eastern tribes. There can be no doubt that the Gypsies have at various times formed alliances with the robbers of particular countries, but that they ever received them in considerable numbers into their fraternity, as Hervas has stated, so as to become confounded with them, the evidence of our eyesight precludes the possibility of believing. If such were the fact, why do the Italian and Spanish Gypsies of the present day still present themselves as a distinct race, differing from the other inhabitants of the west of Europe in feature, colour, and constitution? Why are they, in whatever situation and under whatever circumstances, to be distinguished, like Jews, from the other children of the Creator? But it is scarcely necessary to ask such a question, or indeed to state that the Gypsies of Spain and Italy have kept themselves as much apart as, or at least have as little mingled their blood with the Spaniards and Italians as their brethren in Hungaria and Transylvania with the inhabitants of those countries, on which account they still strikingly resemble them in manners, customs, and appearance. The most extraordinary assertion of Hervas is perhaps his second, namely, that the Gypsies have invented particular words to supply the place of others which they had lost. The absurdity of this supposition nearly induces us to believe that Hervas, who has written so much and so laboriously on language, was totally ignorant of the philosophy of his subject. There can be no doubt, as we have before admitted, that in the robber jargon, whether spoken in Spain, Italy, or England, there are many words at whose etymology it is very difficult to arrive; yet such a fact is no excuse for the adoption of the opinion that these words are of pure invention. A knowledge of the Rommany proves satisfactorily that many have been borrowed from that language, whilst many others may be traced to foreign tongues, especially the Latin and Italian. Perhaps one of the strongest grounds for concluding that the origin of language was divine is the fact that no instance can be adduced of the invention, we will not say of a language, but even of a single word that is in use in society of any kind. Although new dialects are continually being formed, it is only by a system of modification, by which roots almost coeval with time itself are continually being reproduced under a fresh appearance, and under new circumstances. The third assertion of Hervas, as to the Gitanos speaking the allegorical language of which he exhibits specimens, is entitled to about equal credence as the two former. The truth is, that the entire store of erudition of the learned Jesuit, and he doubtless was learned to a remarkable degree, was derived from books, either printed or manuscript. He compared the Gypsy words in the publication of Grellmann with various vocabularies, which had long been in existence, of the robber jargons of Spain and Italy, which jargons by a strange fatuity had ever been considered as belonging to the Gypsies. Finding that the Gypsy words of Grellmann did not at all correspond with the thieves' slang, he concluded that the Gypsies of Spain and Italy had forgotten their own language, and to supply its place had invented the jargons aforesaid, but he never gave himself the trouble to try whether the Gypsies really understood the contents of his slang vocabularies; had he done so, he would have found that the slang was about as unintelligible to the Gypsies as he would have found the specimens of Grellmann unintelligible to the thieves had he quoted those specimens to them. The Gypsies of Spain, it will be sufficient to observe, speak the language of which a vocabulary is given in the present work, and those of Italy who are generally to be found existing in a half-savage state in the various ruined castles, relics of the feudal times, with which Italy abounds, a dialect very similar, and about as much corrupted. There are, however, to be continually found in Italy roving bands of Rommany, not natives of the country, who make excursions from Moldavia and Hungaria to France and Italy, for the purpose of plunder; and who, if they escape the hand of justice, return at the expiration of two or three years to their native regions, with the booty they have amassed by the practice of those thievish arts, perhaps at one period peculiar to their race, but at present, for the most part, known and practised by thieves in general. These bands, however, speak the pure Gypsy language, with all its grammatical peculiarities. It is evident, however, that amongst neither of these classes had Hervas pushed his researches, which had he done, it is probable that his investigations would have resulted in a work of a far different character from the confused, unsatisfactory, and incorrect details of which is formed his essay on the language of the Gypsies.

Having said thus much concerning the robber language in general, we shall now proceed to offer some specimens of it, in order that our readers may be better able to understand its principles. We shall commence with the Italian dialect, which there is reason for supposing to be the prototype of the rest. To show what it is, we avail ourselves of some of the words adduced by Hervas, as specimens of the language of the Gitanos of Italy. 'I place them,' he observes, 'with the signification which the greater number properly have in Italian.'

	Robber jargon of Italy.	Proper signification of the words.
Arm	{ Ale	Wings
	{ Barbacane	Barbican
Belly	Fagiana	Pheasant
Devil	Rabuino	Perhaps RABBIN, which, in Hebrew, is Master
Earth	Calcosa	Street, road
Eye	Balco	Balcony
Father	Grimo	Old, wrinkled
Fire	Presto	Quick
God	Anticrotto	Probably ANTICHRIST
Hair	Prusa[73]	
	{ Elmo	Helmet
Head	{ Borella[74]	
	{ Chiurla[75]	
Heart	Salsa	Sauce
Man	Osmo	From the Italian UOMO, which is man
Moon	Mocoloso di Sant' Alto	Wick of the firmament
Night	Brunamaterna	Mother-brown
Nose	Gambaro	Crab

Sun	Ruffo di Sant' Alto	Red one of the firmament
Tongue	{ Serpentina	Serpent-like
	{ Danosa	Hurtful
Water	{ Lenza	Fishing-net
	{ Vetta[76]	Top, bud

The Germania of Spain may be said to divide itself into two dialects, the ancient and modern. Of the former there exists a vocabulary, published first by Juan Hidalgo, in the year 1609, at Barcelona, and reprinted in Madrid, 1773. Before noticing this work, it will perhaps be advisable to endeavour to ascertain the true etymology of the word Germania, which signifies the slang vocabulary, or robber language of Spain. We have no intention to embarrass our readers by offering various conjectures respecting its origin; its sound, coupled with its signification, affording sufficient evidence that it is but a corruption of Rommany, which properly denotes the speech of the Roma or Gitanos. The thieves who from time to time associated with this wandering people, and acquired more or less of their language, doubtless adopted this term amongst others, and, after modifying it, applied it to the peculiar phraseology which, in the course of time, became prevalent amongst them. The dictionary of Hidalgo is appended to six ballads, or romances, by the same author, written in the Germanian dialect, in which he describes the robber life at Seville at the period in which he lived. All of these romances possess their peculiar merit, and will doubtless always be considered valuable, and be read as faithful pictures of scenes and habits which now no longer exist. In the prologue, the author states that his principal motive for publishing a work written in so strange a language was his observing the damage which resulted from an ignorance of the Germania, especially to the judges and ministers of justice, whose charge it is to cleanse the public from the pernicious gentry who use it. By far the greatest part of the vocabulary consists of Spanish words used allegorically, which are, however, intermingled with many others, most of which may be traced to the Latin and Italian, others to the Sanscrit or Gitano, Russian, Arabic, Turkish, Greek, and German languages.[77] The circumstances of words belonging to some of the languages last enumerated being found in the Gitano, which at first may strike the reader as singular, and almost incredible, will afford but slight surprise, when he takes into consideration the peculiar circumstances of Spain during the sixteenth and seventeenth centuries. Spain was at that period the most powerful monarchy in Europe; her foot reposed upon the Low Countries, whilst her gigantic arms embraced a considerable portion of Italy. Maintaining always a standing army in Flanders and in Italy, it followed as a natural consequence, that her Miquelets and soldiers became tolerably conversant with the languages of those countries; and, in course of time, returning to their native land, not a few, especially of the former class, a brave and intrepid, but always a lawless and dissolute species of soldiery, either fell in or returned to evil society, and introduced words which they had learnt abroad into the robber phraseology; whilst returned galley- slaves from Algiers, Tunis, and Tetuan, added to its motley variety of words from the relics of the broken Arabic and Turkish, which they had acquired during their captivity. The greater part of the Germania, however, remained strictly metaphorical, and we are aware of no better means of conveying an idea of the principle on which it is formed, than by quoting from the first romance of Hidalgo, where particular mention is made of this jargon:-

'A la cama llama Blanda
Donde Sornan en poblado
A la Fresada Vellosa,
Que mucho vello ha criado.
Dice a la sabana Alba
Porque es alba en sumo grado,
A la camisa Carona,
Al jubon llama apretado:
Dice al Sayo Tapador
Porque le lleva tapado.
Llama a los zapatos Duros,
Que las piedras van pisando.
A la capa llama nuve,
Dice al Sombrero Texado.
Respeto llama a la Espada,
Que por ella es respetado,' etc. etc.

HIDALGO, p. 22-3.

After these few remarks on the ancient Germania of Spain, we now proceed to the modern, which differs considerably from the former. The principal cause of this difference is to be attributed to the adoption by the Spanish outlaws, in latter years, of a considerable number of words belonging to, or modified from, the Rommany, or language of the Gitanos. The Gitanos of Spain, during the last half-century, having, in a great degree, abandoned the wandering habit of life which once constituted one of their most remarkable peculiarities, and residing, at present, more in the cities than in the fields, have come into closer contact with the great body of the Spanish nation than was in former days their practice. From their living thus in towns, their language has not only undergone much corruption, but has become, to a slight degree, known to the dregs of society, amongst whom they reside. The thieves' dialect of the present day exhibits, therefore, less of the allegorical language preserved in the pages of Hidalgo than of the Gypsy tongue. It must be remarked, however, that it is very scanty, and that the whole robber phraseology at present used in Spain barely amounts to two hundred words, which are utterly insufficient to express the very limited ideas of the outcasts who avail themselves of it.

Concerning the Germania of France, or 'Argot,' as it is called, it is unnecessary to make many observations, as what has been said of the language of Hidalgo and the Red Italian is almost in every respect applicable to it. As early as the middle of the sixteenth century a vocabulary of this jargon was published under the title of LANGUE DES ESCROCS, at Paris. Those who wish to study it as it at present exists can do no better than consult LES MEMOIRES DE VIDOCQ, where a multitude of words in Argot are to be found, and also several songs, the subjects of which are thievish adventures.

The first vocabulary of the 'Cant Language,' or English Germania, appeared in the year 1680, appended to the life of THE ENGLISH ROGUE, a work which, in many respects, resembles the HISTORY OF GUZMAN D'ALFARACHE, though it is written with considerably more genius than the Spanish novel, every chapter abounding with remarkable adventures of the robber whose life it pretends to narrate, and which are described with a kind of ferocious energy, which, if it do not charm the attention of the reader, at least enslaves it, holding it captive with a chain of iron. Amongst his other adventures, the hero falls in with a Gypsy encampment, is enrolled amongst the fraternity, and is allotted a 'mort,' or concubine; a barbarous festival ensues, at the conclusion of which an epithalamium is sung in the Gypsy language, as it is called in the work in question. Neither the epithalamium, however, nor the vocabulary, are written in the language of the English Gypsies, but in the 'Cant,' or allegorical robber dialect, which is sufficient proof that the writer, however well acquainted with thieves in general, their customs and manners of life, was in respect to the Gypsies profoundly ignorant. His vocabulary, however, has been always accepted as the speech of the English Gypsies, whereas it is at most entitled to be considered as the peculiar speech of the thieves and vagabonds of his time. The cant of the present day, which, though it differs in some respects from the vocabulary already mentioned, is radically the same, is used not only by the thieves in town and country, but by the jockeys of the racecourse and the pugilists of the 'ring.' As a specimen of the cant of England, we shall take the liberty of quoting the epithalamium to which we have above alluded:-

'Bing out, bien morts, and tour and tour
Bing out, bien morts and tour;
For all your duds are bing'd awast,
The bien cove hath the loure.[78]

'I met a dell, I viewed her well,
She was benship to my watch:
So she and I did stall and cloy
Whatever we could catch.

'This doxy dell can cut ben whids,
And wap well for a win,
And prig and cloy so benshiply,
All daisy-ville within.

'The hoyle was up, we had good luck,
In frost for and in snow;
Men they did seek, then we did creep
And plant the roughman's low.'

It is scarcely necessary to say anything more upon the Germania in general or in particular; we believe that we have achieved the task which we marked out for ourselves, and have conveyed to our readers a clear and distinct idea of what it is. We have shown that it has been erroneously confounded with the Rommany, or Gitano language, with which it has nevertheless some points of similarity. The two languages are, at the present day, used for the same purpose, namely, to enable habitual breakers of the law to carry on their consultations with more secrecy and privacy than by the ordinary means. Yet it must not be forgotten that the thieves' jargon was invented for that purpose, whilst the Rommany, originally the proper and only speech of a particular nation, has been preserved from falling into entire disuse and oblivion, because adapted to answer the same end. It was impossible to treat of the Rommany in a manner calculated to exhaust the subject, and to leave no ground for future cavilling, without devoting a considerable space to the consideration of the robber dialect, on which account we hope we shall be excused many of the dry details which we have introduced into the present essay. There is a link of connection between the history of the Roma, or wanderers from Hindustan, who first made their appearance in Europe at the commencement of the fifteenth century, and that of modern roguery. Many of the arts which the Gypsies proudly call their own, and which were perhaps at one period peculiar to them, have become divulged, and are now practised by the thievish gentry who infest the various European states, a result which, we may assert with confidence, was brought about by the alliance of the Gypsies being eagerly sought on their first arrival by the thieves, who, at one period, were less skilful than the former in the ways of deceit and plunder; which kind of association continued and held good until the thieves had acquired all they wished to learn, when they left the Gypsies in the fields and plains, so dear to them from their vagabond and nomad habits, and returned to the towns and cities. Yet from this temporary association were produced two results; European fraud became sharpened by coming into contact with Asiatic craft, whilst European tongues, by imperceptible degrees, became recruited with various words (some of them wonderfully expressive), many of which have long been stumbling-stocks to the philologist, who, whilst stigmatising them as words of mere vulgar invention, or of unknown origin, has been far from dreaming that by a little more research he might have traced them to the Sclavonic, Persian, or Romaic, or perhaps to the mysterious object of his veneration, the Sanscrit, the sacred tongue of the palm-covered regions of Ind; words originally introduced into Europe by objects too miserable to occupy for a moment his lettered attention - the despised denizens of the tents of Roma.

ON THE TERM 'BUSNO'

Those who have done me the honour to peruse this strange wandering book of mine, must frequently have noticed the word 'Busno,' a term bestowed by the Spanish Gypsy on his good friend the Spaniard. As the present will probably be the last occasion which I shall have to speak of the Gitanos or anything relating to them, it will perhaps be advisable to explain the meaning of this word. In the vocabulary appended to former editions I have translated Busno by such words as Gentile, savage, person who is not a Gypsy, and have stated that it is probably connected with a certain Sanscrit noun signifying an impure person. It is, however, derived immediately from a Hungarian term, exceedingly common amongst the lower orders of the Magyars, to their disgrace be it spoken. The Hungarian Gypsies themselves not unfrequently style the Hungarians Busnoes, in ridicule of their unceasing use of the word in question. The first Gypsies who entered Spain doubtless brought with them the term from Hungary, the language of which country they probably understood to a certain extent. That it was not ill applied by them in Spain no one will be disposed to deny when told that it exactly corresponds with the Shibboleth of the Spaniards, 'Carajo,' an oath equally common in Spain as its equivalent in Hungary. Busno, therefore, in Spanish means EL DEL CARAJO, or he who has that term continually in his mouth. The Hungarian words in Spanish Gypsy may amount to ten or twelve, a very inconsiderable number; but the Hungarian Gypsy tongue itself, as spoken at the present day, exhibits only a slight sprinkling of Hungarian words, whilst it contains many words borrowed from the Wallachian, some of which have found their way into Spain, and are in common use amongst the Gitanos.

SPECIMENS OF GYPSY DIALECTS

THE ENGLISH DIALECT OF THE ROMMANY

'TACHIPEN if I jaw 'doi, I can lel a bit of tan to hatch: N'etist I shan't puch kekomi wafu gorgies.'

The above sentence, dear reader, I heard from the mouth of Mr. Petulengro, the last time that he did me the honour to visit me at my poor house, which was the day after Mol-divvus[79], 1842: he stayed with me during the greater part of the morning, discoursing on the affairs of Egypt, the aspect of which, he assured me, was becoming daily worse and worse. 'There is no living for the poor people, brother,' said he, 'the chokengres (police) pursue us from place to place, and the gorgios are become either so poor or miserly, that they grudge our cattle a bite of grass by the wayside, and ourselves a yard of ground to light a fire upon. Unless times alter, brother, and of that I see no probability, unless you are made either poknees or mecralliskoe geiro (justice of the peace or prime minister), I am afraid the poor persons will have to give up wandering altogether, and then what will become of them?'

'However, brother,' he continued, in a more cheerful tone, 'I am no hindity mush,[80] as you well know. I suppose you have not forgot how, fifteen years ago, when you made horseshoes in the little dingle by the side of the great north road, I lent you fifty cottors[81] to purchase the wonderful trotting cob of the innkeeper with the green Newmarket coat, which three days after you sold for two hundred.

'Well, brother, if you had wanted the two hundred instead of the fifty, I could have lent them to you, and would have done so, for I knew you would not be long pazorrhus to me. I am no hindity mush, brother, no Irishman; I laid out the other day twenty pounds in buying ruponoe peamengries;[82] and in the Chonggav,[83] have a house of my own with a yard behind it.

'AND, FORSOOTH, IF I GO THITHER, I CAN CHOOSE A PLACE TO LIGHT AFIRE UPON, AND SHALL HAVE NO NECESSITY TO ASK LEAVE OF THESE HERE GENTILES.'

Well, dear reader, this last is the translation of the Gypsy sentence which heads the chapter, and which is a very characteristic specimen of the general way of speaking of the English Gypsies.

The language, as they generally speak it, is a broken jargon, in which few of the grammatical peculiarities of the Rommany are to be distinguished. In fact, what has been said of the Spanish Gypsy dialect holds good with respect to the English as commonly spoken: yet the English dialect has in reality suffered much less than the Spanish, and still retains its original syntax to a certain extent, its peculiar manner of conjugating verbs, and declining nouns and pronouns.

ENGLISH DIALECT

Moro Dad, savo djives oteh drey o charos, te caumen Gorgio ta Romany Chal tiro nav, te awel tiro tem, te kairen tiro lav aukko prey puv, sar kairdios oteh drey o charos. Dey men to-divvus moro divvuskoe moro, ta for-dey men pazorrhus tukey sar men for-denna len pazorrhus amande; ma muk te petrenna drey caik temptacionos; ley men abri sor doschder. Tiro se o tem, Mi-duvel, tiro o zoozlu vast, tiro sor koskopen drey sor cheros. Avali. Ta-chipen.

SPANISH DIALECT

Batu monro sos socabas ote enre ye char, que camele Gacho ta Romani Cha tiro nao, qu'abillele tiro chim, querese tiro lao acoi opre ye puve sarta se querela ote enre ye char. Dinanos sejonia monro manro de cata chibes, ta estormenanos monrias bisauras sasta mu estormenamos a monrias bisabadores; na nos meques petrar enre cayque pajandia, lillanos abri de saro chungalipen. Persos tiro sinela o chim, Undevel, tiro ye silna bast, tiro saro lachipen enre saro chiros. Unga. Chachipe.

ENGLISH TRANSLATION OF THE ABOVE

OUR Father who dwellest there in heaven, may Gentile and Gypsy love thy name, thy kingdom come, may they do thy word here on earth as it is done there in heaven. Give us to-day our daily bread,[84] and forgive us indebted to thee as we forgive them indebted to us,[85] suffer not that we fall into NO temptation, take us out from all evil.[86] Thine[87] is the kingdom my God, thine the strong hand, thine all goodness in all time. Aye. Truth.

HUNGARIAN DIALECT

The following short sentences in Hungarian Gypsy, in addition to the prayer to the Virgin given in the Introduction, will perhaps not prove unacceptable to the reader. In no part of the world is the Gypsy tongue at the present day spoken with more purity than in Hungary,[88] where it is used by the Gypsies not only when they wish to be unintelligible to the Hungarians, but in their common conversation amongst themselves.

From these sentences the reader, by the help of the translations which accompany them, may form a tolerable idea not only of what the Gypsy tongue is, but of the manner in which the Hungarian Gypsies think and express themselves. They are specimens of genuine Gypsy talk - sentences which I have myself heard proceed from the mouths of the Czigany; they are not Busno thoughts done into gentle Rommany. Some of them are given here as they were written down by me at the time, others as I have preserved them in my memory up to the present moment. It is not improbable that at some future time I may return to the subject of the Hungarian Gypsies.

Vare tava soskei me puchelas cai soskei avillara catari.

Mango le gulo Devlas vas o erai, hodj o erai te pirel misto, te n'avel pascotia l'eras, ta na avel o erai nasvalo.

Cana cames aves pale.

Ki'som dhes keral avel o rai catari?[89]

Kit somu berschengro hal tu?[90]

Cade abri mai lachi e mol sar ando foro.

Sin o mas balichano, ta i gorkhe garasheskri;[91] sin o manro parno, cai te felo do garashangro.

Yeck quartalli mol ando lende.

Ande mol ote mestchibo.

Khava piava - dui shel, tri shel predinava.

Damen Devla saschipo ando mure cocala.

Te rosarow labio tarraco le Mujeskey miro pralesco, ta vela mi anao tukey le Mujeskey miro pralesky.

Llundun baro foro, bishwar mai baro sar Cosvaro.

Nani yag, mullas.

Nasiliom cai purdiom but; besh te pansch bersch mi homas slugadhis pa Baron Splini regimentos.

Saro chiro cado Del; cavo o puro dinas o Del.

Me camov te jav ando Buka-resti - cado Bukaresti lachico tem dur drom jin keri.

Mi hom nasvallo.

Soskei nai jas ke baro ful-cheri?

Wei mangue ke nani man love nastis jav.

Belgra sho mille pu cado Cosvarri; hin oter miro chabo.

Te vas Del l'erangue ke meclan man abri ando a pan-dibo.

Opre rukh sarkhi ye chiriclo, ca kerel anre e chiricli.

Ca hin tiro ker?

Ando calo berkho, oter bin miro ker, av prala mensar; jas mengue keri.

Ando bersch dui chiro, ye ven, ta nilei.

O felhegos del o breschino, te purdel o barbal.

Hir mi Devlis camo but cavo erai - lacho manus o, Anglus, tama rakarel Ungarica; avel catari ando urdon le trin grastensas - beshel cate abri po buklo tan; le poivasis ando bas irinel ando lel. Bo zedun stadji ta bari barba.

Much I ponder why you ask me (questions), and why you should come hither.

I pray the sweet Goddess for the gentleman, that the gentleman may journey well, that misfortune come not to the gentleman, and that the gentleman fall not sick.

When you please come back.

How many days did the gentleman take to come hither?

How many years old are you?

Here out better (is) the wine than in the city.

The meat is of pig, and the gherkins cost a grosh - the bread is white, and the lard costs two groshen.

One quart of wine amongst us.

In wine there (is) happiness.

I will eat, I will drink - two hundred, three hundred I will place before.

Give us Goddess health in our bones.

I will seek a waistcoat, which I have, for Moses my brother, and I will change names with Moses my brother.[92]

London (is) a big city, twenty times more big than Colosvar.

There is no fire, it is dead.

I have suffered and toiled much: twenty and five years I was serving in Baron Splini's regiment.

Every time (cometh) from God; that old (age) God gave.

I wish to go unto Bukarest - from Bukarest, the good country, (it is) a far way unto (my) house.

I am sick.

Why do you not go to the great physician

Because I have no money I can't go

Belgrade (is) six miles of land from Colosvar; there is my son.

May God help the gentlemen that they let me out (from) in the prison.

On the tree (is) the nest of the bird, where makes eggs the female bird.

Where is your house?

In the black mountain, there is my house; come brother with me;let us go to my house.

In the year (are) two seasons, the winter and summer.

The cloud gives the rain, and puffs (forth) the wind.

By my God I love much that gentleman - a good man he, an

Englishman, but he speaks Hungarian; he came[93] hither in a waggon with three horses, he sits here out in the wilderness;[94] with a pencil in his hand he writes in a book. He has a green hat and a big beard.

VOCABULARY OF THEIR LANGUAGE

[This section of the book could not be transcribed as it contained many non-european languages]

APPENDIX -

MISCELLANIES IN THE GITANO LANGUAGE

ADVERTISEMENT

IT is with the view of preserving as many as possible of the monuments of the Spanish Gypsy tongue that the author inserts the following pieces; they are for the most part, whether original or translated, the productions of the 'Aficion' of Seville, of whom something has been said in the Preface to the Spurious Gypsy Poetry of Andalusia; not the least remarkable, however, of these pieces is a genuine Gypsy composition, the translation of the Apostles' Creed by the Gypsies of Cordova, made under the circumstances detailed in the second part of the first volume. To all have been affixed translations, more or less literal, to assist those who may wish to form some acquaintance with the Gitano language.

COTORRES ON CHIPE CALLI / MISCELLANIES

BATO Nonrro sos socabas on o tarpe, manjirificado quejesa tute acnao; abillanos or tute sichen, y querese tute orependola andial on la chen sata on o tarpe; or manrro nonrro de cata chibel dinanoslo sejonia, y estormenanos nonrrias bisauras andial sata gaberes estormenamos a nonrros bisaraores; y nasti nes muques petrar on la bajanbo, bus listrabanos de chorre. - Anarania.

FATHER Our, who dwellest in the heaven, sanctified become thy name; come-to-us the thy kingdom, and be-done thy will so in the earth as in the heaven; the bread our of every day give-us-it to-day, and pardon-us our debts so as we-others pardon (to) our debtors; and not let us fall in the temptation, but deliver-us from wickedness. - Amen.

Panchabo on Ostebe Bato saro-asisilable, Perbaraor de o tarpe y la chen, y on Gresone desquero Beyio Chabal nonrrio Erano, sos guillo sar-trujatapucherido per troecane y sardana de or Chanispero Manjaro, y purelo de Manjari ostelinda debla; Bricholo ostele de or asislar de Brono Alienicato; guillo trejuficao, mule y cabanao; y sundilo a los casinobes,[95] y a or brodelo chibel repurelo de enrre los mules, y encalomo a los otarpes, y soscabela bestique a la tabastorre de Ostebe Bato saro-asisilable, ende aoter a de abillar a sarplar a los Apucheris y mules. Panchabo on or Chanispero Manjaro, la Manjari Cangari Pebuldorica y Rebuldorica, la Erunon de los Manjaros, or Estormen de los crejetes, la repurelo de la mansenquere y la chibiben verable. - Anarania, Tebleque.

I believe in God, Father all-powerful, creator of the heaven and the earth, and in Christ his only Son our Lord, who went conceived by deed and favour of the Spirit Holy, and born of blessed goddess divine; suffered under (of) the might of Bronos Alienicatos;[96] went crucified, dead and buried; and descended to the conflagrations, and on the third day revived[97] from among the dead, and ascended to the heavens, and dwells seated at the right- hand of God, Father all-powerful, from there he-has to come to impeach (to) the living and dead. I believe in the Spirit Holy, the Holy Church Catholic and Apostolic, the communion of the saints, the remission of the sins, the re-birth of the flesh, and the life everlasting. - Amen, Jesus.

OCANAJIMIA A LA DEBLA / PRAYER TO THE VIRGIN

O Debla quirindia, Day de saros los Bordeles on coin panchabo: per los duquipenes sos naquelastes a or pindre de la trejul de tute Chaborro majarolisimo te manguelo, Debla, me alcorabises de tute chaborro or estormen de sares las dojis y crejetes sos menda udicare aquerao on andoba surdete. - Anarania, Tebleque.

Ostebe te berarbe Ostelinda! perdoripe sirles de sardana; or Erano sin sartute; bresban tute sirles enrre sares las rumiles, y bresban sin or frujero de tute po. - Tebleque.

Manjari Ostelinda, day de Ostebe, brichardila per gaberes crejetaores aocana y on la ocana de nonrra beriben! - Anarania, Tebleque.

Chimuclani or Bato, or Chabal, or Chanispero manjaro; sata sia on or presimelo, aocana, y gajeres: on los sicles de los sicles. - Anarania.

O most holy Virgin, Mother of all the Christians in whom I believe; for the agony which thou didst endure at the foot of the cross of thy most blessed Son, I entreat thee, Virgin, that thou wilt obtain for me, from thy Son, the remission of all the crimes and sins which I may have committed in this world. - Amen, Jesus.

God save thee, Maria! full art thou of grace; the Lord is with thee; blessed art thou amongst all women, and blessed is the fruit of thy womb. - Jesus.

Holy Maria, mother of God, pray for us sinners, now and in the hour of our death! - Amen, Jesus.

Glory (to) the Father, the Son, (and) the Holy Ghost; as was in the beginning, now, and for ever: in the ages of the ages. - Amen.

OR CREDO / THE CREED SARTA LO CHIBELARON LOS CALES DE CORDOVATI / TRANSLATED BY THE GYSPIES OF CORDOVA

Pachabelo en Un-debel batu tosaro-baro, que ha querdi el char y la chique; y en Un-debel chinoro su unico chaboro erano de amangue, que chalo en el trupo de la Majari por el Duquende Majoro, y abio del veo de la Majari; guillo curado debajo de la sila de Pontio Pilato el chinobaro; guillo mulo y garabado; se chale a las jacharis; al trin chibe se ha sicobado de los mules al char; sinela bejado a las baste de Un-debel barrea; y de ote abiara a juzgar a los mules y a los que no lo sinelan; pachabelo en el Majaro; la Cangri Majari barea; el jalar de los Majaries; lo meco de los grecos; la resureccion de la maas, y la ochi que no marela.

I believe in God the Father all-great, who has made the heaven and the earth; and in God the young, his only Son, the Lord of us, who went into the body of the blessed (maid) by (means of) the Holy Ghost, and came out of the womb of the blessed; he was tormented beneath the power of Pontius Pilate, the great Alguazil; was dead and buried; he went (down) to the fires; on the third day he raised himself from the dead unto the heaven; he is seated at the major hand of God; and from thence he shall come to judge the dead and those who are not (dead). I believe in the blessed one; in the church holy and great; the banquet of the saints; the remission of sins; the resurrection of the flesh, and the life which does not die.

REJELENDRES / PROVERBS

Or soscabela juco y terable garipe no le sin perfine anelar relichi. Bus yes manupe cha machagarno le pendan chuchipon los brochabos. Sacais sos ne dicobelan calochin ne bridaquelan. Coin terelare trasardos e dinastes nasti le buchare berrandanas a desquero contique. On sares las cachimanes de Sersen abillen reches. Bus mola yes chirriclo on la ba sos gres balogando. A Ostebe brichardilando y sar or mochique dinelando. Bus mola quesar jero de gabuno sos manpori de bombardo. Dicar y panchabar, sata penda Manjaro Lillar. Or esorjie de or narsichisle sin chismar lachinguel. Las queles mistos grobelas: per macara chibel la piri y de rachi la operisa. Aunsos me dicas vriardao de jorpoy ne sirlo braco. Chachipe con jujana - Calzones de buchi y medias de lana. Chuquel sos pirela cocal terela. Len sos sonsi bela pani o reblandani terela.

He who is lean and has scabs needs not carry a net.[98] When a man goes drunk the boys say to him 'suet.'[99] Eyes which see not break no heart. He who has a roof of glass let him not fling stones at his neighbour. Into all the taverns of Spain may reeds come. A bird in the hand is worth more than a hundred flying. To God (be) praying and with the flail plying. It is worth more to be the head of a mouse than the tail of a lion. To see and to believe, as Saint Thomas says. The extreme[100] of a dwarf is to spit largely. Houses well managed:- at mid-day the stew-pan,[101] and at night salad. Although thou seest me dressed in wool I am no sheep. Truth with falsehood-Breeches of silk and stockings of Wool.[102] The dog who walks finds a bone. The river which makes a noise[103] has either water or stones.

ODORES YE TILICHE / THE LOVER'S JEALOUSY

Dica Calli sos linastes terelas, plasarandote misto men calochin desquinao de trinchas punis y canrrias, sata anjella terelaba dicando on los chorres naquelos sos me tesumiaste, y andial reutila a men Jeli, dinela gao a sos menda orobibele; men puni sin trincha per la quimbila nevel de yes manu barbalo; sos saro se muca per or jandorro. Lo sos bus prejeno Calli de los Bengorros sin sos nu muqueis per yes manu barbalo... On tute orchiri nu chismo, tramisto on coin te araquera, sos menda terela men nostus pa avel sos me camela bus sos tute.

Reflect, O Callee![104] what motives hast thou (now that my heart is doting on thee, having rested awhile from so many cares and griefs which formerly it endured, beholding the evil passages which thou preparedst for me;) to recede thus from my love, giving occasion to me to weep. My agony is great on account of thy recent acquaintance with a rich man; for every thing is abandoned for money's sake. What I most feel, O Callee, of the devils is, that thou abandonest me for a rich man... I spit upon thy beauty, and also upon him who converses with thee, for I keep my money for another who loves me more than thou.

OR PERSIBARARSE SIN CHORO / THE EVILS OF CONCUBINAGE

Gajeres sin corbo rifian soscabar yes manu persibarao, per sos saro se linbidian odoros y beslli, y per esegriton apuchelan on sardana de saros los Benjes, techescando grejos y olajais - de sustiri sos lo resaronomo niquilla murmo; y andial lo fendi sos terelamos de querar sin techescarle yes sulibari a or Jeli, y ne panchabar on caute manusardi, persos trutan a yesque lili.

It is always a strange danger for a man to live in concubinage, because all turns to jealousy and quarrelling, and at last they live in the favour of all the devils, voiding oaths and curses: so that what is cheap turns out dear. So the best we can do, is to cast a bridle on love, and trust to no woman, for they[105] make a man mad.

LOS CHORES / THE ROBBERS

On grejelo chiro begoreo yesque berbanilla de chores a la burda de yes mostipelo a oleba rachi - Andial sos la prejenaron los cambrais presimelaron a cobadrar; sar andoba linaste changano or lanbro, se sustino de la charipe de lapa, utilo la pusca, y niquillo platanando per or platesquero de or mostipelo a la burda sos socabelaba pandi, y per or jobi de la clichi chibelo or jundro de la pusca, le dino pesquibo a or langute, y le sumuquelo yes bruchasno on la tesquera a or Jojerian de los ostilaores y lo techesco de or grate a ostele. Andial sos los debus quimbilos dicobelaron a desquero Jojerian on chen sar las canrriales de la Beriben, lo chibelaron espusifias a los grastes, y niquillaron chapescando, trutando la romuy apala, per bausale de las machas o almedalles de liripio.

On a certain time arrived a band of thieves at the gate of a farm- house at midnight. So soon as the dogs heard them they began to bark, which causing[106] the labourer to awake, he raised himself from his bed with a start, took his musket, and went running to the court-yard of the farm-house to the gate, which was shut, placed the barrel of his musket to the keyhole, gave his finger its desire,[107] and sent a bullet into the forehead of the captain of the robbers, casting him down from his horse. Soon as the other fellows saw their captain on the ground in the agonies of death, they clapped spurs to their horses, and galloped off fleeing, turning their faces back on account of the flies[108] or almonds of lead.

COTOR YE GABICOTE MAJARO / SPECIMEN OF THE GOSPEL OR SOS SARO LO HA CHIBADO EN CHIPE CALLI OR RANDADOR DE OCONOS PAPIRIS AUNSOS NARDIAN LO HA DINADO AL SURDETE. FROM THE AUTHOR'S UNPUBLISHED TRANSLATION OF THE NEW TESTAMENT

Y soscabando dicando dico los Barbalos sos techescaban desqueros mansis on or Gazofilacio; y dico tramisto yesque pispiricha chorrorita, sos techescaba duis chinorris saraballis, y penelo: en chachipe os penelo, sos caba chorrorri pispiricha a techescao bus sos sares los aveles: persos saros ondobas han techescao per los mansis de Ostebe, de lo sos les costuna; bus caba e desquero chorrorri a techescao saro or susalo sos terelaba. Y pendo a cormunis, sos pendaban del cangaripe, soscabelaba uriardao de orchiris berrandanas, y de denes: Cabas buchis sos dicais, abillaran chibeles, bus ne muquelara berrandana costune berrandana, sos ne quesesa demarabea. Y le prucharon y pendaron: Docurdo, bus quesa ondoba? Y sos simachi abicara bus ondoba presimare? Ondole penclo: Dicad, sos nasti queseis jonjabaos; persos butes abillaran on men acnao, pendando: man sirlo, y or chiro soscabela pajes: Garabaos de guillelar apala, de ondolayos: y bus junureis barganas y sustines, ne os espajueis; persos sin perfine sos ondoba chundee brotobo, bus nasti quesa escotria or egresiton. Oclinde les pendaba: se sustinara sueste sartra sueste, y sichen sartra sichen, y abicara bareles dajiros de chenes per los gaos, y retreques y bocatas, y abicara buchengeres espajuis, y bareles simachis de otarpe: bus anjella de saro ondoba os sinastraran y preguillaran, enregandoos a la Socreteria, y los ostardos, y os legeraran a los Oclayes, y a los Baquedunis, per men acnao: y ondoba os chundeara on chachipe. Terelad pus seraji on bros garlochines de ne orobrar anjella sata abicais de brudilar, persos man os dinare rotuni y chanar, la sos ne asislaran resistir ne sartra pendar satos bros enormes. Y quesareis enregaos de bros batos, y opranos, y sastris, y monrrores, y queraran merar a cormuni de averes; y os cangelaran saros per men acnao; bus ne carjibara ies bal de bros jeros. Sar bras opachirima avelareis bras orchis: pus bus dicareis a Jerusalen relli, oclinde chanad sos, desquero petra soscabela pajes; oclinde los soscabelan on la Chutea, chapesguen a los tober-jelis; y los que on macara de ondolaya, niquillense; y lo sos on los oltariques, nasti enrren on ondolaya; persos ondoba sen chibeles de Abillaza, pa sos chundeen sares las buchis soscabelan libanas; bus isna de las araris, y de las sos dinan de oropielar on asirios chibeles; persos abicara bare quichartura costune la chen, e guillara pa andoba Gao; y petraran a surabi de janrro; y quesan legeraos sinastros a sares las chenes, y Jerusalen quesa omana de los suestiles, sasta sos quejesen los chiros de las sichenes; y abicara simaches on or orcan, y on la chimutia, y on las uchurganis; y on la chen chalabeo on la suete per or dan sos bausalara la loria y des-queros gulas; muquelando los romares bifaos per dajiralo de las buchis sos costune abillaran a saro or surdete; persos los solares de los otarpes quesan sar- chalabeaos; y oclinde dicaran a or Chaboro e Manu abillar costune yesque minrricla sar baro asislar y Chimusolano: bus presimelaren a chundear caba buchis, dicad, y sustinad bros jeros, persos pajes soscabela bras redencion.

And whilst looking he saw the rich who cast their treasures into the treasury; and he saw also a poor widow, who cast two small coins, and he said: In truth I tell you, that this poor widow has cast more than all the others; because all those have cast, as offerings to God, from that which to them abounded; but she from her poverty has cast all the substance which she had. And he said to some, who said of the temple, that it was adorned with fair stones, and with gifts: These things which ye see, days shall come, when stone shall not remain upon stone, which shall not be demolished. And they asked him and said: Master, when shall this be? and what sign shall there be when this begins? He said: See, that ye be not deceived, because many shall come in my name, saying: I am (he), and the time is near: beware ye of going after them: and when ye shall hear (of) wars and revolts do not fear, because it is needful that this happen first, for the end shall not be immediately. Then he said to them: Nation shall rise against nation, and country against country, and there shall be great tremblings of earth among the towns, and pestilences and famines; and there shall be frightful things, and great signs in the heaven: but before all this they shall make ye captive, and shall persecute, delivering ye over to the synagogue, and prisons; and they shall carry ye to the kings, and the governors, on account of my name: and this shall happen to you for truth. Keep then firm in your hearts, not to think before how ye have to answer, for I will give you mouth and wisdom, which all your enemies shall not be able to resist, or contradict. And ye shall be delivered over by your fathers, and brothers, and relations, and friends, and they shall put to death some of you; and all shall hate you for my name; but not one hair of your heads shall perish. With your patience ye shall possess your souls: but when ye shall see Jerusalem surrounded, then know that its fall is near; then those who are in Judea, let them escape to the mountains; and those who are in the midst of her, let them go out; and those who are in the fields, let them not enter into her; because those are days of vengeance, that all the things which are written may happen; but alas to the pregnant and those who give suck in those days, for there shall be great distress upon the earth, and it shall move onward against this people; and they shall fall by the edge of the sword; and they shall be carried captive to all the countries, and Jerusalem shall be trodden by the nations, until are accomplished the times of the nations; and there shall be signs in the sun, and in the moon, and in the stars; and in the earth trouble of nations from the fear which the sea and its billows shall cause; leaving men frozen with terror of the things which shall come upon all the world; because the powers of the heavens shall be shaken; and then they shall see the Son of Man coming upon a cloud with great power and glory: when these things begin to happen, look ye, and raise your heads, for your redemption is near.

THE ENGLISH DIALECT OF THE ROMMANY

'TACHIPEN if I jaw 'doi, I can lel a bit of tan to hatch: N'etist I shan't puch kekomi wafu gorgies.'

The above sentence, dear reader, I heard from the mouth of Mr. Petulengro, the last time that he did me the honour to visit me at my poor house, which was the day after Moldivvus,[109] 1842: he stayed with me during the greatest part of the morning, discoursing on the affairs of Egypt, the aspect of which, he assured me, was becoming daily worse and worse. 'There is no living for the poor people, brother,' said he, 'the chok-engres (police) pursue us from place to place, and the gorgios are become either so poor or miserly, that they grudge our cattle a bite of grass by the way side, and ourselves a yard of ground to light a fire upon. Unless times alter, brother, and of that I see no probability, unless you are made either poknees or mecralliskoe geiro (justice of the peace or prime minister), I am afraid the poor persons will have to give up wandering altogether, and then what will become of them?

'However, brother,' he continued, in a more cheerful tone, 'I am no hindity mush,[110] as you well know. I suppose you have not forgot how, fifteen years ago, when you made horse-shoes in the little dingle by the side of the great north road, I lent you fifty cottors[111] to purchase the wonderful trotting cob of the innkeeper with the green Newmarket coat, which three days after you sold for two hundred.

'Well, brother, if you had wanted the two hundred, instead of the fifty, I could have lent them to you, and would have done so, for I knew you would not be long pazorrhus to me. I am no hindity mush, brother, no Irishman; I laid out the other day twenty pounds in buying rupenoe peam-engries;[112] and in the Chong-gav,[113] have a house of my own with a yard behind it.

'AND, FORSOOTH, IF I GO THITHER, I CAN CHOOSE A PLACE TO LIGHT A FIRE UPON, AND SHALL HAVE NO NECESSITY TO ASK LEAVE OF THESE HERE GENTILES.'

Well, dear reader, this last is the translation of the Gypsy sentence which heads the chapter, and which is a very characteristic specimen of the general way of speaking of the English Gypsies.

The language, as they generally speak it, is a broken jargon, in which few of the grammatical peculiarities of the Rommany are to be distinguished. In fact, what has been said of the Spanish Gypsy dialect holds good with respect to the English as commonly spoken: yet the English dialect has in reality suffered much less than the Spanish, and still retains its original syntax to a certain extent, its peculiar manner of conjugating verbs, and declining nouns and pronouns. I must, however, qualify this last assertion, by observing that in the genuine Rommany there are no prepositions, but, on the contrary, post-positions; now, in the case of the English dialect, these post-positions have been lost, and their want, with the exception of the genitive, has been supplied with English prepositions, as may be seen by a short example:-

Hungarian Gypsy.(114)	English Gypsy.	English.
Job	Yow	He
Leste	Leste	Of him
Las	Las	To him
Les	Los	Him
Lester	From leste	From him
Leha	With leste	With him

PLURAL.

Hungarian Gypsy	English Gypsy.	English
Jole	Yaun	They
Lente	Lente	Of them
Len	Len	To them
Len	Len	Them
Lender	From Lende	From them

The following comparison of words selected at random from the English and Spanish dialects of the Rommany will, perhaps, not be uninteresting to the philologist or even to the general reader. Could a doubt be at present entertained that the

Gypsy language is virtually the same in all parts of the world where it is spoken, I conceive that such a vocabulary would at once remove it.

	English Gypsy.	Spanish Gypsy.
Ant	Cria	Crianse
Bread	Morro	Manro
City	Forus	Foros
Dead	Mulo	Mulo
Enough	Dosta	Dosta
Fish	Matcho	Macho
Great	Boro	Baro
House	Ker	Quer
Iron	Saster	Sas
King	Krallis	Cralis
Love(I)	Camova	Camelo
Moon	Tchun	Chimutra
Night	Rarde	Rati
Onion	Purrum	Porumia
Poison	Drav	Drao
Quick	Sig	Sigo
Rain	Brishindo	Brejindal
Sunday	Koorokey	Curque
Teeth	Danor	Dani
Village	Gav	Gao
White	Pauno	Parno
Yes	Avali	Ungale

As specimens of how the English dialect maybe written, the following translations of the Lord's Prayer and Belief will perhaps suffice.

THE LORD'S PRAYER

Miry dad, odoi oprey adrey tiro tatcho tan; Medeveleskoe si tiro nav; awel tiro tem, be kairdo tiro lav acoi drey pov sa odoi adrey kosgo tan: dey mande ke-divvus miry diry morro, ta fordel man sor so me pazzorrus tute, sa me fordel sor so wavior mushor pazzorrus amande; ma riggur man adrey kek dosch, ley man abri sor wafodu;

tiro se o tem, tiro or zoozli-wast, tiro or corauni, kanaw ta ever-komi. Avali. Tatchipen.

LITERAL TRANSLATION

My Father, yonder up within thy good place; god-like be thy name; come thy kingdom, be done thy word here in earth as yonder in good place. Give to me to-day my dear bread, and forgive me all that I am indebted to thee, as I forgive all that other men are indebted to me; not lead me into any ill; take me out (of) all evil; thine is the kingdom, thine the strong hand, thine the crown, now and evermore. Yea. Truth.

THE BELIEF

Me apasavenna drey mi-dovvel, Dad soro-ruslo, savo kedas charvus ta pov: apasavenna drey olescro yeck chavo moro arauno Christos, lias medeveleskoe Baval-engro, beano of wendror of medeveleskoe gairy Mary: kurredo tuley me-cralliskoe geiro Pontius Pilaten wast; nasko pre rukh, moreno, chivios adrey o hev; jas yov tuley o kalo dron ke wafudo tan, bengeskoe stariben; jongorasa o trito divvus, atchasa opre to tatcho tan, Mi-dovvels kair; bestela kanaw odoi pre Mi-dovvels tacho wast Dad soro-boro; ava sig to lel shoonaben opre mestepen and merripen. Apasa-venna en develeskoe Baval-engro; Boro develeskoe congri, develeskoe pios of sore tacho foky ketteney, soror wafudu-penes fordias, soror mulor jongorella, kek merella apopli. Avali, palor.

LITERAL TRANSLATION

I believe in my God, Father all powerful, who made heaven and earth; I believe in his one Son our Lord Christ, conceived by Holy Ghost,[117] born of bowels of Holy Virgin Mary, beaten under the royal governor Pontius Pilate's hand; hung on a tree, slain, put into the grave; went he down the black road to bad place, the devil's prison; he awaked the third day, ascended up to good place, my God's house; sits now there on my God's right hand Father-all-powerful; shall come soon to hold judgment over life and death. I believe in Holy Ghost; Great Holy Church, Holy festival of all good people together, all sins forgiveness, that all dead arise, no more die again. Yea, brothers.

SPECIMEN OF A SONG IN THE VULGAR OR BROKEN ROMMANY

As I was a jawing to the gav yeck divvus, I met on the dron miro Rommany chi: I puch'd yoi whether she com sar mande; And she penn'd: tu si wafo Rommany,

And I penn'd, I shall ker tu miro tacho Rommany, Fornigh tute but dui chave: Methinks I'll cam tute for miro merripen, If tu but pen, thou wilt commo sar mande.

TRANSLATION

One day as I was going to the village, I met on the road my Rommany lass: I ask'd her whether she would come with me, And she said thou hast another wife.

I said, I will make thee my lawful wife, Because thou hast but two children; Methinks I will love thee until my death, If thou but say thou wilt come with me.

Many other specimens of the English Gypsy muse might be here adduced; it is probable, however, that the above will have fully satisfied the curiosity of the reader. It has been inserted here for the purpose of showing that the Gypsies have songs in their own language, a fact which has been denied. In its metre it resembles the ancient Sclavonian ballads, with which it has another feature in common - the absence of rhyme.

FOOTNOTES:

1. QUARTERLY REVIEW, Dec. 1842
2. EDINBURGH REVIEW, Feb. 1843.
3. EXAMINER, Dec. 17, 1842.
4. SPECTATOR, Dec. 7, 1842.
5. Thou speakest well, brother!
6. This is quite a mistake: I know very little of what has been written concerning these people: even the work of Grellmann had not come beneath my perusal at the time of the publication of the first edition OF THE ZINCALI, which I certainly do not regret: for though I believe the learned German to be quite right in his theory with respect to the origin of the Gypsies, his acquaintance with their character, habits, and peculiarities, seems to have been extremely limited.
7. Good day.
8. Glandered horse.
9. Two brothers.
10. The edition here referred to has long since been out of print.
11. It may not be amiss to give the etymology of the word engro, which so frequently occurs in compound words in the English Gypsy tongue:- the EN properly belongs to the preceding noun, being one of the forms of the genitive case; for example, Elik-EN boro congry, the great Church or Cathedral of Ely; the GRO or GEIRO (Spanish GUERO), is the Sanscrit KAR, a particle much used in that language in the formation of compounds; I need scarcely add that MONGER in the English words Costermonger, Ironmonger, etc., is derived from the same root.
12. For the knowledge of this fact I am indebted to the well-known and enterprising traveller, Mr. Vigne, whose highly interesting work on Cashmire and the Panjab requires no recommendation from me.

13. Gorgio (Spanish GACHO), a man who is not a Gypsy: the Spanish Gypsies term the Gentiles Busne, the meaning of which word will be explained farther on.
14. An Eastern image tantamount to the taking away of life.
15. Gentes non multum morigeratae, sed quasi bruta animalia et furentes. See vol. xxii. of the Supplement to the works of Muratori, p. 890.
16. As quoted by Hervas: CATALOGO DE LAS LENGUAS, vol. iii. p. 306.
17. We have found this beautiful metaphor both in Gypsy and Spanish; it runs thus in the former language:-'LAS MUCHIS. (The Sparks.) 'Bus de gres chabalas orchiris man dique a yes chiro purelar sistilias sata rujias, y or sisli carjibal dinando trutas discandas.
18. In the above little tale the writer confesses that there are many things purely imaginary; the most material point, however, the attempt to sack the town during the pestilence, which was defeated by the courage and activity of an individual, rests on historical evidence the most satisfactory. It is thus mentioned in the work of Francisco de Cordova (he was surnamed Cordova from having been for many years canon in that city):-'Annis praeteritis Iuliobrigam urbem, vulgo Logrono, pestilenti laborantem morbo, et hominibus vacuam invadere hi ac diripere tentarunt, perfecissentque ni Dens O. M. cuiusdam BIBLIOPOLAE opera, in corum, capita, quam urbi moliebantur perniciem avertisset.' DIDASCALIA, Lugduni, 1615, I vol. 8VO. p. 405, cap. 50.
19. Yet notwithstanding that we refuse credit to these particular narrations of Quinones and Fajardo, acts of cannibalism may certainly have been perpetrated by the Gitanos of Spain in ancient times, when they were for the most part semi-savages living amongst mountains and deserts, where food was hard to be procured: famine may have occasionally compelled them to prey on human flesh, as it has in modern times compelled people far more civilised than wandering Gypsies.
20. England.
21. Spain.
22. MITHRIDATES: erster Theil, s. 241.
23. Torreblanca: DE MAGIA, 1678.
24. Exodus, chap. xiii. v. 9. 'And it shall be for a sign unto thee upon thy hand.' Eng. Trans.

25. No chapter in the book of Job contains any such verse.
26 'And the children of Israel went out with an high hand.' Exodus, chap. xiv. v. 8. Eng. Trans.
27. No such verse is to be found in the book mentioned.
28. Prov., chap. vii. vers. 11, 12. 'She is loud and stubborn; her feet abide not in her house. Now is she without, now in the streets, and lieth in wait at every corner.' Eng. Trans.
29. HISTORIA DE ALONSO, MOZO DE MUCHOS AMOS: or, the story of Alonso, servant of many masters; an entertaining novel, written in the seventeenth century, by Geronimo of Alcala, from which some extracts were given in the first edition of the present work.
30. O Ali! O Mahomet! - God is God! - A Turkish war-cry.
31. Gen. xlix. 22.
32. In the original there is a play on words. - It is not necessary to enter into particulars farther than to observe that in the Hebrew language 'ain' means a well, and likewise an eye.
33. Gen. xlviii. 16. In the English version the exact sense of the inspired original is not conveyed. The descendants of Joseph are to increase like fish.
34. Exodus, chap. xii. v. 37, 38.
35. Quinones, p. 11.
36. The writer will by no means answer for the truth of these statements respecting Gypsy marriages.
37. This statement is incorrect.
38. The Torlaquis (idle vagabonds), Hadgies (saints), and Dervishes (mendicant friars) of the East, are Gypsies neither by origin nor habits, but are in general people who support themselves in idleness by practising upon the credulity and superstition of the Moslems.
39. In the Moorish Arabic, [Arabic text which cannot be reproduced] - or reus al haramin, the literal meaning being, 'heads or captains of thieves.'
40. A favourite saying amongst this class of people is the following: 'Es preciso que cada uno coma de su oficio'; I.E. every one must live by his trade.
41. For the above well-drawn character of Charles the Third I am indebted to the pen of Louis de Usoz y Rio, my coadjutor in the editing of the New Testament in Spanish (Madrid, 1837). For a

further account of this gentleman, the reader is referred to THE BIBLE IN SPAIN, preface, p. xxii.

42. Steal a horse.
43. The lame devil: Asmodeus.
44. Rinconete and Cortadillo.
45. The great river, or Guadalquiver.
46. A fountain in Paradise.
47. A Gypsy word signifying 'exceeding much.'
48 'Lengua muy cerrada.'
49 'No camelo ser eray, es Calo mi nacimiento;No camelo ser eray, eon ser Cale me contento.'
50. Armed partisans, or guerillas on horseback: they waged a war of extermination against the French, but at the same time plundered their countrymen without scruple.
51. The Basques speak a Tartar dialect which strikingly resembles the Mongolian and the Mandchou.
52. A small nation or rather sect of contrabandistas, who inhabit the valley of Pas amidst the mountains of Santander; they carry long sticks, in the handling of which they are unequalled. Armed with one of these sticks, a smuggler of Pas has been known to beat off two mounted dragoons.
53. The hostess, Maria Diaz, and her son Joan Jose Lopez, were present when the outcast uttered these prophetic words.
54. Eodem anno precipue fuit pestis seu mortalitas Forlivio.
55. This work is styled HISTORIA DE LOS GITANOS, by J. M-, published at Barcelona in the year 1832; it consists of ninety-three very small and scantily furnished pages. Its chief, we might say its only merit, is the style, which is fluent and easy. The writer is a theorist, and sacrifices truth and probability to the shrine of one idea, and that one of the most absurd that ever entered the head of an individual. He endeavours to persuade his readers that the Gitanos are the descendants of the Moors, and the greatest part of his work is a history of those Africans, from the time of their arrival in the Peninsula till their expatriation by Philip the Third. The Gitanos he supposes to be various tribes of wandering Moors, who baffled pursuit amidst the fastnesses of the hills; he denies that they are of the same origin as the Gypsies, Bohemians, etc., of other lands, though he does not back his denial by any proofs, and is confessedly ignorant of the Gitano language, the grand criterion.

56. A Russian word signifying beans.
57. The term for poisoning swine in English Gypsy is DRABBING BAWLOR.
58. Por medio de chalanerias.
59. The English.
60. These words are very ancient, and were, perhaps, used by the earliest Spanish Gypsies; they differ much from the language of the present day, and are quite unintelligible to the modern Gitanos.
61. It was speedily prohibited, together with the Basque gospel; by a royal ordonnance, however, which appeared in the Gazette of Madrid, in August 1838, every public library in the kingdom was empowered to purchase two copies in both languages, as the works in question were allowed to possess some merit IN A LITERARY POINT OF VIEW. For a particular account of the Basque translation, and also some remarks on the Euscarra language, the reader is referred to THE BIBLE IN SPAIN, vol. ii. p. 385-398.
62. Steal me, Gypsy.
63. A species of gendarme or armed policeman. The Miquelets have existed in Spain for upwards of two hundred years. They are called Miquelets, from the name of their original leader. They are generally Aragonese by nation, and reclaimed robbers.
64. Those who may be desirous of perusing the originals of the following rhymes should consult former editions of this work.
65. For the original, see other editions.
66. For this information concerning Palmireno, and also for a sight of the somewhat rare volume written by him, the author was indebted to a kind friend, a native of Spain.
67. A very unfair inference; that some of the Gypsies did not understand the author when he spoke Romaic, was no proof that their own private language was a feigned one, invented for thievish purposes.
68. Of all these, the most terrible, and whose sway endured for the longest period, were the Mongols, as they were called: few, however, of his original Mongolian warriors followed Timour in the invasion of India. His armies latterly appear to have consisted chiefly of Turcomans and Persians. It was to obtain popularity amongst these soldiery that he abandoned his old religion, a kind of fetish, or sorcery, and became a Mahometan.

69. As quoted by Adelung, MITHRIDATES, vol. i.

70. Mithridates.

70. For example, in the HISTORIA DE LOS GITANOS, of which we have had occasion to speak in the first part of the present work: amongst other things the author says, p. 95, 'If there exist any similitude of customs between the Gitanos and the Gypsies, the Zigeuners, the Zingari, and the Bohemians, they (the Gitanos) cannot, however, be confounded with these nomad castes, nor the same origin be attributed to them; . . . all that we shall find in common between these people will be, that the one (the Gypsies, etc.) arrived fugitives from the heart of Asia by the steppes of Tartary, at the beginning of the fifteenth century, while the Gitanos, descended from the Arab or Morisco tribes, came from the coast of Africa as conquerors at the beginning of the eighth.' He gets rid of any evidence with respect to the origin of the Gitanos which their language might be capable of affording in the following summary manner: 'As to the particular jargon which they use, any investigation which people might pretend to make would be quite useless; in the first place, on account of the reserve which they exhibit on this point; and secondly, because, in the event of some being found sufficiently communicative, the information which they could impart would lead to no advantageous result, owing to their extreme ignorance.' It is scarcely worth while to offer a remark on reasoning which could only emanate from an understanding of the very lowest order, - so the Gitanos are so extremely ignorant, that however frank they might wish to be, they would be unable to tell the curious inquirer the names for bread and water, meat and salt, in their own peculiar tongue - for, assuredly, had they sense enough to afford that slight quantum of information, it would lead to two very advantageous results, by proving, first, that they spoke the same language as the Gypsies, etc., and were consequently the same people - and secondly, that they came not from the coast of Northern Africa, where only Arabic and Shillah are spoken, but from the heart of Asia, three words of the four being pure Sanscrit.

72. As given in the MITHRIDATES of Adelung.

73. Possibly from the Russian BOLOSS, which has the same signification.

74. Basque, BURUA.

75. Sanscrit, SCHIRRA.
76. These two words, which Hervas supposes to be Italian used in an improper sense, are probably of quite another origin. LEN, in Gitano, signifies 'river,' whilst VADI in Russian is equivalent to water.
77. It is not our intention to weary the reader with prolix specimens; nevertheless, in corroboration of what we have asserted, we shall take the liberty of offering a few. Piar, to drink, (p. 188,) is Sanscrit, PIAVA. Basilea, gallows, (p. 158,) is Russian, BECILITZ. Caramo, wine, and gurapo, galley, (pp. 162, 176,) Arabic, HARAM (which literally signifies that which is forbidden) and GRAB. Iza, (p. 179,) harlot, Turkish, KIZE. Harton, bread, (p. 177,) Greek, ARTOS. Guido, good, and hurgamandera, harlot, (pp. 177, 178,) German, GUT and HURE. Tiple, wine, (p. 197,) is the same as the English word tipple, Gypsy, TAPILLAR.
78. This word is pure Wallachian ([Greek text which cannot be reproduced]), and was brought by the Gypsies into England; it means 'booty,' or what is called in the present cant language, 'swag.' The Gypsies call booty 'louripen.'
79. Christmas, literally Wine-day.
80. Irishman or beggar, literally a dirty squalid person.
81. Guineas.
82. Silver teapots.
83. The Gypsy word for a certain town.
84. In the Spanish Gypsy version, 'our bread of each day.'
85. Span., 'forgive us our debts as we forgive our debtors.'
86. Eng., 'all evil FROM'; Span., 'from all ugliness.'
87. Span., 'for thine.'
88. By Hungary is here meant not only Hungary proper, but Transylvania.
89. How many days made come the gentleman hither.
90. How many-year fellow are you.
91. Of a grosh.
92. My name shall be to you for Moses my brother.
93. Comes.
94. Empty place.
95. V. CASINOBEN in Lexicon.
96. By these two words, Pontius Pilate is represented, but whence they are derived I know not.
97. Reborn.

98. Poverty is always avoided.
99. A drunkard reduces himself to the condition of a hog.
100. The most he can do.
101. The puchero, or pan of glazed earth, in which bacon, beef, and garbanzos are stewed.
102. Truth contrasts strangely with falsehood; this is a genuine Gypsy proverb, as are the two which follow; it is repeated throughout Spain WITHOUT BEING UNDERSTOOD.
103. In the original WEARS A MOUTH; the meaning is, ask nothing, gain nothing.
104. Female Gypsy,
105. Women UNDERSTOOD.
106. With that motive awoke the labourer. ORIG.
107. Gave its pleasure to the finger, I.E. his finger was itching to draw the trigger, and he humoured it.
108. They feared the shot and slugs, which are compared, and not badly, to flies and almonds.
109. Christmas, literally Wine-day.
110. Irishman or beggar, literally a dirty squalid person.
111. Guineas.
114. Silver tea-pots.
115. The Gypsy word for a certain town.
116. As given by Grellmann.
117. The English Gypsies having, in their dialect, no other term for ghost than mulo, which simply means a dead person, I have been obliged to substitute a compound word. Bavalengro signifies literally a wind thing, or FORM OF AIR.

532200

Made in the USA